KENNETH LONERGAN

Kenneth Lonergan was born in New York City in 1962. Plays include *This Is Our Youth* (The New Group, 1996), *The Waverly Gallery* (Promenade Theatre, 2000), *Lobby Hero* (Playwrights Horizons, 2001), *The Starry Messenger* (The New Group, 2009), *Medieval Play* (Signature Theatre, 2012) and *Hold on to Me Darling* (Atlantic Theater Company, 2016).

Work for the cinema includes *You Can Count on Me* (2000), *Gangs of New York* (co-written with Jay Cocks and Steve Zaillian, 2002), *Margaret* (2011) and *Manchester by the Sea* (2016). He also adapted E.M. Forster's *Howards End* for the BBC in 2017.

Awards include the Academy Award for Best Original Screenplay and BAFTA Award for Best Original Screenplay for *Manchester by the Sea*; the Sundance Film Festival Grand Jury Prize and Writers Guild of America Award for Best Original Screenplay for *You Can Count On Me*; while *The Waverly Gallery* was a finalist for the 2001 Pulitzer Prize for Drama.

Kenneth Lonergan

THREE PLAYS

This Is Our Youth
The Waverly Gallery
Lobby Hero

introduced by the author

NICK HERN BOOKS

London
www.nickhernbooks.co.uk

A Nick Hern Book

Kenneth Lonergan: Three Plays first published in Great Britain as a paperback original in 2019 by Nick Hern Books Limited, The Glasshouse, 49a Goldhawk Road, London W12 8QP

Cover image: iStock.com/shuoshu

Designed and typeset by Nick Hern Books, London
Printed in Great Britain by Mimeo Ltd, Huntingdon, Cambridgeshire PE29 6XX

A CIP catalogue record for this book is available from the British Library

ISBN 978 1 84842 875 1

Contents

Preface
Kenneth Lonergan

The plays in this edition were written in the 1990s and first produced in 1996, 2000 and 2001, respectively, in various Off-Broadway theatres in New York. Two of them, *This Is Our Youth* and *Lobby Hero*, were subsequently produced in London in 2002, and all three were recently revived on Broadway over the last three years. This edition gives me the opportunity to say a little something about them. But I'm really not sure I can add much to what I've already said elsewhere, and it's always a bit tricky talking about your own work because there are a lot of good arguments against doing it at all.

For one thing, discussing what you are doing, have done, and would like to do is one of the best ways there is to stop doing it. Ernest Hemingway, who was if anything over-aware of what he was doing and how he did it, said somewhere that when you talk about your work you always run the risk of talking it away. This seems true enough. George Orwell, who was much less interested in himself than Hemingway was, shied away from discussing his books because he felt they ought to speak for themselves; i.e. if you need to clarify or expand on what you've written in a preface (like this one) there's probably something missing from it that no preface can hope to provide.

Still, all kinds of wonderful writers have told us many fascinating things about their work, and the way they work, and it doesn't seem to have done them any harm. Robert A. Caro just published a book called, aptly enough, *Working*, about how he approached his monumental biography of Robert Moses, and his still unfinished multi-volume *The Years of Lyndon Johnson*. Having read thousands of pages in these amazing books I was almost desperate to know how he went about writing them, and I wish he'd write three more books about how he does it. Many of George Bernard Shaw's prefaces are as interesting as the plays they preface, which is saying a lot. I won't say the preface to *Saint Joan* is better than *Saint Joan*, but it's a pleasure to read even if you haven't read or seen *Saint Joan*, or don't intend to – which would be a mistake, of course. We have nothing at all from Shakespeare about his plays that is not contained in them, unless you count some very simple stage directions which he may or may not have written. This has obviously done the plays no harm. But it would be nice to have had a word or two from him anyway.

Of course, there are lots of writers who say things about their work you wish they hadn't. Either they spoil your fun by telling you what they're really writing about, when you thought they were writing about something more interesting, or they seem to insist that the only way to write anything at all is their way. 'All really good plays start with X,' they say. Or, 'Without A, your play can attain a sort of B, but it will never reach the heights of C.' This kind of thing is very annoying, especially since A always turns out to be the advice-giver's specialty. They never say that flat-out, but nobody goes around explaining why true merit can only be found in others.

There is, however, one saving grace shared by the writer who lets the air out of her own balloon by showing you what's inside it, and the writer who insists that his way is the only way: They're both wrong. Because neither one knows, or could know, everything about him or herself, what he or she has written, or anything else for that matter. 'No surprise in the writer, no surprise in the reader,' said Robert Frost, rather bossily.

When Samuel Johnson, no actor, derided the notion that great acting requires genuine feeling and spontaneity, insisting rather that every gesture and inflection be carefully chosen and rigorously rehearsed without the smallest variation, it's enough to make you shrivel up with boredom just thinking about it. Imagine if his famous sense of humour had been suffocated by the same strictures he laid on poor Garrick; strictures which encumbered his own prose, nearly but not quite to the point of obscuring the light cast by his extraordinary mind through those winding, epigrammatic, aggressively impersonal sentences.

Two hundred years later, Noël Coward was making equally snooty pronouncements about his own acting, and acting generally. 'The actor can't afford real emotions; he must be in complete control from the moment he steps onstage, etc.' The truth, perhaps, but not the whole truth. Far be it from me to knock Noël Coward, but if his best acting had really been as devoid of spontaneous feeling as he claimed, nobody would have been listening to him say so forty years into his career. The same goes for his sixty plays, three hundred songs, twenty-five film scripts, twenty short stories, cabaret act, autobiography, diaries, letters, and novel.

So while it can be entertaining and instructive to hear something from the creator about his or her creation, the author's opinions, interesting or not, are more or less beside the point. What the author sees is always more interesting than what he or she thinks about it. And if it's something nobody else has ever seen, or ever seen in quite that way, or described from quite that angle, our author has something immensely more valuable to offer the rest of us than what he or she thinks about anything.

Which is why respect for the autonomy of what has been created is something worth cultivating. It's also an idea worth inculcating in theatre audiences, who can't help but approach every play they attend encumbered by their own slew of opinions, most of which have little or no bearing on what they are about to watch. But we get more out of the theatre when our eyes are open to more of what the theatre has to offer; and it's better for our souls. It's also better for the theatre. Not every insight is backed by energy sufficient to bash itself into the general consciousness. Not every idea is favoured by winds sufficient to succesfully navigate the choppy sea of our opinions, good, bad and indifferent. And everybody knows from personal experience that energy and favourable winds sustain a lot of ideas that are totally horrible. Survival of the fittest, a concept routinely misunderstood and misapplied as if it were some sort of mechanism for the general improvement of just about everything, has no bearing whatsoever on the health of the arts, which prosper better under cultivation than competition – like a farm or garden as opposed to, say, a jungle. I guess you could argue that the violent, open competition for survival in the jungle produces extraordinary life forms you just don't see on a farm. But the truth is, the inside of your mind and the difficulties pursuing any line of work are jungle enough for the propagation of interesting life forms. Maybe a better model for the theatre would be a zoo. But whatever model you choose, I would certainly argue for the cultivation of experience over opinion.

It's a hard row to hoe, and of course every sentence I've written here expresses an opinion. But it's the value of maintaining a little scepticism about one's opinions and one's competence to define the life flickering in a play, or novel, or any work of art, that I would argue for – both in the artist and the audience.

The late Christopher Hitchens cautioned that the problem with open-mindedness is that it can lead to empty-mindedness. Maybe so. But no rational person can argue against flexibility of mind, any more than you can argue that it's better for your muscles to be atrophied than supple. Minds, like muscles, shrink and stiffen if you don't keep stretching them. The theatre is supposed to help us do just that. A theatre with more in it can stretch our minds farther than one constrained and constricted by what we think should be in it, or what we think is in it now.

There's not much you can do about the influence of opinion over experience except to temper it as best you can. Maybe it's better to separate them altogether. Or if you can't do that, at least put them in their proper relation to each other. It was presumably on this principle that Shaw, writer of copious prefaces, recommended waiting to read the introduction until after reading the book.

July 2019

Simultaneous Dialogue

For characters speaking to each other, double dialogue laid out in side-by-side columns is meant to be spoken *simultaneously*: i.e., the actor saying the dialogue in the right-hand column is *not* to wait for the actor saying the dialogue in the left-hand column to finish, but to speak at the exact same time, taking his cue from the *vertical* placement of the text.

For example:

CHARACTER A.
What do you mean, speak at
the same time? Didn't we –   CHARACTER B.
I *am* speaking at the same   They mean speak
time.   *simultaneously.*
Well *you* didn't do it.   Don't wait for – That's not
the point.

In the above, Character B says the word 'They' at the same time that Character A says the word 'I' and the word 'Don't' at the same time Character A says the word 'Well.'

However, for double columns in which *two sets* of characters are having separate but simultaneous conversations, the speakers *start* at the same time, but continue along only in reference to their own column.

For example:

CHARACTER A.   CHARACTER C.
I saw that movie yesterday.   What time does the bus
get in?
CHARACTER B.
Oh yeah? Was it good?   CHARACTER D.
Five o'clock.
CHARACTER A.
No, not especially.   CHARACTER C.
The bus gets in at five
o'clock?

In the above, Characters A and C start speaking at the same time, but then each column proceeds at its own pace, without reference to the other column.

While in some cases absolute precision is neither possible nor necessary, in general, the more precisely the actors try to stick to these rules, the better the double dialogue will work.

THIS IS OUR YOUTH

This Is Our Youth was first produced by The New Group (Scott Elliott, Artistic Director; Claudia Catania, Executive Producer) and performed at the INTAR Theatre, New York City, in October 1996. The cast was as follows:

DENNIS ZIEGLER   Josh Hamilton
WARREN STRAUB   Mark Ruffalo
JESSICA GOLDMAN   Missy Yager

Director   Mark Brokaw

This Is Our Youth was revived by Second Stage Theater (Carole Rothman, Artistic Director; Carol Fishman, Managing Director; Alexander Fraser, Executive Director), by special arrangement with Barry and Fran Weissler and The New Group (Scott Elliott, Artistic Director; Claudia Catania, Executive Producer) and performed in New York City in November 1998. The production subsequently transferred to the Douglas Fairbanks Theatre under the auspices of Barry and Fran Weissler and Eric Krebs. The cast was as follows:

DENNIS ZIEGLER   Mark Rosenthal
WARREN STRAUB   Mark Ruffalo
JESSICA GOLDMAN   Missy Yager

Director   Mark Brokaw
Set Designer   Allen Moyer
Costume Designer   Michael Krass
Lighting Designer   Mark McCullough
Sound Designer   Robert Murphy
Fight Director   Rick Sordelet
Production Stage Manager   William H. Lang

This Is Our Youth received its UK premiere, produced by
Phil Cameron for Background, Clare Lawrence and Anna
Waterhouse for Out of the Blue (for and on behalf of Back to
Blue Ltd), at the Garrick Theatre, London, on 15 March 2002.
The cast was as follows:

DENNIS ZIEGLER   Hayden Christensen
WARREN STRAUB   Jake Gyllenhaal
JESSICA GOLDMAN   Anna Paquin

Director   Laurence Boswell
Set Designer   Jeremy Herbert
Costume Designer   Iona Kenrick
Lighting Designer   Adam Silverman

From 2 April 2002, the cast was as follows:

DENNIS ZIEGLER   Matt Damon
WARREN STRAUB   Casey Affleck
JESSICA GOLDMAN   Summer Phoenix

The production was revived at the Garrick Theatre
on 20 November 2002. The cast was as follows:

DENNIS ZIEGLER   Colin Hanks
WARREN STRAUB   Kieran Culkin
JESSICA GOLDMAN   Alison Lohman

From 16 January 2003, the cast was as follows:

DENNIS ZIEGLER   Chris Klein
WARREN STRAUB   Freddie Prinze Jr.
JESSICA GOLDMAN   Heather Burns

This is Our Youth was revived by Steppenwolf Theatre
Company (Martha Lavey, Artistic Director; David Hawkanson,
Executive Director) and performed at the Upstairs Theatre in
Chicago in June 2014. The cast was as follows:

DENNIS ZIEGLER	Kieran Culkin
WARREN STRAUB	Michael Cera
JESSICA GOLDMAN	Tavi Gevinson
Director	Anna D. Shapiro
Set Designer	Todd Rosenthal
Costume Designer	Ann Roth
Lighting Designer	Brian MacDevitt
Sound Designer	Rob Milburn
	Michael Bodeen
Fight Director	Thomas Schall
Production Stage Manager	Cambra Overend

The production transferred to the Cort Theatre, New York City, in
September 2014, produced by Scott Rudin, Eli Bush, Roger
Berlind, William Berlind, Jon B. Platt, Roy Furman, The Shubert
Organization, Ruth Hendel, Scott M. Delman, Stephanie P.
McClelland, Sonia Friedman, Tulchin Bartner, The Araca Group,
Heni Koenigsberg, Daryl Roth, Joan Raffe & Jhett Tolentino,
Catherine & Fred Adler, with executive producers, Joey Parnes,
Sue Wagner, and John Johnson.

Characters

DENNIS ZIEGLER, *twenty-one years old*
WARREN STRAUB, *nineteen years old*
JESSICA GOLDMAN, *nineteen years old*

Place

The play takes place in Dennis's one-room apartment
on the Upper West Side of Manhattan.

Time

Late March, 1982.

ACT ONE

A cold Saturday night in March, 1982, after midnight. A small, impersonal pillbox studio apartment on the second or third floor of a somewhat run-down postwar building on the Upper West Side of Manhattan between Broadway and West End, lived in by DENNIS ZIEGLER. *There are a TV and stereo, a lot of records, some arbitrary furniture, a little-used kitchenette, and a mattress on the floor in the corner. Scattered around the room are piles of the* New York Post, *sports magazines, and a lot of underground comic books. There is sports equipment in the apartment, if not actually in view. The room looks lived-in, but aside from a wall of photographs from* DENNIS*'s life, no effort whatsoever has been made to decorate it. It looks like it could be packed up and cleared out in half an hour.*

DENNIS *is watching an old black-and-white movie on TV. He is a grungy, handsome, very athletic, formerly long-haired kid, just twenty-one years old, wearing baggy chino-type pants and an ancient polo shirt. He is a very quick, dynamic, fanatical, and bullying kind of person; amazingly good-natured and magnetic, but insanely competitive and almost always successfully so; a dark cult god of high school only recently encountering, without necessarily recognizing, the first evidence that the dazzling, aggressive hipster techniques with which he has always dominated his peers might not stand him in good stead for much longer.*

The buzzer buzzes. DENNIS *is too cool to answer it right away. It buzzes again. He gets up and goes to the intercom.*

DENNIS. Yeah?

WARREN (*over the intercom*). Yo, Dennis. It's me, Warren.

DENNIS. What do you want?

WARREN (*over the intercom*). Yo, lemme up.

DENNIS *hits the buzzer. Sits down and watches TV. There is a knock at the door. Again, he doesn't answer it right away. Another knock.*

(*Off.*) Yo, Denny.

DENNIS *gets up and unlocks the door without opening it, then plops down again to watch TV.*

WARREN STRAUB *comes in the front door. He is a skinny nineteen-year-old – an odd, kicked dog of a kid with large tracts of thoughtfulness in his personality that are not doing him much good at the moment, probably because they so infrequently influence his actions. He has spent most of his adolescence in hot water of one kind or another, but is just beginning to find beneath his natural eccentricity a dogged self-possession his friends may not all share. Despite his enormous self-destructiveness, he is above all things a trier, easily beaten back but hard to knock down. His language and wardrobe are heavily influenced by* DENNIS *– but only up to a point, and he would be a good-looking kid if he eased up on his personal style a little.*

He comes into the apartment lugging a very big suitcase and an overloaded heavy-duty hiking backpack.

Hey.

DENNIS. What's with the suitcase?

WARREN. Nothing… What are you doing?

DENNIS. Nothing.

WARREN *closes the door and puts down his stuff. Sits down next to* DENNIS *on the mattress and looks at the TV.*

WARREN. What are you watching?

DENNIS. Lock the door.

WARREN *gets up and locks the door. He sits down as before.*

WARREN. What are you watching?

DENNIS *flashes off the TV with the remote control.*

DENNIS. Nothing. What do you want?

WARREN. Nothing.

DENNIS. I don't have any pot.

WARREN. I don't want any. I got some.

DENNIS. Let me see it.

WARREN *produces a ziplock plastic bag carefully wrapped around a small amount of dark green marijuana.* DENNIS *opens it and smells it.*

This is good. Where'd you get it?

WARREN. From Christian.

DENNIS. Can we smoke it?

WARREN. I'm saving it.

DENNIS. For what?

DENNIS *takes the pot out of the bag and reaches for a record album.*

He starts to crumble the pot onto the album cover.

WARREN. Just half.

DENNIS. Shut up.

WARREN. Just *half*, man.

DENNIS *looks at him and crumbles the rest of the pot onto the album.*

DENNIS. You got papers?

WARREN. You're a fuckin' asshole.

He gets up. DENNIS *laughs.*

DENNIS. There's some papers on the table. Gimme one.

WARREN *does not comply.*

DENNIS (*sharply*). Hey! Give me a *rolling* paper. Do you know how much *money* you owe me?

WARREN *takes out a small wad of bills, peels off a few, and drops them on the bed.*

Where'd you get this?

WARREN. What do you care?

DENNIS. Well if you're so rich then you can get more pot from Christian tomorrow, so give me the fucking rolling papers before I beat the shit out of you.

WARREN *goes to the table and throws a packet of Club or Zig-Zag rice papers to* DENNIS.

What happened, Jasonius kicked you out?

WARREN. No, man, I left.

DENNIS. You can't stay here.

WARREN. I don't want to stay here.

DENNIS. Why'd he kick you out? What'd you do?

WARREN. Nothing. I got stoned and he comes home and he's like, 'This apartment smells like pot *all the time*.' And I'm like, 'Yeah, 'cause I'm always *smoking* it.' So then he's like, 'I want that smell out of this house.' And then he's like, 'No, actually, I want *you* out of this house.' Then he throws a few bills on the floor and is like, 'There's some cash, now pack up your shit and get out before I beat your fuckin' head in.' And I was like, 'Whatever.' So he went on a date with his whore, and I packed up my stuff and left.

DENNIS. Where are you going to stay?

WARREN. I don't know. Maybe I'll stay with Christian. I don't know. Maybe I'll stay in a hotel. Who the hell knows?

DENNIS. How are you going to stay in a hotel?

WARREN. I got money.

DENNIS. How much did he give you?

WARREN. He gave me some money.

DENNIS. Why? Like to thank you for leaving?

WARREN. I guess.

DENNIS. How much is this?

Putting the beautifully rolled joint in his mouth, DENNIS *counts the money* WARREN *threw on the bed.*

WARREN. Two hundred.

DENNIS *finishes counting. From under the mattress he pulls a beat-up school composition notebook and flips through it till he finds* WARREN*'s name.*

DENNIS. 'Warren.'

He writes something in the book.

(*Writing.*) '*Cleared*, with stolen funds.'

WARREN. They're not stolen, man, he gave it to me.

DENNIS *closes the book, finds a match, and lights up.*

DENNIS (*holding in the smoke*). Where did Christian get this from?

WARREN. I don't know.

DENNIS *slaps* WARREN *in the face, playfully but hard.*

DENNIS. Don't fuckin' lie to me – where'd he get it?

WARREN *tries to hit* DENNIS *back. They scuffle, but* DENNIS *is much bigger and stronger and stops him.*

WARREN. Don't fuckin' hit me –

DENNIS. Where did he get it from?

WARREN. Why don't you ask him?

DENNIS. Did he get it from Philip?

WARREN. No, he said he got it from some fuckin' Rastafarian.

DENNIS. That guy Wally?

WARREN. I don't know.

DENNIS. That guy Kresko?

WARREN. I don't know. I don't keep track of where you guys perform your criminal activities. Who cares? Gimme that.

DENNIS *doesn't move. He keeps smoking,* WARREN *reaches for the joint.* DENNIS *allows him to take it.*

DENNIS. How much money did you steal?

WARREN. A lot.

DENNIS. Let me see.

WARREN *opens his backpack and takes out a felt shoe bag stuffed with thousands of dollars in small bills. He loosens the ties and shows it to* DENNIS.

That's a lot.

WARREN. It's fifteen thousand dollars.

DENNIS. Are you *fucking* crazy? (*Pause*) Give me half.

WARREN. No.

DENNIS. Give me five.

WARREN. I'm not giving you anything.

DENNIS. No. Give me five, we'll go to *France*, and we'll mail the rest back to your dad with a note. 'Took five. Went to *France*.'

WARREN. I'm keeping it.

DENNIS. Are you kidding? He'll send large men after you with *guns*.

WARREN. He doesn't even know I have it.

DENNIS. What do you mean?

WARREN. I mean he –   DENNIS. Where did you *get* it from?

WARREN. It was in his room.

DENNIS. It was in his *room*?

WARREN. Yeah.

DENNIS. Your father keeps fifteen thousand dollars cash in his *room*? For what? *Tips?*

WARREN. I don't know. I guess he's got some kind of illicit lingerie deal in the works or something, I don't know.

DENNIS. Your father is so heavy, man…

WARREN. Yeah, so after he threw me out and went to *supper*, I was just roaming the house looking for liftable objects, if that was gonna be his attitude. So I go in his bedroom and there's this sinister-looking *brief*case just *sitting* on his *bed*. So I jimmied open the lock and there's like rows and rows of cash just starin' at me. Like totally full of money.

DENNIS. Jason.

WARREN. Yeah! So I'm like, '*Dad…!*' And then I'm like, 'Should I take this? This is some serious money.' And then I'm like, 'Fuck yeah. Make him *pay*.' So I take out the cash, and I fill the briefcase with all these old *National Geographics* and lock it up again. So it'll probably sit there for the weekend, and then when he goes to deposit it, or bribe whoever he was planning on bribing, he'll open it up and hopefully he'll think like one of his *cohorts* ripped him off. Or like, his *slut* did it.

DENNIS. No he *won't*.

WARREN. Why not?

DENNIS. Of *course* he won't.

WARREN. Why not?

DENNIS. Because he's not a *moron*.

WARREN. Yes he is.

DENNIS. You really think after he throws you out of the house he's gonna open his briefcase and find twenty copies of his own *National Geographics* where his *money* should be, and he's not gonna know you did it? You're a fuckin' moron. Now get that shit outta here.

WARREN. I'm telling you –

DENNIS. Take it over to Christian's house and let your father's bodyguards break *his* fuckin' legs.

WARREN. He doesn't *have* any bodyguards.

DENNIS. That guy who drives his car is not a bodyguard?

WARREN. No, he's a *driver*.

DENNIS. That guy like shows me his *gun*, like every time I *see* him.

WARREN. Yeah, because he's *insane*. But my father is not a *criminal*. He's just in *business* with criminals.

DENNIS. I don't give a shit *what* he is. I can't believe you cart that kind of money across town and like bring it to my *doorstep*. No – no – I mean you are so stupid, man, you are so incredibly stupid. He kicks you out so you steal fifteen thousand *dollars* from him?

WARREN. I was pissed.

DENNIS. Okay: Get it out of here. Take it to Christian's house.

WARREN. He's not home.

DENNIS. Take it to Yoffie's house; go to Leonard's house. I don't care.

WARREN. Nobody's home. Everyone's parents are home. I'm not allowed in their houses. Come on. I don't want to be wandering around the streets with all that money. Come on.

Pause.

DENNIS. This is so typical of you, man, I mean this is like...

WARREN. Yeah yeah yeah.

DENNIS. This is like the prototype moronic move we've all
    come to expect from your corner. You drive the guy *crazy*
    because you're such a sniveling little obnoxious punk, you
    grate on the guy until he finally throws you out – arguably
    the most dangerous lingerie manufacturer in the *world* – And
    then you steal his money and bring it to my *house*, and
    expect me to like *hide* you or something?

    WARREN *starts to speak.*

    No – no – That's why nobody likes you, man, because you're
    always provoking people. Okay, now everybody's provoked,
    only *you're* the one they all fuckin' hate! Listen to me. I'm
    trying to tell you something. This is good for you.

WARREN. Oh, yeah.

DENNIS. No it is. It's good for you. Listen. You're a fuckin'
    idiot. You never have any money. Nobody can stand to have
    you around. And you can't get laid. I mean, man, you cannot
    get laid. You *never* get laid. Like the last girlfriend you had
    was in like ninth grade and it lasted for two weeks, and that
    bitch probably still hasn't recovered.

WARREN. She hasn't. I freaked her out.

DENNIS. What kind of *life* do you lead? You live with your
    father – a psycho. He beats the shit out of you on like this
    regular *basis*, you habitually owe me hundreds of dollars,
    you never pay me – until now, but we won't even discuss
    that – Nobody can stand to have you around because you're
    such an annoying loudmouthed little creep, and now you're
    like some kind of fugitive from *justice*? What is gonna
    happen to you, man?

WARREN. What's gonna happen to anybody? Who cares?

    DENNIS *shrugs, sits. Relights the joint, which has gone out.*

    Like you're so independent?

DENNIS. Yeah, because my parents *pay* for this apartment.
    They don't throw me *out* of it. Because they're so grateful
    I don't wanna live with them. Because I don't *goad* them

into *making* me dependent. I'm just like, '*Don't* send me to college. Just spring for my rent, I'll be a fuckin' *bike* messenger till I decide what I wanna do, and we'll never have to deal with each other.' And they're like, '*Fine*.'

Pause.

WARREN. Why do you say that shit?

DENNIS. Because it's true.

| WARREN. Why do you – | DENNIS. Because you |
| | deserve it. |

WARREN *is close to tears*.

DENNIS. Are you *crying* now?

WARREN. No. (*Pause*) *I* don't know what to do. (*Pause*) *I* don't know where to go.

DENNIS. Well – for one thing you should give me five thousand dollars and then you should return that money.

WARREN. I'm not giving you five thousand dollars.

DENNIS. I'm telling you. *France*.

Pause.

WARREN. You want some money?

DENNIS. No, I don't want any money.

WARREN *opens the bag and holds out two bricks of cash*.

WARREN. Take some money. Go to fuckin' France.

DENNIS. I don't wanna go to France. Like I want your father *stalking* me for the rest of my life? Now put that shit back in the bag and take it back to where you found it. It *scares* me.

WARREN *puts the money back and closes the ties*.

WARREN. I can't return it because he's home by now. He's *asleep*. The shit is in his bedroom and he's gonna be home all day tomorrow because he's having some associates over for *brunch*.

DENNIS. Brunch. (*Pause*) That's a wild concept: It's not breakfast and it's not lunch. It's *brunch.* (*Rolls the word around in his mouth.*) 'Brunch.' 'Let's serve *brunch...*' It's something you serve. (*Long pause.*) This is strong pot.

WARREN. I know.

DENNIS. All right: You know what you should tell your father?

WARREN. It doesn't matter what I do. He's gonna kill me anyway, so what's the difference?

DENNIS. No. Let's figure this out. It's gonna be okay. I'm a total mathematical genius. Now how much of this cash did you spend?

WARREN. Not much. I paid you back... I took a cab... I ate sushi... Two hundred and fifty bucks. But he gave me fifty.

DENNIS. Okay. So don't spend any more, hang out till Monday, and then return it on Monday when he goes to work. If the briefcase is already gone, then just like, leave the cash in his bedroom with a note of explanation – and like, leave town.

WARREN. I don't know.

DENNIS. That's a sound plan. And if he still hasn't even opened the briefcase you're like home free. Except for two hundred bucks.

WARREN. Can I get the two hundred back from you?

DENNIS. No, man, that's like, *paid.* I can't release that cash.

WARREN. Where am I gonna stay?

DENNIS. Stay with Christian.

WARREN. Why can't I stay here?

DENNIS. 'Cause I don't want you.

WARREN. It's just two days.

DENNIS. I don't care.

WARREN. Come on. Nothing is gonna happen. He's not gonna know I came here. He definitely won't open the briefcase till Monday, and I'll be gone by then.

DENNIS. You are so stupid, man. I mean this definitely crowns your career as an idiot.

WARREN. Just let me stay here for Christ's sakes! I do shit for you all the time –

DENNIS. Like what?

WARREN. Like when your girlfriend kicked you out, you stayed at my house for two *weeks* –

DENNIS. That was your *father's* house.

WARREN. So *what*?

DENNIS. This is *my* house.

WARREN. And I got in a lotta trouble for that, too. I hang out with you whenever you want, I play sports with you all the time, I buy pot from you, I take all your fuckin' abuse and I'm a good fuckin' friend. So why can't you help me out when I'm in trouble and not be such a fuckin' asshole?

DENNIS. 'Cause you're *always* in trouble. You have like no sense of *differentiation*.

WARREN. It's just two days!

DENNIS. All right, all right, shut up.

WARREN. Thanks.

DENNIS. But if your father shows up here I'm givin' you up immediately.

WARREN. I'm sure you will. But he's not gonna.

Silence.

So what's up? What do you wanna do?

DENNIS. No, I don't wanna *do any*thing. Don't *needle* me, Warren. If you wanna stay here you can stay here, but you gotta shut up.

DENNIS *turns on the TV and watches it wholeheartedly.*

WARREN. Hey, where's that chick Jessica? (*Pause*) Denny. Have you seen that chick Jessica recently?

DENNIS. No. What about her?

WARREN. I'm into her.

DENNIS. She's out of your league, man.

WARREN. I think she likes me.

DENNIS. No she doesn't.

WARREN. I think she does.

DENNIS. Shut up.

WARREN. She's really cute, man.

DENNIS. She is cute. That's why it'll never happen.

WARREN *wanders over to the fridge.*

There's nothing in there.

WARREN *opens the fridge and looks in. It's pretty bare.*

Get *outta* there, Warren! I just told you there's nothing in there.

WARREN. How come you never have any food in here?

DENNIS *doesn't answer. He watches TV.*

Let's go play football.

DENNIS *doesn't answer.*

Where's your girlfriend?

DENNIS. We had a fight.

WARREN. Why?

DENNIS. Because she's a cunt.

WARREN. Tell her to come over and bring that girl Jessica.

DENNIS. Tell her yourself.

WARREN (*going to the phone*). Where's she at?

DENNIS. You can't call her. We had a fight.

> WARREN *picks up* DENNIS'*s football and makes phantom passes*.

WARREN. Let's go outside and play.

DENNIS. Forget it.

WARREN. Let's call your girlfriend and tell her to call that girl Jessica, and we'll take a few thousand bucks out of the shoe bag and rent a really nice hotel suite and get a lot of champagne and shit and have a wild party. What do you think?

> WARREN *throws* DENNIS *the football*. DENNIS *throws it back*. DENNIS *knows how to throw a football*.

DENNIS. You can't spend that money.

WARREN. I'll spend some of it. Big deal.

> *They toss the football back and forth.*

Come on, I'll get laid. It'll be good.

DENNIS. Let's just get a couple of prostitutes.

WARREN. Okay.

DENNIS. You want to? We can call this Japanese place Philip goes to, and they'll send over like two incredibly beautiful and obedient Oriental hostesses to entertain and delight us.

WARREN. Let's do it.

DENNIS. How much will you spend?

WARREN. I don't know. How much is it?

DENNIS. Like two hundred apiece.

WARREN. I'd be into that.

DENNIS. What'll you tell your dad?

WARREN. Fuck my dad. I took his *money*!

DENNIS. You *robbed* him!

WARREN *throws a hard pass that goes wide and smashes into some breakables.*

WARREN. Whoa. Sorry.

DENNIS. What is your problem!?

WARREN. I lost control of the ball.

DENNIS *gets the ball out of the smashed shelfware.*

Yo. Denny. Toss it back.

DENNIS. You broke my girlfriend's sculpture!

WARREN. Whoa… Really? I'm sorry.

DENNIS. What is your *problem*?

WARREN. I don't know. I really broke it?

DENNIS. *Yeah*, you really *broke* it.

WARREN *comes over and examines the broken clay sculpture.*

WARREN. What was it?

DENNIS. It was two girls, makin' out.

WARREN. Intense.

DENNIS. Now it's like, half of two girls.

WARREN. I'm really sorry, man, it was an accident.

DENNIS. It's a piece of shit anyway.

WARREN. Yo, lemme see it. Maybe I can glue it back together.

DENNIS. Get away from it.

WARREN. Lemme see.

WARREN *tries to get a hand on the broken sculpture.* DENNIS *roughly blocks him out with his body and elbows.*

DENNIS. Go sit in the *corner*, Warren, you're a fuckin' menace. Look what you *did*.

WARREN. Let me repair it.

DENNIS *can't do anything with it. He lets* WARREN *look at it.*

No problem. You just get some Krazy Glue and glue it together. Do you have any?

DENNIS. No I don't have any *Krazy* Glue.

WARREN. I can fix this.

DENNIS *wanders away from the shelves.*

DENNIS. I'm *wasted...*

WARREN. Look. See?

He has propped the two halves of the broken sculpture together so it looks whole.

Just glue it like that and it'll be fine. You probably don't even need a clamp.

WARREN *picks up the football and makes phantom passes at* DENNIS.

Yo, heads up. Yo, Denny – go out.

DENNIS. Would you put that *down*?

WARREN. Go long!

DENNIS. The fuck am I gonna go *long*?

WARREN. Yo, go out!

WARREN *throws the football hard, a little out of* DENNIS*'s reach, and it smashes into a bunch of other stuff.*

DENNIS. What is *with* you, Warren?

WARREN. Come on, you *had* it!

DENNIS *grabs the football, rears back, and wings a viciously hard pass at* WARREN*'s head.* WARREN *ducks and the football smashes into the sculpture again, totally demolishing it.*

DENNIS. *Catch* it, you *moron*! Don't *duck*! This is my *house*!

WARREN. You tried to kill me, man!

DENNIS. What is the matter with you?

WARREN. I didn't *do* anything!

DENNIS *stalks the room toward* WARREN, *grabs him in
a headlock and flings him down on the floor. They are both
half-laughing.*

DENNIS. Get outta my *house*!

WARREN. Come on, man, I didn't do anything!

DENNIS *rains open-handed blows down on* WARREN*'s
head and body.* WARREN *covers up.* DENNIS *drops onto
his gut, knee first.* WARREN *groans in pain.* DENNIS *gets
up and looks at the wreckage.*

DENNIS. Look what you did.

WARREN. Oh my stomach.

DENNIS. Oh, forget *this*...

*He starts tossing the pieces of the sculpture, basketball-style,
into the wastepaper basket across the room. He's a good
shot. Most of them go in.*

She's gonna freak out.

The last piece goes into the wastepaper basket. DENNIS
walks over to it and boots it into the wall. He goes to
WARREN, *who is covering his head.*

You all right?

WARREN *uncovers his head.* DENNIS *slaps him in the face.*

WARREN. Cut it out.

DENNIS. That's for breaking her shit.

WARREN. You murdered my stomach.

Long silence.

I'm restless.

DENNIS *gives him a look.*

So, you don't wanna call any Japanese hostesses?

DENNIS. You couldn't handle it. You'd go limp and be depressed about it for like a year and a half.

WARREN. Let's call 'em!

DENNIS. Shut up. It's two hundred dollars apiece. You wanna spend that cash?

WARREN. No, man, I can't.

DENNIS. What are you gonna do about the two hundred bucks?

WARREN. I don't know. I'll sell something.

DENNIS. What, from like your little faggot memorabilia collection?

WARREN. Yeah.

DENNIS. So why don't you ever sell any of that shit to pay *me*? You should let me call Adam Saulk's brother, man. He makes a fortune buying and selling that shit.

WARREN. I pay you.

DENNIS. You do not.

WARREN. Besides, paying you isn't like life and death. Anyway, you make so much money off all of us already it's like completely ridiculous.

DENNIS. Yeah, and I always smoke pot with you, all of you, *my* pot, all the time, like hundreds and hundreds of dollars' worth. So why shouldn't I make some money offa you? You fuckin' guys like *gripe* at me all the time, and I'm providing you schmucks with such a crucial service. Plus I'm developing valuable entrepreneurial skills for my future. *Plus* I'm like providing you with precious memories of your *youth*, for when you're fuckin' *old*. I'm like the basis of half your personality. All you do is imitate me. I turned you onto *The Honeymooners*, Frank *Zappa*, Ernst *Lubitsch*, *sushi*. I'm like a one-man youth culture for you pathetic assholes. You're gonna remember your youth as like a gray stoned haze punctuated by a series of beatings from your fuckin' dad, and like, *my* jokes. God *damn*! You know how much *pot* I've thrown out the *window* for you guys in the middle of the night when you're wandering around the street like *junkies* looking for half a joint so you can go to sleep, because you scraped all the *resin* out of your pipes? And you bitch about the fact that along the way I turn a little profit? You should thank God you ever *met* me, you little fuckin' hero-worshipping little *fag*.

WARREN. You are out of your mind, man.

DENNIS *laughs.* WARREN *opens his big suitcase and start removing the first items in an extensive collection of toys and memorabilia from the 1950s and '60s: Mint condition mid-'60s Mattel toys, first release albums, a 1950s toaster, etc.*

DENNIS. Don't take that stuff out in here.

WARREN. Why not? I wanna see what I can sell.

DENNIS. No – no – Don't take that stuff out in my apartment. It depresses me.

WARREN. Why?

DENNIS. Don't take all that cutesy kitschy fuckin' retro-Sixties bullshit out in my apartment. I don't wanna look at it.

WARREN. I can get a couple of hundred bucks for any of these albums.

DENNIS. Lemme see.

WARREN *hands him an obscure early Frank Zappa album.*

Where'd you get this?

WARREN. From this buddy of mine in Seattle.

DENNIS. This is an amazing album.

DENNIS *looks through some of the stuff.*

What is this shit? What's with the little *spacemen*? You are weird, man.

WARREN. This is Major Matt Mason. Don't you remember this?

DENNIS. No.

WARREN. They had these when we were little. They're really cool, and these are in really good condition. I could get like a hundred fifty, two hundred bucks for this.

DENNIS. Seriously?

WARREN. Yeah.

DENNIS. So how do you always owe me money?

WARREN. 'Cause I don't wanna sell them.

DENNIS. You are a depressing little man. Now put that shit away.

WARREN (*holding it out to him*). Look, he's got a little space helmet. The visor moves up and down.

DENNIS. Get that shit *away* from me!

The phone rings. DENNIS *lets it ring twice, then picks up.*

(*Into the phone*). Yeah?... Because you're bein' a cunt.

The line goes dead. DENNIS *hangs up and laughs, suddenly energized.*

WARREN. You're intense, man.

DENNIS. I'm the best! I don't let people freak me out. I freak *them* out.

WARREN. You're an amazing man.

DENNIS. Hey – listen: That girl you like: what's her name?

WARREN. Jessica.

DENNIS. She's friends with that other girl, Natalie. You know her?

WARREN. Yeah?

DENNIS. Okay, check it out: That girl Natalie likes me, okay? Last summer when Valerie was in Sweden with her family, I was like making out with her all the time, but that's all she ever let me do. But I saw her last week and she was coming onto me all over the place. So look: new plan: We'll take a thousand bucks out of the shoe bag, cab it over to Philip's house, pick up an ounce of blow, call Natalie, tell her and Jessica to come over here, we'll get them wired, I'll fuck Natalie – you do your best to fuck Jessica – Then tomorrow we make a few calls, sell the rest of the blow, turn a tidy little profit, and return the whole fifteen grand to your psychotic father intact on Monday. That's a great plan.

WARREN. How do you figure?

DENNIS. Because we extract a quarter ounce for ourselves, throw back in a quarter ounce of cut, sell it for like a hundred twenty-five a gram, clear around thirty-six hundred bucks, return the thousand-dollar investment to the bag along with the two hundred you already owe him, and you're still gonna end up making like six hundred dollars.

WARREN (*slowly*)....All right...

DENNIS. Okay?

WARREN. Yeah.

DENNIS (*grabbing the phone*). Okay –

WARREN. But like... what's the basic margin of profit?

DENNIS. Like eighteen hundred each.

WARREN. So but... if we're making eighteen hundred each, how come I only end up with *six*?

DENNIS (*still holding the phone*). You *don't* end up with six: you end up with *eighteen*, minus the thousand you're investing and the two hundred you already *owe*. Plus a free eighth of blow, which you can snort or sell as you see fit. Get it?

WARREN. Um, not really. But whatever.

DENNIS. What don't you get?

WARREN. I don't really get the whole thing.

DENNIS *hangs up the phone.*

DENNIS. Look: We're buying a Z for a *thousand dollars*...

WARREN. No, I get *that* part. I just – I mean, theoretically, we're making a joint investment, right?

DENNIS. Yeah...?

WARREN. Only in terms of the actual cash outlay, it's all coming from my area. Right? So in a way, I'm the only actual investor.

DENNIS. Yeah...?

WARREN. So then why aren't I making all the money?

DENNIS. Because it's my connect and my customers and I'm gonna have the shit in my house.

WARREN. Yeah, but –

DENNIS. What do you *mean* why aren't you making all the money?

WARREN. I'm not saying I *should*. But you're saying we should split the profits *before* I put back the thousand dollars, and I'm saying like, why aren't we doing it *afterwards*?

DENNIS. Because it's my *connect*. I'm providing the *connect*.

WARREN. I'm providing the *cash*.

DENNIS. So what?

WARREN....So I figure the odds be fifty-fifty.

DENNIS. You do, huh? All right. Whatever... But that's fucked up, because I'm doing all the work, and all you did was steal some money from your father which you're getting back in like ten *minutes*.

WARREN. All right, so what do you want to do?

DENNIS. I don't know. I just – I should definitely get some kind of *service* fee. So look – we'll split the twenty-six hundred net: thirteen hundred each. And then you pay me two hundred more for doing all the *work* – that leaves me with fifteen and you with eleven hundred. Out of which you can pay your father back the two hundred dollars or not. Whatever you want. Okay?

WARREN. I guess.

DENNIS. Is that all *right* with you? Can I *call* him now?

WARREN. Yeah. Call him up.

DENNIS. Don't *ever* try to out-Jew me, little man. I'm twice the Jew you'll ever be. I'm like a Jewish *god*. I'm like – *Jooooo*lius *Caesar*!

WARREN. You're a fuckin' *mental* case, man.

DENNIS. Way to take care of *business*, little Warren!

DENNIS *pinches* WARREN *very hard*.

WARREN. Ow!

DENNIS *dials the phone. Waits*.

DENNIS (*to* WARREN). He's not there. (*Into the phone*.) Philly. Dennis. Call me. I'm looking for some fun.

He hangs up.

Shit.

The phone rings. He lets it ring twice, then picks up.

(*Into the phone*.) Yeah?... No!... 'Cause I don't know!... 'Cause I don't *give* a shit... Yeah... Yeah, okay... (*To* WARREN.) Go in the bathroom.

WARREN. Come on...

DENNIS. Go in the bathroom!

WARREN *goes in the bathroom*.

(*Into the phone*.) I'm sorry, baby. I know I messed up... I know! As soon as I start arguing, I immediately snap into attack mode and just become as insanely brutal as I possibly can. It's because of my fuckin' *mother*... All right, why don't you come over?... Warren's here, but I'll get rid of him... Yeah... Oh, *really*?... No, totally *bring* her: Warren's like, in *love* with her… Would she be into that?… What if we got some blow?… She might. All right. See if she'll come over. I'll work on it.

DENNIS *hangs up*.

Hey!

WARREN *comes out of the bathroom*.

WARREN. What's up?

DENNIS. Nothin'. I got good news for you, so get your little boner ready, 'cause my girlfriend's on her way over with your favorite teenage prostitute.

WARREN. What do you mean?

DENNIS. What do you think I mean?

WARREN. She's with Jessica?

DENNIS. Yeah.

WARREN. They're coming over here?

DENNIS. That's right, my little love machine.

WARREN. Excellent.

DENNIS. Only I told 'em we'd get drugs, so shut up for a second and let me think.

Pause. He picks up the phone and dials.

WARREN. Who are you calling?

DENNIS *ignores him*.

DENNIS (*into the phone*). Stuey. Hey. What are you doing?… You are too much, man. You shoulda been like, a Roman *senator*. Let me ask you something: Have you seen this weed Christian's been selling? It's like an olive-colored dark-green heavy sense with like a medium amount of fuzz, very wet and sticky, in like long oblong-shaped little buds, shaped like beef sate… Oh you got some?… Do you know where he got it?… All right: Let me ask you something else. Do you know where Philip is?… Yeah. Have you seen it?… How is it?…

Really. How much did you get?… What's he asking?…
I did. He's *not home*… No, I just *tried* him, you fat fuck, he's
not home. Why do you have to aggravate me all the time?

WARREN. What's up?

DENNIS (*into the phone*). So listen. Stuey. Baby: If I can't get
ahold of Philip in like twenty, I'm comin' over there and
taking an eighth offa you, all right?… No, *Stuart*, I'm not
buying it from you, I'm *taking* it, at cost. I'll give you cash
up front, whatever you paid Philip, and you can get more
from him tomorrow… *Yeah*, as a *favor*… Because I'm
asking you to, that's why. Because I fuckin' *introduced* you
to him in the first place, you fuckin' globulous *fuck*. You
wouldn't even *know* him if it wasn't for me: you'd still be
dealing commercial pot outside some Long Island mall to a
bunch of dyed-blonde Great Neck *bimbettes*, you fat fuckin'
asshole. I *created* you, Stuey, and I can destroy you just as
easily! I don't care how many syphilis-ridden Dutch
backpackers are blowing you, man. Why do you always have
to like, try to have some mincing little bullshit *advantage*
over me all the time? So you don't feel like such a fat, ugly
man or something?… No, man, because you're like totally
uncivilized. You have like no sense of protocol, like
whatsoever… All right all right. I'll call you back.

He hangs up.

WARREN. What's up?

DENNIS. Nothin'. He's sitting on his waterbed doing *speed*balls
with some naked Dutch *hitch*hiker he picked up at the *bus*
stop, and he wants to like *dicker* with me over the price of an
eighth of coke, like I can't go over to Philip's myself
tomorrow and pick it up for *less* than what *he* paid, and like
I haven't turned him on to tons of business and tons of my
own customers – just so he can be holding some kind of *cards*
on me or something. Plus he's so stoned out of his mind to
begin with you can't understand a word he's saying anyway.

WARREN. So… what are we gonna do?

DENNIS. I don't know. See if Philip calls back, and if he doesn't, we'll just have to deal with the Fat Man. Maybe we should just forget it. It's late anyway. I don't wanna be lying in bed grinding my teeth all night. Unless you wanna just stay up and watch *H.R. Pufnstuff* at 5.30 in the morning.

WARREN. I can't watch that show, man. It freaks me out.

DENNIS. So what do you wanna do?

WARREN. Well... Are they coming over?

DENNIS. Yeah they're coming over.

WARREN. I'm into it.

DENNIS. All right. Should we get heroin? No, too much, right?

WARREN. Let's do speedballs.

DENNIS. Shut up. Do you even *know* what a speedball *is*? No.

WARREN. Yeah I know what a speedball is. It's like half-heroin half-cocaine. Right?

DENNIS. Yeah, but we can't give these girls *speed*balls. What are you, a maniac? Anyway, Valerie won't do heroin. *You* won't do heroin. So what are you talking about?

WARREN. I've done it.

DENNIS. Yeah, *once*. You'd be throwing up all night. That'd make a good impression. Speedballs are *sick*, man. They get you so fucked up you're like, really sorry.

WARREN. Let's do it!

DENNIS. Shut up.

Long pause.

WARREN. What's up?

DENNIS. No, nothing's *up*. How can you sit in a room with somebody for hours with nothing going on, and keep asking 'What's up?' every ten minutes like something *new* happened all of a sudden that you didn't know about?

WARREN. I don't know. It's just an expression.

WARREN *is walking around the room, picking things up and looking at them.*

So what's up? Where are they?

DENNIS. They're coming. Take it easy. And get away from my shit.

WARREN *keeps looking through* DENNIS*'s stuff.*

WARREN. But do they know I'm here?

DENNIS. Yeah, yeah, I told 'em you're here, I totally set it up for you. Just don't get weird and bizarre and start talking about your dead sister, and you'll do fine.

WARREN. I'm not gonna talk about anything.

Pause.

DENNIS. Yeah, just don't   WARREN. You're really
be like –   harsh, man.

DENNIS. *I'm* harsh?

WARREN. Yeah.

DENNIS. Why? You should *face* that shit.

WARREN. I face it all the time.

DENNIS. Well why do you have like her childhood *pictures* up all over your room, and like articles about her *murder* in your fuckin' *drawer*, like ten years after the fact? You're gonna let that shit dominate your life? You gotta like, get *on* with it.

WARREN. I am getting on with it. That's why I have her picture up. So I can get on with it. (*Pause*) She's fuckin' lucky she's dead anyway.

DENNIS. She is not. Shut up.

Pause. DENNIS *gets up and goes to his stereo and puts on a record. It is a slow song, e.g., Frank Zappa's 'Anyway the*

Wind Blows' from Cruising with Ruben & the Jets. *He holds out his arms and walks toward* WARREN, *singing along to him loudly.*

WARREN. Get away from me.

DENNIS *keeps coming, looming over* WARREN, *who tries to escape.*

Get away from me, man.

DENNIS *falls on top of him, crushing him with his body, still singing.*

Get *off* me, man!

DENNIS *laughs, screams.* WARREN *struggles to get out from under him.* DENNIS *gives him a loud wet kiss on the cheek and sits back.*

WARREN *pushes him over and sits up.* DENNIS *flops onto his back.*

WARREN *walks around.*

DENNIS. I love Warren, man. He plays with me all day and all night for as long as I want and he never complains.

He sits up, grabs the phone, and dials.

(*Into the phone.*) Stuey. It's me. I'm comin' over: What are you telling me?… Okay, *forget* it.

WARREN. What's up?

DENNIS (*covering the phone*). He'll only sell us an ounce for fifteen hundred if you give him the cash up front. So I'm not doing that. I don't buy retail. But you can, if you want. But I'm not paying this *pork* loin fifteen hundred bucks for an ounce of blow. It's not worth my while.

WARREN. So let's –

DENNIS. *Unless*, we just keep an *eighth* for ourselves, instead of a quarter. That way you still make your eleven hundred and I make my fifteen. We just keep less blow for ourselves. (*Into the phone.*) HOLD ON A SECOND! (*Covers the phone.*) So what do you want to do?

WARREN. I'd go for it.

DENNIS (*into the phone*). All right, I'm comin' over. Get dressed.

He hangs up and starts looking for his sneakers.

WARREN. So should we get some champagne or something?

DENNIS. All right. But I'm not payin' for that either.

WARREN. Nobody's asking you to.

DENNIS. What do you want, like Dom Perignon?

WARREN. There is no other brand.

DENNIS. How many should I get? One bottle? Two?

WARREN. Let's get two.

DENNIS. They're expensive.

WARREN. That's no problem.

DENNIS. All right.

WARREN. So... how much do you need?

DENNIS. Gimme fifteen hundred for the blow and like two hundred for the champagne.

WARREN. The champagne's not gonna cost two hundred dollars.

DENNIS. Just gimme enough to cover it. Or let's just forget the whole thing. I don't wanna do any coke. It's a terrible drug. It's for chumps. It sucks. I'll fuck my girlfriend and go to sleep, and you can go sleep in the park.

Pause. WARREN *goes to the shoe bag and starts counting out the money.* DENNIS *starts putting on his sneakers.*

WARREN. So but... should I come with you, or what's the deal?

DENNIS. No, you gotta let Valerie in. She threw her key down the trash chute.

WARREN. No, man... I don't wanna deal with your girlfriend.

DENNIS. It's all right. We made up. Just stay here. I won't be long.

WARREN. Whatever.

DENNIS *finishes tying his sneakers and looks at him.*

DENNIS. See – this is no good. You're already like freaked out and nervous. Forget it. That girl's gonna smell it the minute she comes in. What is the *matter* with you?

WARREN. What do you mean?

DENNIS. What are you, like, worried about what to *say*? Don't say *any*thing. Just sit there and look handsome, you Greek *god*. She should be worried about *you*. You're a handsome guy. You're like an intelligent fuckin' interesting guy. You don't have to *do* anything. Just don't get freaked out. We're gonna break this stupefying losing streak of yours wide open. Now gimme the money.

WARREN. All right. (*Pointedly.*) This is *seventeen hundred.*

DENNIS (*mocking his grave tone*). 'All right.'

DENNIS *takes the money and shuffles into his coat.*

So just let 'em up and I'll be back in like twenty.

WARREN. Cool.

DENNIS. Be *glad*, man! She's really cute and she's got a great body and maybe you can actually fuck her.

WARREN. I'm gonna give it the old college try.

DENNIS *goes out.* WARREN *locks the door after him. Steps back into the room, alone. He looks at himself in the mirror. He tries to make his appearance more casual, but it's a challenge. He untucks his shirt, musses his hair, etc. He finds the half-smoked joint, lights it, and takes one huge hit.*

He sits there without moving.

The buzzer buzzes. He waits for it to buzz again before getting up to press the intercom button.

Hello?

JESSICA (*on the intercom*). It's Jessica.

WARREN. Okay.

WARREN buzzes her in and moves away from the intercom. He waits. There is a knock on the door. He goes to the door, opens it, and steps back.

You may enter.

Enter JESSICA GOLDMAN. *She is the same age as* WARREN – *around nineteen. She wears effective make-up, big shoes, and a slightly pricey little dress that shows off her figure to good advantage. She is dressed up for the night, not down, and definitely looks a little out of place in* DENNIS*'s grunge palace. She is a fairly cheerful but very nervous girl, whose self-taught method of coping with her nervousness consists of seeking out the nearest available oasis of self-assurance and entrenching herself there with a watchful defensiveness that sweeps away anything that might threaten to dislodge her, including her own chances at happiness and the opportunity of gaining a wider perspective on the world that might eventually make her less nervous to begin with.*

Despite her prickliness, she is basically friendly, definitely interested in WARREN, *and trying to make a good impression.*

JESSICA. Hi, Warren. How are you?

WARREN. I'm okay.

He hesitates, then leans in to kiss her hello, on the cheek. She is not expecting this, so it's a little physically embarrassing.

Um… Where's Valerie?

JESSICA. She went with *Dennis*. We ran into him downstairs, and they said I should just come *up*.

She stands by the door, not sure where to go or what's appropriate.

WARREN. So how you doing, Jessica? You're looking very automated tonight.

JESSICA. What the fuck is *that* supposed to mean?

WARREN. Nothing. It's just a fashion concept.

JESSICA. What?

WARREN. Um – nothing. You wanna come in?

She steps into the room. He closes the door.

JESSICA. So how long do you think they're gonna be?

WARREN. I don't know. Maybe a half-hour?

JESSICA. What? What do you mean? Where do they have to go?

WARREN. Like, the East Fifties.

JESSICA. Well... okay. (*Pause*) I don't mean to be paranoid. I just don't want to be the victim of some teenage matchmaking scheme.

WARREN. Noted.

JESSICA. You know? If I'm gonna get set up, I'm gonna do it myself.

WARREN. Well nobody's setting you up, so why don't you calm down?

JESSICA. Oh you can't see why I would *think* that?

WARREN. I don't know or care what you think, Jessica. I'm just staying here because my *dad* threw me out of the *house*. But go *home*. It's fine with me.

JESSICA (*not an apology*). Okay, *sorry*.

She comes in.

You probably think I'm like a total bitch now, right?

WARREN. I don't think anything. I don't even know what you're *talking* about.

He locks the door.

And now... you're *mine*!

JESSICA. No *way*!

WARREN. I'm kidding! Calm *down*!

JESSICA (*on 'calm'*). That's not funny at *all*!

WARREN. Noted.

JESSICA sits down and takes out her cigarettes and lighter.

JESSICA. Is it okay if I smoke in here?

WARREN. Go ahead. It's not my house.

JESSICA. Well is there an ashtray or something I can use?

WARREN. I'm sure there's one somewhere.

He looks for an ashtray and finds one at the same time she finds an empty soda can.

Here you go.

JESSICA. No, it's okay. I can use this. Thanks, though.

WARREN puts down the ashtray and sits down across the room from her. She smokes.

Long silence.

WARREN. So are you like a really big cigarette smoker?

JESSICA. I guess so.

WARREN. How many cigarettes would you say you smoke in the average day?

JESSICA. I don't know. Like a pack and a half a day, on a really heavy smoking day. Maybe like a half a pack a day if I'm like, in the country.

WARREN.... Yeah... I never really got into the whole cigarette scene myself. But I hear great things about it.

JESSICA. Well, but if you smoke pot all the time, it's much worse on your lungs than cigarettes.

WARREN. I guess my lungs are pretty severely damaged.

JESSICA. I'm sure they are.

Long silence.

So did those guys go to get, um, to get coke?

WARREN. That's the plan.

JESSICA. I don't want to do very much.

WARREN. Well, we're getting like, a *lot*.

JESSICA. I'll do *some...*

WARREN. And we're getting some Dom Perignon to top it off. So it should be pretty good.

JESSICA. Sounds good...

Long silence.

So why'd your dad throw you out of the house? What did you *do*?

WARREN. We just had a slight policy dispute. It's no big deal.

JESSICA. Are you staying here? Where are you gonna sleep?

WARREN. I don't know. It wasn't like a really detailed plan. I was just planning to crash on the floor for a few days till I figure out what I'm doing.

JESSICA. What *are* you gonna do?

WARREN. I don't know. I was thinking I might just buy a bus ticket and head out West. I have a buddy who lives in Seattle, so I might just do that... I definitely wanna get out of *this* – *pit*. That's for sure.

JESSICA. You mean New York? You don't like living here?

WARREN. What's to like? You go outside and it *smells* bad. You know? And I live on Central Park *West*.

JESSICA. Well –

WARREN. I like the *out*doors.

JESSICA. I know, but –

WARREN. Like last winter I went to visit this buddy of mine who lives in Jackson Hole? In Wyoming? And we'd just *ski* every day, you know? And bus tables at night. And when you get up in the morning and open the front door it's like, *silent*. You know? You go outside and it's like, the *mountains*. And *snow*. And nobody around for miles. And like the whole... *sky* over your head. You know? So what the fuck am I doing languishing on *this* trash heap for? The intellectual stimulation? I'm not getting any. All I do is smoke pot. I can do that anywhere. I can just bring that *with* me, you know?

JESSICA. Yeah... I don't really take advantage of the city's facilities either, and it just seems like such a total waste.

WARREN. Yeah. I mean... yeah.

Pause.

JESSICA. But – you're not planning on going to school at all? Didn't you *go* to school somewhere or something?

WARREN. Um, briefly.

JESSICA. So...?

WARREN. I... It just wasn't happening.

JESSICA. Where were you?

WARREN. Ohio.

JESSICA. Where, Oberlin?

WARREN. Whatever. You're at FLT, right?

JESSICA. Yeah. I really like it there. It's a little Jappy for me, but there's a lot of really great people there if you know where to look for them. But it's kind of weird, because I'm living at home – Which is great: like my mom and I get along incredibly well – but a lot of my formerly closest 'friends' are out of the city now, and sometimes I wonder, you know, if I should've... I don't know.

WARREN. So are you heavily into fashion development?

JESSICA. Yeah. I've been doing a lot of designing. I've always done it. It's what I want to do.

WARREN. Well… My basic philosophy about clothes is that they should be comfortable, and not look like too many people had to slave over their creation. But then again, I'm not very fashion-oriented.

JESSICA. Yeah, but, you know, you will be someday.

WARREN. I doubt it.

JESSICA. Yeah, but you will. Your whole personality'll be different.

WARREN. You think?

JESSICA. Sure. What you're like now has nothing to do with what you're gonna *be* like. Like right now you're all like this rich little pot-smoking burnout rebel, but ten years from now you're gonna be like a plastic *surgeon* reminiscing about how wild you used to be…

WARREN. Well, I don't want to make any rash predictions at this point… but I seriously doubt I'm gonna be going in for plastic surgery.

JESSICA. Well, okay, whatever, but you'll definitely be a completely different person. Everything you think will be different, and the way you act, and all your most passionately held beliefs are all gonna be completely different, and it's really depressing.

WARREN. How do you figure?

JESSICA. Because it just basically invalidates whoever you are right *now*. You know what I mean? It just makes your whole self at any given point in your life seem so completely *dismissable*. So it's like, what is the point?

WARREN. I don't really know about that…

JESSICA. Well it's *true*.

WARREN. Maybe so, but I don't really *agree* with it.

JESSICA. Well, I've thought about this a lot.

WARREN. So have I.

JESSICA. I mean look who our *President* is now if you don't believe me.

WARREN. I'm not sure I follow you.

JESSICA. No, like the classic *example* is all those kids from the Sixties who were so righteous about changing the face of civilization, and then the minute they got older they were all like, 'Actually, you know what? Maybe I'll just be a *lawyer*.'

WARREN. I guess that's one interpretation...

JESSICA. But it's totally true! And now like Ronald *Reagan* is President of the United States. I mean, how embarrassing is *that*?

WARREN. It's pretty embarrassing... Although I have to say, I definitely know some people who are still seriously into civic activities. Like my mother does a fair amount of volunteer work for some kind of grape-picking civil-liberties organization in California...

JESSICA. I know people who do that too. But I'm not talking about the last pathetic remnants of Upper West Side Jewish... *liberalism*. I'm talking about the *main*stream, and it is such a *joke*. I mean, I definitely feel that *evil* has like, triumphed in our time.

WARREN. So do I. But I still don't know if I would really ascribe all that to the theory that people's personalities undergo some kind of fundamental *alteration* when they get older.

JESSICA. Well, they do. And it's a big factor.

WARREN. I mean they obviously do to a *degree* –

JESSICA. Yeah!

WARREN. And things definitely happen to alter your general *trajectory* –

JESSICA. Yeah! And no matter –

WARREN (*on 'And'*). But I think that... you basically get a set of characteristics, and then they pretty much just develop in different ways. Like –

JESSICA. But can I just –

WARREN (*on 'can'*). Like the last year of high school,
I suddenly realized that all these weird kids I grew up with
were like well on their way to becoming really weird *adults*.
And it was pretty *scary*, you know? Like you see a crazy kid,
and you realize, he's never gonna grow *out* of it. He's a
fucked-up crazy kid and he's just gonna be a fucked-up crazy
adult with like a ruined life.

Pause.

JESSICA. Are you done now?

WARREN. I'm done with *that* thought.

JESSICA. Well can I please say something?

WARREN. Go ahead.

JESSICA. Thank you: I'm not saying anything about whether
you're quote unquote 'fucked up' or not. I don't mean it as
a *moral* issue –

WARREN. Neither do I.

JESSICA. I just –

WARREN. I think that personality components are like protons
and electrons. Like in science: Every molecule is made
of the same basic components, like the difference between
a hydrogen molecule and a calcium molecule is like *one
proton* or something...

JESSICA. Yeah? That's wrong, but yeah?

WARREN. So my theory is that people's *personalities* are
basically constructed the same way. None of them are
exactly the same, but they're all made of the same thing.

JESSICA. That's interesting.

WARREN. Thank you.

JESSICA. Unfortunately it has nothing to do with what I'm
talking about...

WARREN. That is unfortunate.

JESSICA. I'm not talking about the chemical structure of your *brain*, I'm talking about – It's like, when you find an old *letter* you wrote, that you don't remember writing. And it's got all these thoughts and opinions in it that you don't remember having, and it's written to somebody you don't even remember having ever written a letter *to*.

WARREN. I've never found a letter like that.

JESSICA. Well I have. Like, a lot of them. And it just makes you realize that there's just these huge swaths of time in your life that didn't register at *all*, and that you might just as well have been *dead* during them for all the difference they make to you now.

WARREN. That seems like a fairly nihilistic viewpoint, Jessica.

JESSICA. Well, I am so completely the opposite of nihilistic it's amazing that anyone could even *say* that about me.

WARREN. Well –

JESSICA. But we don't agree. So that's okay. You think what you think, and I think what I think, and there's no way we're ever going to convince each other, so my suggestion is we just drop it.

WARREN. All right.

Silence.

JESSICA. Hey, is there anything to drink in here? I've got this really bad taste in my mouth.

WARREN (*getting up*). I think there's some water.

JESSICA (*starts to get up*). I can get it.

WARREN. That's all right, 'Chivalry is not dead. It just smells funny.'

JESSICA does not know how to respond to this, so she just looks at him. He gives up and goes to the fridge, finds a juice jar full of cold water, pours some in a glass, and brings it to her.

JESSICA. Thanks a lot.

She takes the glass and drinks.

God, I was so thirsty.

WARREN *sits down, this time right next to her on the bed. He is sitting next to her, but not looking at her. It's making them both very nervous.*

JESSICA *gets up and goes to the wall of photographs.*

So who are all these photos of? Are you on this wall?

WARREN. Yeah, I'm represented.

He follows her to the wall. She finds a photo with him in it.

JESSICA. Wow, is this *you*?

WARREN. Yep.

JESSICA. God, what a little *stoner*. You look so different with long hair...

WARREN. Yeah. Everybody definitely went for the traditional post-high-school chop.

JESSICA. Valerie says you just cut your hair when Dennis cut his hair.

WARREN *does not respond.*

Well, you definitely look better with it short.

WARREN. That seems to be the general consensus. But it makes me wanna like *instantly* have long hair.

JESSICA *scans the photographs.*

JESSICA. Wow. What a great picture of Dennis. I mean, he definitely has a slight cleanliness problem, but if he didn't, he'd be seriously gorgeous.

WARREN. You think?

JESSICA. Oh my God, are you *kidding*?

WARREN. I guess.

JESSICA. So his dad's like a really famous painter, right?

WARREN. I guess he's pretty famous.

JESSICA. Wow. So is that like, really hard for Dennis to deal with?

WARREN. I have no idea.

JESSICA. And his father's really sick or something?

WARREN. Uh... He's definitely having some pretty dire prostate problems.

JESSICA. His mom is beautiful...

WARREN. It's an incredibly attractive family.

JESSICA. What does she do?

WARREN. She's like a big-city social-worker administrator of some kind. She's always like installing swimming pools for the poor or something.

JESSICA. What?

WARREN. Nothing. She runs these programs for the city government or something. She designs social-work programs for street kids and drug addicts and stuff like that. But she's a fuckin' psycho.

JESSICA (*bristling*). Why do you say that? Just because she's a social worker?

WARREN. No – because of her *behavior*.

JESSICA. Why? What does she do?

WARREN. I don't know. She's just really *strident*. She's like a bleeding-heart dominatrix with like a *hairdo*. She –

JESSICA. 'Bleeding heart?'   WARREN. I don't know.
                                                          Yeah!

JESSICA. What are you like a big *Republican* or something?

WARREN. Not at all. I'm a total Democrat. I just –

JESSICA. So why do you *say* that about her?

WARREN. Because that's what's she's *like*. But I don't really *care*. Maybe she's really nice. I don't really want to get into an argument about it.

JESSICA. No, it's just – my sister is a social worker, and I really –

WARREN. I didn't say anything *about* your sister.

JESSICA. I know you didn't. I just th–	WARREN. I didn't know you *had* a sister.
I know – but I just think it's like a really good thing to do with your life and I j– Okay, I *know*! I just admire people who dedicate themselves like that, and I –	And I was not attempting to vilify the entire social-worker community!

WARREN. So do *I*. What she *does* is fine. It's just how she *is*. I think it's totally brave to do that kind of work. Unless you're just –

JESSICA. Unless what?

WARREN. Unless you just have no sense of people. No – Like if your *mission* overrides your actual moral *opinion*, but – forget it. It's not – it doesn't matter.

JESSICA. All right. I certainly didn't mean to offend you.

WARREN. I'm not offended.

A moment. JESSICA looks at the stuff in WARREN's open suitcase.

JESSICA. Hey – what's this stuff?

WARREN. Those are just some of my belongings.

JESSICA (*looking through*). What are these?

WARREN. It's just some fuckin' shit.

JESSICA. What are these, like antique toys or something?

WARREN. Um, for the most part…

JESSICA. These are really cool.

WARREN. You think?

JESSICA. Yeah, they remind me of the stuff my cousins had when I was a little kid. I always wanted to play with their toys, and they were like, 'Go play with dolls, you little bitch.' And I was like, 'Fuck *you*!'… I *love* old toys.

WARREN. I have a fair amount of this kind of thing.

JESSICA. Do you know how many toys I had – I mean how much, of the stuff I had when I was little, I wish I had now? Like, I think of some of those toys and I just look back on them with this *longing*… You know?

WARREN. Definitely.

JESSICA (*takes out the Major Matt Masons*). Who are these guys?

WARREN. That's my Major Matt Mason collection. You know Major Matt Mason?

She shakes her head.

Come on, Major Matt Mason, when we were kids – Aw, he's the best! Check him out, he's like, ready for his *mission*. I have a complete set, all in prime condition. I could actually sell them for a lot of money, but I'm hanging onto them.

JESSICA. Really cool.

He shows her his heavy-duty 1950s toaster.

WARREN. And this is my amazing toaster. Toaster Amazing, I call it. Look at this. It's really something.

She looks.

Yeah, GE made only like a few hundred of this model like in the Fifties, and then they recalled them because they were like exploding in people's kitchens at breakfast and burning down their homes. (*Laughs, sobers.*) So only a few hundred actually exist. I got one from this dealer I know in Colorado and he had no idea what he was selling me.

JESSICA. Huh.

WARREN. I have made toast with it, but nothing bad happened
   to me. But I don't really use it too much because it really
   depreciates in value. But it's great to know I have one of the
   only ones in existence.

JESSICA. What's your favorite thing in this collection?

WARREN. Definitely my Wrigley Field Opening Day baseball
   cap my grandfather gave me. No contest.

JESSICA. What's that?

   WARREN *takes out an ancient blue-and-white baseball cap.*

WARREN. This is a real collectors' item, like an *amazing*
   collectors' item, actually. My mom's dad got it the first day
   at Wrigley Field when he was totally like a little kid, in 1914.

   JESSICA *reads what's embroidered on the cap.*

JESSICA, 'Wrigley Field, Home of the Chicago Cubs, Opening
   Day.' (*Reads off the other side.*) 'True Value.'

WARREN. True Value Hardware, all *right*.

   She puts the hat on.

   Looks good, Jessica…

   She smiles. A moment.

JESSICA. I didn't know your family was from Chicago.

WARREN. They're not. Just my grandfather. He was actually
   really cool. When he was a young man, he was like a fairly
   well-known aviator. You know, with like the fur-lined leather
   cap with the earflaps, and the whole bit. He actually set a
   couple of early endurance records in the 1920s…

JESSICA. Wow… I didn't know that…

WARREN. Yeah… he was pretty interesting. (*Laughs.*) Like
   whenever he would meet one of my friends, I'd be like,
   'Grampa, this is my friend Neil.' And my grampa'd be like,
   'Nice to meet you, Neil. Are you Jewish?' And my friend

Neil would be like, 'Um... Yeah?' And my grampa'd be like, 'Neil, in the year 1923 I was the greatest Jewish aviator in this country. That's because I was the *only* Jewish aviator in this country. You wanna see a picture?' And then he would break out his clippings, which had these photos of himself in his fuckin' Sopwith Camel that he carried with him *all the time*. He was pretty amusing.

JESSICA. Is he still alive?

WARREN. Nah, nah...

JESSICA. Where does your mom live?

WARREN. Santa Barbara.

JESSICA. God, so why don't you go stay with her? That's supposed to be pretty nice.

WARREN. I don't particularly want to live in California, for one thing.

JESSICA. Why not?

WARREN. Because of the *people* in it. Plus my mom lives with her boyfriend... And anyway, she's kind of freaked out generally, so it's kind of tough to be around her for very long at one stretch.

JESSICA. Did you... didn't you have a sister that died? Or something?

WARREN. Um...

He hesitates for a long moment.

...Yeah. I did.

JESSICA. So – I mean – is that why you say your mom, your mom is freaked out?

WARREN. I would say it was definitely a prominent factor.

JESSICA. What did your sister die of?

WARREN. Um, she was murdered.

JESSICA. Oh my God, is that true?

WARREN. No, that's just a little joke we have about it in the family.

JESSICA. What?

WARREN. Yeah it's *true*.

JESSICA. I'm sorry: I didn't mean, 'Is that true?' I just meant… You know, 'Oh my God.'

WARREN. Yeah…

JESSICA. How did it happen? Do you mind talking about it…?

WARREN. Not really. Do you want any pot?

He picks up the roach.

JESSICA. No, no thanks. But you go ahead.

WARREN. Um – That's all right.

He puts down the roach.

JESSICA. So what happened? That is so horrible.

WARREN. Um, nothing. She was living with this guy named Julian. And my parents were kind of freaked out that she was living with this guy because she was only nineteen, and he was much older. (*Very long pause.*) It's really not my favorite topic.

JESSICA (*blushing*). I'm sorry!…

WARREN. That's okay…

JESSICA.…I'm, sorry…

WARREN. It's okay…

Long silence. She is very embarrased. He holds out the roach to her.

Do you want any of this?

JESSICA. Okay.

He lights the roach and gives it to her. She takes a hit, doesn't get much, or coughs, but doesn't relight it or try again. Silence.

The Wild City.

She turns and looks at him thoughtfully for a moment.

Are those your records?

WARREN. Um, yeah. These are my authentic first-release Sixties albums, all in perfect condition. Got the whole thing here: Early Mothers, Captain Beefheart, Herman's Hermits, everything. You wanna hear one?

JESSICA. Sure.

He puts on a high-velocity Frank Zappa song, e.g., 'Mystery Roach' from 200 Motels.

All *right!*

She nods and starts dancing.

Wake this dump *up!*

WARREN. All right!

WARREN starts dancing in his own separate space.
He takes a few tentative steps toward her, then she moves
unambiguously to him, and they start dancing more or less
together.

JESSICA. Uh-*huh*, uh-*huh*, uh-*huh* uh-*huh* uh-*huh*.

She opens her arms, and WARREN *steps into them. The*
music abruptly segues into a Zappa-esque confusion of
sound that is impossible to dance to.

WARREN. Um – I don't know. I guess you can't really dance to this next song too well.

JESSICA. Well...

WARREN. Hold on.

He hurries to the stereo and puts on a slow, romantic song,
e.g., 'Lucille Has Messed My Mind Up' from Joe's Garage
Act II.

JESSICA. Oh. Okay. Goes for the slow song. I get it.

WARREN. Of course.

JESSICA. Okay. I'm game.

She starts to take his hands.

Wait. (*Lets go.*) I've got a hair in my mouth.

She extracts the hair from her mouth, shakes it off her finger, and puts her hands back up. They dance, not entirely gracelessly.

WARREN. I'm definitely into actual dancing.

JESSICA. Yeah, I think our generation definitely missed out in the dancing department.

WARREN. Yeah... I guess like, whoever the genius was who decided you didn't need *steps* should have come up with something else instead.

JESSICA. Yeah, right?

He dips her.

Check him *out*. Mr *Dip*.

He brings her back up again.

You could be a really good dancer.

WARREN. Thanks. So could you. (*A joke:*) If only society would give us a chance.

JESSICA. Yeah, man!

They dance.

WARREN. Listen –

JESSICA. Yeah?

WARREN. I just gotta say, I find you incredibly attractive.

JESSICA. Okay – Relax, will you?

WARREN. But listen – would you be mortally offended if I kissed you for just a second?

JESSICA. Well, I mean, what's the rush?

WARREN. No rush. I'd just like to get rid of this knot in my stomach.

JESSICA. Oh – Sure, I mean – whatever's expedient.

WARREN (*moving closer*). No – It's just...

JESSICA (*letting him*). Yeah...?

WARREN kisses her. She kisses back. It quickly turns into heavy teenage-style making-out. JESSICA breaks away.

They're gonna walk in, and I'm gonna be really embarrassed.

WARREN (*a blatant lie*). Yeah – me too.

She takes a few steps away and looks back at him sharply.

JESSICA. They *are* coming back, right?

WARREN. Yeah...!

JESSICA. Okay. Just checking. (*Pause*) But I mean... do you like me, Warren, or what?

WARREN. Of course I do! Can't you tell?

JESSICA. I don't know. Not really. Maybe you just want to mess around or something.

WARREN. Um, I do. *And* I like you. I completely enjoy talking to you...

JESSICA. Well, okay, which would you prefer if you had to choose?

Pause.

WARREN. That would depend on which one we'd already been doing more *of*.

JESSICA. All right. Never mind. Stupid question. I'm sorry. It's just, I'm always getting drawn into these situations and then getting hurt really badly. So...

WARREN. Noted.

JESSICA. You wanna close your eyes for a second?

WARREN. Yes.

He closes his eyes. JESSICA *crosses to him and kisses him, until they are both sprawled inelegantly on* DENNIS*'s horrible mattress, feeling each other up and getting so worked up that* JESSICA *pulls away again, not out of coquetry but just to put on the brakes.*

JESSICA. Okay, gotta take a break.

WARREN. Well... I mean – if you want to, we could go someplace else.

JESSICA. What do you mean? Like, to your house or something?

WARREN. Um – no, my house wouldn't work out too well right now...

JESSICA. Well, we can't go to *my* house.

WARREN. Well, look, why don't we – Why don't we just go rent the penthouse suite at The *Plaza* or something, and like hang out and order room service and like watch the sun come up over the park.

JESSICA. How could we do that?

WARREN. Because I happen to be extremely liquid at the moment.

JESSICA. Are you serious?

WARREN. Yeah...!

JESSICA. Well... what about Dennis and Valerie?

WARREN. I'll leave them a note. Or, we can just tell them where we are, and have them meet us there, or we can just hang out by ourselves... Whatever we feel like doing.

JESSICA. Um – all right.

WARREN. Really?

JESSICA. Sure. I mean… yeah.

WARREN. All right. Let me just get some funding.

He goes to the shoe bag and takes out a couple of bricks of cash.

JESSICA. Oh my *God*. Is that *money* in there?

WARREN. I'm afraid so.

JESSICA. Where did you get that?

WARREN. These are the proceeds from my unhappy childhood.

JESSICA. The what…?

WARREN. I'll tell you about it later. Are you ready?

JESSICA. I'm ready.

She slings her purse over her shoulder. Stops.

Shit! I should've called my mother.

WARREN. What for?

JESSICA. I'm just supposed to call her if I'm gonna be out after 12.30.

WARREN. Doesn't that wake her?

JESSICA. She doesn't care, she goes right back to sleep.

WARREN. Do you want to call her now?

JESSICA. No. She's just gonna freak out 'cause I didn't call earlier. I don't know. I'll just deal with it later… I don't know why the fuck she's always so *worried* about me.

They go out.

ACT TWO

The next day, a little after noon. On the little table is a small laboratory scale, a brown paper bag, an unopened jar of Mannitol, a tablespoon, an upside-down porcelain dinner plate, a nearly unfurled ten-dollar bill, and a straight-edged razor.

DENNIS *is sprawled out asleep on his mattress in a crazy tangle of sheets, wearing only a T-shirt and a pair of boxer shorts. The buzzer buzzes.* DENNIS *stirs but does not wake. The buzzer buzzes again. He sits up, then staggers to the intercom and presses the Talk button.*

DENNIS. What?

WARREN (*on the intercom*). It's Warren.

> DENNIS *buzzes him in, unlocks the door and leaves it ajar, then collapses back onto the bed.* WARREN *comes in looking chipper. He carries a small deli bag with a coffee in it.*

> Hey.

DENNIS. Where've you been? What happened to you?

WARREN. Nothing. I was with Jessica.

DENNIS. You were with her this whole time?

WARREN. Pretty much.

DENNIS. What time is it?

WARREN. Around noon.

> DENNIS *goes into the bathroom, leaving the door open. Over the following, we hear him pee and flush the toilet. He comes out.*

> So… Did you get that Z from Stuey?

DENNIS (*off*). Yeah. It's *great*. Me and Valerie were doing lines with him and *Bergita* for like two and a half hours. Plus he says the heroin he has is like really amazing too.

WARREN. Who's Bergita? The Dutch girl?

DENNIS comes back out.

DENNIS. Yeah. She was pretty cute. I don't understand how that guy gets girls, man. He is like a classically ugly man.

He collapses on the bed again.

WARREN. Where's Valerie?

DENNIS. Oh, *Valerie*. Valerie walked in here and took one look at the shards of her sculpture lying in the garbage and went completely insane. She was screaming at me so loud it literally hurt my *ears*. She was like, 'You're totally selfish, you do whatever you want, you never apologize to anyone, you have no idea how to deal with people, and you're gonna die alone.' Then she burst into tears and fled to her aunt's house in Connecticut. I totally blame you.

WARREN. Sorry about that, man.

DENNIS. I don't give a shit. She's out of her mind.

WARREN. So – is this it?

DENNIS. Yeah.

WARREN picks up a brown paper bag off the table and very carefully takes out of it a double-wrapped ziplock baggy containing an ounce of cocaine.

WARREN. That's a lot of blow.

DENNIS. Yeah. Now put it down before you break it.

WARREN puts down the bag of cocaine.

So what happened with you and that girl?

WARREN. Nothing. I had a nice time.

DENNIS. Did you fuck her?

WARREN. Um... Yeah. I did.

DENNIS. You did? As in actual penetration?

WARREN. Basically.

DENNIS. No – what do you mean 'basically'? Did you or didn't you?

WARREN. No – I did.

DENNIS. So that's amazing.

WARREN. I'm pretty pleased.

DENNIS. *Warren*. Breaks the losing streak.

WARREN. Yeah. I kind of like her. She really likes to argue. But I'm into that.

DENNIS. So where did you go? Her house?

WARREN. No, man, I took her to the fuckin' Vanderbilt Suite at The Plaza Hotel.

DENNIS. No you didn't.

WARREN. Yes I did.

DENNIS. You took her to The *Plaza*?

WARREN. Yeah. I got this really beautiful suite, and we just drank champagne and looked out over the park and made love on the *balcony*. It was pretty intense.

Pause.

DENNIS. You should have gone to The Pierre.

WARREN. Why do you say that?

DENNIS. Because The Plaza is a dump. My old man says it used to be amazing, but now it's totally run-down and rancid and The Pierre is just a much, much better hotel. You gotta stay at The Pierre or The Carlton or like The Carlyle.

WARREN. Well – I never stayed at any of them, but I definitely thought The Plaza was pretty cool.

DENNIS. So were you actually able to do anything with her? Or did you just like come immediately?

WARREN. I came pretty fast.

DENNIS. Naturally. You only did it once?

WARREN. Well… I think she kind of freaked out a little bit afterwards.

DENNIS. What do you mean? What'd she do?

WARREN. Well, she didn't really freak out, but she definitely got pretty quiet. And I was like, 'What's the matter? We just had an amazing time together, and I really like you.' And she was like, 'But I don't even *know* you.' So I was like, 'Well you know me now.' But I don't really know if she agreed with that interpretation.

DENNIS *crosses to the table and starts opening up the bag of cocaine to show* WARREN.

DENNIS. Yeah. Don't worry about that. A lot of times your average girl teen will bug out immediately following a swift and manly conquest. It's no big deal. You didn't do anything to her that she didn't do to you. Just call her up and, you know, take her to the *zoo* or something. Only don't sit here and start getting depressed after you finally got laid with a completely good-looking girl after a *drought* like the fucking Irish *potato* famine of *1848*, because you're bringing me down. You should be totally proud of yourself and not get into your usual self-flagellating stew just because you came too fast and she freaked out afterwards. (*Laughs.*) Now come here and look at the crystal formation on this rock. It's unbelievable.

WARREN *looks*.

WARREN. That's a big rock.

DENNIS. It's a big rock. This baby alone would probably pay for your whole *night* at The Plaza. You know?

WARREN. I doubt it.

DENNIS. Why? How much did you spend?

WARREN. I guess it was around a thousand bills all told, but I didn't really tally it up yet.

DENNIS. You spent a *thousand dollars* on that girl when she was totally ready to fuck you for free?

WARREN. I wasn't so sure, man. She seemed kinda skittish.

DENNIS. So, what, now you're in the hole for twenty-five hundred bucks?

WARREN. Twenty-seven.

DENNIS. What is the *matter* with you? How did you spend that much *money*?

WARREN. I'm not really sure.

DENNIS. Okay: You're outta control. You are like hell bent for destruction and I want nothing more to fuckin' *do* with it! I can't sell twenty-seven hundred dollars worth of blow before tomorrow *morning*.

WARREN. Why not?

DENNIS. Because it's totally *impossible*! I'll make the *calls*, but I can't speed the natural pace of the market. It's just not gonna happen. Besides, your share of the profits only comes to thirteen hundred minus my fuckin' service fee! And even if it *didn't*, I'm not letting you stay here all week with that money, Warren, because when your father finds out you spent that money on drugs, he's gonna think I'm in *cahoots* with you, and then he's gonna forgive you and kill *me*.

WARREN. No he's not.

DENNIS. Yes he is! How could you spend another thousand dollars?!

WARREN. It was surprisingly easy.

DENNIS. All right: That's it. Get on the phone, call Christian, tell him we need distribution help. Tell him you'll give him whatever he wants out of your half and if he can't help us move all twenty grams by tonight you're comin' over there to stay with *him*. Because I am officially closing the Dennis Ziegler Home for Runaway Boys. You understand me?

WARREN. Who am I calling? Christian?

DENNIS. Yeah, Christian!

WARREN. All right…!

As WARREN *picks up the phone,* DENNIS *roams around the room.*

DENNIS. Oh you are so stupid, man. You are so stupid. If your father finds you here, man, he's gonna sic that fuckin' *driver* on me and I am totally gonna have to leave town. And this is such a bad time for me.

WARREN (*holding the phone*). Did you have breakfast yet?

DENNIS. No I didn't have breakfast. I just got up.

WARREN. Let's take a run over to Zabars and pick up a smoked salmon.

DENNIS. DIAL THE PHONE!

WARREN *dials the phone.*

WARREN (*into the phone*). Hello Mr Berkman, is Christian there?… Oh, okay. Could you please tell him that Warren Straub called?… I'm fine, how are you?… Not too much. How's *Mrs* Berkman?

DENNIS. GET OFF THE PHONE!

WARREN (*into the phone*). Anyway – could you just tell him I called, and he can call me at Dennis Ziegler's house?

DENNIS *makes a wild, negative, cut-off gesture.*

Actually, just tell him I'll try him later… Thanks a lot.

He hangs up.

DENNIS. What's the *matter* with you?

WARREN. Nothing. Why don't you calm down?

DENNIS. Oh you are really asking for it. Maybe I can get ahold of Philip.

The phone rings. They look at it fearfully. It keeps ringing.
DENNIS *picks it up tentatively.*

(*Into the phone.*) Yeah?... BECAUSE I DIDN'T *BREAK* YOUR FUCKIN' SCULPTURE, *WARREN* BROKE IT!

He slams the phone down as hard as he possibly can. Runs his raging fingers through his hair.

WARREN *starts to speak.*

DENNIS *grabs the phone and dials furiously. Waits.*

(*Into the phone.*) I just want you to think about what a sick, unhappy person you are that after all the serious problems we've been having for the last three months over your relentless identity crisis – *which has nothing to fuckin' do with me!* – we're finally getting along together like we fuckin' love each other, and you freak out at me *this much* and get me *this angry* at you, because one of my *friends* accidentally broke your semi-lesbian progressive-school clay *sculpture*!... It was on the *shelf* so I could *look* at it! Will you *listen* to yourself! Will you listen to what you're *saying*?... YOU TORTURE ME ABOUT A *SCULPTURE*, YOU PSYCHOTIC MONSTER!? I'D LIKE TO RIP YOUR FUCKIN' HEAD OFF!

He slams the phone down and kicks it as hard as he can across the room.

WARREN. You have a nice touch, man.

DENNIS. Shut up! (*Starts laughing.*) I'm sick, *sick*! All right: Christian's not home and I ain't callin' Philip. What about this shit? Could you sell any of this?

He rattles WARREN'*s open suitcase full of toys.*

WARREN. Um – yeah. I can sell *all* of it.

DENNIS. Really? For how much? Could you get two thousand dollars for what's in here?

WARREN. I don't know. I never really tallied it up, but I'm fairly sure I could get considerably *more* than that.

DENNIS. Oh, we are selling this *today*. I'm calling Adam
  Saulk's brother right now.

He picks up the phone. Stops.

Is that okay?

WARREN. Go ahead.

DENNIS *dials the phone*.

DENNIS. All right. Maybe this'll solve everything. (*Into the
  phone*.) Is that Donald?… Dennis Ziegler, man, what's goin'
  on?… I'm all right. Listen, do you know Warren *Straub*?…
  Yeah. So he's got like a lot of really high-quality toys and
  shit from like the Fifties and Sixties, and about thirty really
  rare first-release albums – (*Covers the phone. To* WARREN,
  who is signalling him.) *What?*

WARREN. I think you should mention the toaster.

DENNIS. No, he doesn't care about your *toaster*, Warren. (*Into
  the phone*.) One second, man.

WARREN. Yes he does. It's really rare.

DENNIS (*covers the phone*). It's worth money?

WARREN. *Yeah.*

DENNIS (*into the phone*). Sorry, man – he's also got this
  incredibly rare toaster from like… *1847*.

WARREN. 1955.

DENNIS (*into the phone*).
  From *1955*. Like a
  completely rare edition of
  toaster. I'm not sure what the   WARREN. Tell him they
  actual model is, but – I said   recalled it.
  I'm not sure what
  the actual *model* is, but I   Tell him they recalled it.
  definitely know it is
  one fine toaster. (*Covers the*   D. Tell him they recalled it.
  phone.) Would you shut up!

WARREN *shuts up*.

DENNIS (*into the phone*). Yeah, man – anyway – he was gonna
sell some of this shit to his regular boy, but I told him I had
a friend who could probably come up with a much better
price, and I wanted to try to give you the business if you were
interested. But the thing is, Donald? Donald? This stuff is like
really good, so I don't wanna waste my time if you're not
totally prepared to step up to the plate. You know what I mean
there, Donald?… Yeah?… All right… No, this afternoon's not
so good for me, man: I'm going to a ball game with my
brother… No, man, Warren's like ready to *go*… Well what are
you doing right now?… All right, gimme your address.
(*Writes down the address*.) All right, man, see you in a few.

He hangs up.

I am a total business *genius*. I don't even know what this shit
is *worth* and I'm already getting you like the best possible
price for it. I am just like completely naturally gifted at
business.

WARREN. Well… There is my usual *guy*, who's definitely
offered me decent money for the whole collection at various
times, so –

DENNIS. No, never mind your usual guy. You should totally let
me handle this transaction for you, Warren, because this guy
is like completely intimidated by me, and I'm just gonna get
you much more money. All right?

WARREN. Whatever.

DENNIS. All right. Now before I go over there, tell me what
would be the best possible money you could *possibly* get for
this shit.

WARREN. I don't know. If you include the records, I guess the
best price you could hope to get would be like, I don't know,
like *maybe* twenty-five at the very outside.

DENNIS. You're seriously telling me this *junk* is worth
twenty-five hundred bucks?

WARREN. Yeah. Because it's a really good collection. But you
probably won't get that.

DENNIS. All right. Now listen to me, Warren. I am not selling
your *baby* toys if you don't tell me it's okay, because I don't
want you *guilting* it over my head for the rest of my life.
Okay? But if you don't want me to, I am totally throwing you
out of here right now. Because I have no desire to incur the
Wrath of Jason, and you can't just walk in here and dump your
situation on me and then obstruct every possible solution
I come up with just because you're a destructive little *freak*
who has to like *wreck* everything so you can get everybody
whipped into a *frenzy* over you all the time. But I don't want
you telling me later that I forced you into selling your precious
belongings, because it's totally up to you. All right?

WARREN. No. Go ahead and sell 'em. I don't know what else
to do.

DENNIS *starts getting dressed.*

DENNIS. All right. If this stuff is worth twenty-five bills then
I probably won't have to sell *all* of it, so tell me which of
these I should try to hang onto and which I should
immediately toss into the gaping maw of Donald Saulk.

WARREN. I guess... save the Major Matt Masons for last...
And if you can, I guess I'd prefer it if you didn't sell the
toaster.

Pause.

DENNIS. I just totally humiliated myself talking up this fuckin'
toaster, now you're telling me I can't *sell* it?

WARREN. Not if you don't have to, no. I don't know how
much he's gonna offer –

DENNIS. All right. I'll try.

WARREN. And give me the hat.

DENNIS *picks up the baseball cap.*

DENNIS. We can't sell this?

WARREN. I don't think so.

DENNIS. Why not? You could get money for this, couldn't you?

WARREN. I know I could, but I'm not selling it.

DENNIS. All right.

> DENNIS *gives* WARREN *the baseball cap and starts packing up the suitcase.*
>
> *The buzzer buzzes.*
>
> It's Jason!

WARREN. It's not Jason!

DENNIS. It's totally Jason! I'm going across the roof!

WARREN. It's not Jason, he doesn't even know I'm here!

DENNIS. He knows who your *friends* are! You think he didn't figure out where you *went*? You only *have* two friends! All *right*!

WARREN. But it's not him, you fuckin' *socio*path: he's throwing a *brunch*!

> *Pause.*

DENNIS. You answer it.

WARREN. No way.

DENNIS. Why not?

WARREN. Because it's not my house, man.

DENNIS. So what?

WARREN. I don't wanna answer it. What if it's him?

DENNIS. All right. Shut *up*.

WARREN. I wasn't talking.

DENNIS. Shut up!

> DENNIS *goes to the intercom and hits the Talk button.*
>
> Yeah?

JESSICA (*on the intercom*). It's Jessica Goldman. Is Warren there?

DENNIS (*to* WARREN). I'm gonna *kill* you, Warren.

WARREN. I didn't know she was coming here.

DENNIS. That scared the shit out of me.

WARREN. Why? Just buzz her in.

DENNIS hits the buzzer and goes to the suitcase.

DENNIS. All right. Saulk's only on Eighty-First, so I won't be long. I'll do my best, and I'll try to save Major Matt Mason if I can. But he might be called upon to make the ultimate Outer Space sacrifice.

WARREN. I understand, man... Farewell, Toaster Amazing.

WARREN unhappily watches DENNIS pack away the last of the collection and zip up the suitcase.

DENNIS. All right. Cheer up, man. Your troubles are almost over.

WARREN. I'm cheerful.

There is a knock on the door. DENNIS is nearest the door and opens it.

JESSICA stands in the doorway.

JESSICA. Hi, Dennis. How are you?

DENNIS. I'm fine, Jessica. How are *you*?

JESSICA. Fine.

DENNIS. Are you from the Leg Embassy?

He is referring to her short skirt.

JESSICA. Yeah, I'm the Ambassador.

DENNIS. Stay with it.

JESSICA comes into the room.

JESSICA (*to* WARREN). Hey. I was just around the corner so I thought I'd buzz up.

WARREN (*bizarrely, to* JESSICA). Good Morgen to all good Norsemen.

JESSICA. Excuse me?

WARREN. How many Norse Horsemen does it take to Smoke a Herring?

DENNIS laughs rudely and loudly at WARREN's awkward attempt at eccentric humor and goes into the bathroom, closing the door behind him. We hear the sink running. WARREN crosses with awkward confidence toward JESSICA.

All Norse Horsemen smoke Morgen Cigarettes.

JESSICA. Am I supposed to know what you're talking about?

WARREN. I'm not talking about anything. It's just something to say. Don't you want to kiss me Good Morgen?

He comes to her to kiss her. It doesn't go too well. She turns her face or ducks her head so he can't kiss her.

JESSICA (*low, referring to* DENNIS *in the bathroom*). Um, can we please not, like...

WARREN. Sorry.

JESSICA. That's okay...

She moves away from him. DENNIS comes out of the bathroom. He sits on the floor to put on his sneakers.

WARREN. So D. How long you think you're gonna be?

DENNIS (*looking at* JESSICA). I don't know. How much time do you need?

WARREN (*confused*). Um... We were gonna get some food...

JESSICA. How much *time* do we need?

DENNIS (*to* WARREN). So who's stoppin' you?

WARREN. I was actually wondering about the *key*.

JESSICA (*to* DENNIS). How much time do we need for *what*?

DENNIS. For whatever dastardly deed you're planning to *indulge* in, Jessica.

JESSICA. I don't think we're gonna be indulging in anything very dastardly, to tell you the truth, Dennis.

WARREN. I thought we were gonna be indulging in some *brunch*.

DENNIS. So *that's* your story, eh? (*À la Snidely Whiplash*.) Yeh heh heh heh…!

JESSICA. What is he *talking* about?

WARREN. Denny, man, you're my *best friend*.

DENNIS (*getting up*). All right, kids, I'm outta here. Try to find some way to entertain yourselves.

JESSICA. Don't leave on my account.

DENNIS. Don't worry about it. (*To* WARREN.) Be back in a half.

DENNIS *exits, with the suitcase*.

JESSICA. Where's he going?

WARREN. He just has a business transaction to perform.

JESSICA. What is he, like the big drug dealer or something?

WARREN. He's the big everything.

JESSICA. Well… Sorry to bust in on you like this –

WARREN. That's okay.

JESSICA. – but I actually just wanted to tell you I can't have brunch.

WARREN. Why not?

JESSICA. Well, when I got home this morning I had this really huge fight with my mom and I think I'd better just be at home today. She kind of freaked out that I never called last night, so now she wants to have some big landmark discussion about how we're gonna handle my living there this year…

WARREN. Well… Thanks for cancelling in person.

JESSICA. Well, I'm sorry, but my mom is really upset and getting along with her is a really big priority for me right now. I tried to call before, but the line was busy.

WARREN. Do you want to make a plan for any time this week?

JESSICA. I think I'd better just chill out a little bit this week, actually.

WARREN. All right.

Silence.

JESSICA. Well… You seem like you're really angry…

WARREN. I'm not.

JESSICA. Well, that's not the impression you're *conveying*, but…

WARREN. No – I guess I just don't understand why you walked ten blocks out of your way so you could be around the corner so you could buzz up and tell me you can't have brunch with me.

JESSICA. Uh, no: I told you I tried to call…

WARREN. Yeah – he was on the phone for like two *minutes*.

JESSICA. All right, I'm *sorry*.

WARREN. There's nothing to be sorry about.

JESSICA. All right.

She goes slowly to the door and puts her hand on the knob.

So… can I ask you something?

WARREN. Go ahead.

JESSICA. Did you tell Dennis what happened last night?

Pause.

WARREN. Um… I guess.

JESSICA. Really. What did you say?

WARREN. Nothing. I said we had a nice time.

JESSICA. That's all?

WARREN. Pretty much.

JESSICA. I find that really hard to believe.

WARREN. Why?

JESSICA. I don't know. Don't you guys get into like comparing *notes* and stuff?

WARREN. I'm not really into that.

JESSICA. Well... okay... It's just – This is getting a little weird now, because when I talked to Valerie, she asked *me* if anything happened with us last night. And for some reason, I guess I didn't really tell her that anything did. So now she's gonna talk to *Dennis*, and I'm gonna look like a total *liar* to someone I'm just starting to be close friends with and who I really care about...

WARREN. Um... So... I don't really get... You're mad at me because you lied to Valerie?

JESSICA. No... I just should have figured that you would like rush off to tell your friends that you *fucked* me –

WARREN. Whoa!

JESSICA. – whereas I might be more inclined to be a little more *discreet* about it till I found out where I stood with you.

WARREN. I didn't fuckin' rush off *any*where!

JESSICA. Yeah, whatever, you know what? It doesn't matter –

WARREN. I came *back* here 'cause I'm *staying* here –

JESSICA. Okay, but you know what? It really doesn't matter –

WARREN. And the minute I walked in he like totally *grilled* me –

JESSICA. Oh so you just tell him whatever he wants to know no matter what the consequences are for somebody else?

WARREN. No! Will you let me finish my –

JESSICA (*on 'let'*). But honestly, Warren? I really don't care who you told, or what you told them, because people are gonna think whatever they think and you know what? There's nothing I can do about it.

WARREN. What people? What are you talking about!

JESSICA. I don't know, but whatever it is I must be wrong because of the way you're *yelling*.

WARREN. You're not anything!

JESSICA. Well, it really – I should just really listen to my instincts, you know? Because your instincts are never wrong. And it was totally against my instinct to come over here last night, and it was definitely against my instinct to *sleep* with you, but I did and it's too late. And now my mom is totally furious at me, I probably ruined my friendship with Valerie, and now like Dennis *Ziegler* thinks I'm like, easy *pickins*, or something –

WARREN. Nobody thinks anything –

JESSICA. And it's not like I even care what he thinks, okay? Because I don't actually *know* him. Or you. Or *Valerie*, for that matter! So it doesn't really matter! I've made new friends before, I can make more new friends now if I have to. So let's just forget the whole thing ever happened, you can chalk one up in your *book*, or whatever –

WARREN. I don't *have* a *book*.

JESSICA. – and I'll just *know* better next time! Hopefully. Okay?

Pause.

WARREN. I don't really get what you're so upset about.

JESSICA. Well: I guess I'm just *insane*.

WARREN. I thought we had a really good time together, and I was actually in a fairly *up* state of mind for once.

JESSICA. I'm sure you were.

WARREN. Well, I didn't mean that in any kind of lascivious way, so I don't know why you want to take it like that. I really like you.

JESSICA. Yeah, whatever.

WARREN. No not whatever! I'm sorry I said anything to Dennis. I definitely caved in to the peer pressure. But I also definitely said as little as possible and was totally respectful of you in the way I talked about you. Even though I was pretty excited about what happened last night, and also about like, maybe like, the prospect of like, I don't know, like, going *out* with you – which I would be very into, if you were. But if you want to think the whole thing meant nothing to me, then go ahead, because that's not the case.

JESSICA. Well… You know, I really –

WARREN. It's totally weird, like taking all your clothes off and having sex with someone you barely know, and then being like, 'What's up *now*?' You know? Like it's such an intense experience, but then nobody knows what to fuckin' say, even though nothing really bad actually happened. You know?

JESSICA. …Well… I don't know…

WARREN. But I really like you… I don't really agree with most of your *opinions*…

JESSICA. Oh, thank you.

WARREN. …but I don't meet a lot of people who can actually make me *think*, you know? And who can hold their own in an interesting discussion. And who I'm totally hot for at the same time. You know? It's a fairly effective combination.

Pause.

JESSICA. I don't know, Warren. Things are just really weird in my life right now. And everything you're saying is really sweet, but I have literally no idea whether you mean it or not. It's like my instinct is just *broken*… And I guess sometimes actions speak louder than words…

WARREN. But what action could I possibly take except to say I'm sorry for whatever it is you think I've done?

JESSICA (*a joke:*). Presents are always nice. Just kidding.

WARREN. You want a present?

JESSICA. I'm just kidding.

WARREN. Why? I'm sitting on twelve thousand *dollars*. I'll buy you a *sports* car. Okay?

JESSICA. That's okay. I don't have a license yet.

WARREN. Well, what do you want?

Pause.

JESSICA....Are you serious?

WARREN. *Name it.*

JESSICA. Okay... (*Pause*) Um... Could I have the hat?

Pause.

WARREN. Definitely.

Pause.

JESSICA. Really?

WARREN. It's yours.

He picks up the baseball cap and holds it out to her.

Here.

Pause. JESSICA *looks at him uncertainly.*

JESSICA....Don't if you don't want to.

WARREN. I really want to.

JESSICA. Why?

WARREN. Because I really like you.

Pause. She reaches out slowly and takes the hat.

JESSICA. Well – I don't know what to say...

WARREN *does not respond.*

I mean – I can't believe it…! I can't believe that you would give me something that means this much to you – I don't even know what to say.

WARREN. Good.

She puts it on her head and self-consciously 'models' it for him.

JESSICA. What do you think?

WARREN….Looks great on you…

JESSICA. You think?

WARREN. Definitely.

She looks at him. He is clearly in distress and can't hide it.

JESSICA. Well, you look totally miserable.

WARREN. I'm not.

She takes off the hat.

JESSICA. Well I'm sorry, but I feel really weird taking your grandfather's hat.

WARREN. Then why'd you fucking ask me for it?

JESSICA *flushes a deep mortified red.*

JESSICA. I was *totally kidding*
when I asked you for   WARREN. No you weren't!
something –

JESSICA. – Yes I was! But then you *insisted* I pick something! Only why did you *give* it me if you don't want me to *have* it?

WARREN. Because I really want you to have it!

JESSICA. But why do you keep *saying* that when you obviously DON'T?

WARREN. NO! God *damn*! What do I have to do, like BEG you to take it from me?

A long moment.

JESSICA. Okay. Sorry.

She puts the hat back on her head. Silence.

Well… I mean… Should I just go home?

WARREN (*looking at the floor*). I don't know… Do whatever.

JESSICA. Well, then I guess I will.

She goes to the door.

Should I assume you no longer want to go out this week?

WARREN. I don't think we can. I'm all out of baseball hats.

JESSICA *takes off the hat.*

JESSICA. Can I please say something?

WARREN. You try to give me that hat back one more time,
I swear to God I'll fuckin' *burn* it…!

Pause. JESSICA *puts the baseball cap down on the table.*

JESSICA. Well… That would be up to you.

She turns and exits. WARREN *sits very still for a minute.
Then he gets up and carefully puts the hat away with his
stuff. He sits at the table and carefully dumps all the cocaine
on the dinner plate and looks at it.*

*He spoons some Mannitol onto the plate, and starts mixing
the two powders together, concentrating intensely.*

*The phone rings. He reaches for it and knocks the entire
plate of cocaine onto the floor. He doesn't know what to do
for a minute. He laughs. The phone keeps ringing. He
answers it.*

WARREN (*into the phone*). Hello?

*He stands up like he just got an electric shock. He listens for
a moment.*

Well, Dad, I guess the jig is up… W– Well I – Could I – I
was planning on *returning* it… Thank you… Well, you're
actually gonna have to wait like an hour… Do whatever you
want, but I won't be here… Why don't you punch me in the

face and throw me out of the apartment?... That is definitely my intention... Uh-huh... I don't know, Dad: What kind of world do *you* think I'm living in?...

Pause. He sits down. More quietly:

Yeah. I think about her all the time... I don't really know, Dad. I just see her in my imagination, I guess... Well, I feel pretty strongly about the fact that I have a lot better judgment than she did at my age, and it's also not too likely that I'm gonna move in with some thirty-five-year-old guy who beats me up all the time. So I don't really think it's an appropriate comparison. Although I will say that it's a totally obvious one. By which I mean I don't think it's all that clever... All right: I know your brunching companions await... Well, it is really hard to fully appreciate what your girlfriend has to go through, but it's really fucking fortunate that she has both the good looks and the intelligence to see her through all the rough spots... Sounds good... Do whatever you want... I hate you too.

His father hangs up. WARREN *hangs up too.*

He looks at the cocaine on the floor. He starts to scrape what he can off the floor and onto the plate. But it's an impossible job. He suddenly stomps on the cocaine, smearing it all over the floor with wild kicks. After a moment of this, he stops.

DENNIS *comes in, very freaked out. He puts down the suitcase, now empty.*

DENNIS. What are you doing? What happened?

WARREN. I knocked the drugs on the floor.

DENNIS. You did *what*?

WARREN. I was trying to mix in the cut.

DENNIS. What? How bad is it?

WARREN. It's pretty bad.

DENNIS. Oh – GOD! Okay – All right – I can't even deal with this right now – Listen to me, Warren. Something terrible has happened.

WARREN. What's the matter? Somebody's dead?

DENNIS. Yeah.

WARREN. Who, my mother?

DENNIS (*furious*). No, not your fuckin' *mother*, you idiot –

WARREN. Okay –

DENNIS. It's *Stuey*.

WARREN. Who?

DENNIS. Stuey! Stuey! It's fuckin' Stuey!

WARREN. Stuey who?

DENNIS. Stuart! The Fat Man. Stuart Grossbart. What's the matter with you?

WARREN. Oh shit. *That* Stuey.

DENNIS. Yeah 'that Stuey!'
How many fuckin' Stueys   WARREN. All right!
do you know?   I couldn't place the name
                                 for a second! What
                                 happened to him?

DENNIS. I don't know, man. I guess he did too many speedballs. He was with that Dutch chick all night, and they went to sleep and when she woke up this morning she couldn't wake him up, so she turned him over and there was blood coming out of his nose and his *eyes*, and he was dead.

WARREN. Whoa.

DENNIS. I mean I just *saw* the guy last *night*. I am so freaked out. I can't even believe it.

WARREN. How did you find out about it?

DENNIS. 'Cause when I got to Donald Saulk's house he was on the phone with Yoffie. So I got on the phone and Yoffie told me he went over to Stuey's this morning and there were all these cops there, and that girl was sitting there freaked out of her mind crying and screaming and like smoking cigarettes and

talking half in English and half in Dutch, and Yoffie told the
cops he was Stuey's friend and they told him what happened.

WARREN. *Stuey.*

DENNIS. I guess it's a good thing we didn't do any speedballs.
You know?

WARREN. But did we buy bad shit, or what?

DENNIS. I don't think so. I was doing it all night and I didn't
wake up with fuckin' blood coming out of *my* nose. Did you?

WARREN. No. But I didn't do any of it yet.

DENNIS. And the *girl* was okay. So I guess he just overdid it.
But I am so freaked out. I mean the guy is *dead*. Do you
know what that *means*? It's like, he's not gonna be *around*
any more, like at *all*. And it's just got me really fuckin'
scared. I mean we are such assholes to be doing all this shit,
man. At some point in the near future, I am totally stopping.
I know he was a big fat slob who totally overdid everything
and all he ever ate was like sirloin drenched in butter and
sour cream, but the guy was like twenty-three years old and
now he's just *gone*. You know? Like he is no more.

WARREN. Yeah.

DENNIS. I don't know, man. I guess there's only a certain
amount of time you can keep doing this shit before shit starts
to happen to you. I mean I am really scared.

WARREN. So did you sell my stuff?

DENNIS. Yeah.

WARREN. Did you have to sell everything?

DENNIS. Oh yeah.

WARREN. How much did you get for it?

DENNIS. I only got nine hundred.

WARREN. What do you mean?!

DENNIS. I mean you had a totally inflated idea of what that shit
was worth, so don't make me feel *bad* about it –

WARREN. I know exactly what it was worth and that guy just *rooked* you.

DENNIS *turns white with rage.*

DENNIS. I am really gonna fuckin' hit you, man! I totally got the best possible deal I could!

WARREN. Then you shouldn't have sold it!

DENNIS. You told me to sell it! At least I didn't knock the fuckin' *coke* on the floor, so don't make me feel *bad* about this, man, all right? I'm freaked out of my mind. So maybe I didn't do so well. I don't know. I'm sorry. It's better than nothing.

WARREN. I guess.

Silence.

DENNIS. What happened to that girl?

WARREN. She left.

DENNIS. You already had a fight with her?

WARREN. I'm not really sure what happened.

DENNIS. How could you mess that up so fast? What kind of talent for misery do you have, man?

WARREN. I don't know. I guess I'm pretty advanced.

DENNIS. Did my girlfriend call back?

WARREN. No.

DENNIS. I think I went too far with her before. But I can't even deal with it right now. I'm too freaked out.

DENNIS *lies down on his back.*

I just can't believe this, man, it's like so completely bizarre. And it's not like I even liked the guy that much, you know? I just *knew* him. You know? But if we had been doing those speedballs last night we could both be *dead* now. Do you understand how *close* that is? I mean… It's *death. Death.* It's so incredibly heavy, it's like so much heavier than like

ninety-five percent of the shit you deal with in the average day
that constitutes your supposed life, and it's like so totally off to
the *side* it's like completely ridiculous. I mean that was *it*. That
was his *life*. Period. The Life of Stuart. A fat Jew from Long
Island with a grotesque accent who sold drugs and ate steak
and did nothing of note like whatsoever. (*Gets up and starts
moving around*.) I don't know, man. I'm like, high on fear.
I feel totally high on fear. I'm like – I don't even know what to
do with myself. I wanna like go to *cooking* school in *Florence*,
or like go into *show* business. I could so totally be a
completely great chef it's like ridiculous. Or like an actor or
like a director. I should totally direct movies, man, I'd be
a genius at it. Like if you take the average person with the
average sensibility or sense of humor or the way they look at
the world and what thoughts they have or what they think, and
you compare it to the way *I* look at shit and the shit I come up
with to say, or just the *slant* I put on shit, there's just like no
comparison at all. I could totally make movies, man, I would
be like one of the greatest movie makers of all time. Plus I am
like so much better at sports than anyone I know except Wally
and those big black basketball players, man, but I totally
played with those guys and completely earned their respect,
and Wally was like, 'Denny, man, you are the only white
friend I have who I can take uptown and hang out with my
friends and not be *embarrassed*.' Because I just go up there
and hang out with them and like get them so much more
stoned than they've ever been in their *life* and like am
completely not intimidated by them at all. You know?

WARREN. Yeah.

DENNIS. I'm high on fear, man. I am completely stoned out of
my mind on fear. And like you guys think I'm like totally
confident and on top of it, but it's not true at all. My fuckin'
mother is so fuckin' harsh and wildly extreme that I just got
trained to snap back twice as hard the minute anybody starts
to fuck with me. That's how I fight with Valerie. Like the
minute we get into an argument whatever she says to me
I just double it and totally get in her face until she backs
down or like has to like, leave the *room*. And it completely

works too, because I don't have to take any of the shit I see
all my male friends taking from their fuckin' girlfriends, or
like the shit my father takes from my mother. I mean all he
does is fuckin' lord it over everybody man, over all my
brothers and sisters and like all his fuckin' assistants and his
dealers and agents and like all these celebrities who buy his
art, because he totally knows that he's like a complete living
genius and so he's like, 'Why should I spend two minutes
talking to anybody I don't *want* to?' Except now he's like
torturing everyone constantly because he basically never
doesn't have to pee, and my mother is freaking out because
she's working fourteen hours a day because they cut the
money out of all her programs and she's totally predicting
major inner-city catastrophe in years to come, and she
completely has his balls in a vice. She's like, 'Eddie, you're
an asshole. Eddie, nobody gives a shit if you have to pee:
You always have to pee, so shut up.' She just *tramples* him,
man. She's like, 'No matter what you do it doesn't matter,
because all you do is sell a bunch of paintings to like, one
percent of the population and I'm out there every day like,
saving children's *lives* and trying to help real people who are
being destroyed by Ronald *Reagan* – So whatever you do
and however famous you are it's just a total tissue of conceit,
because it's got nothing to do with anybody but rich people.'
She just makes total emasculated mincemeat out of him and
the only thing he can do to fight back is go fuck some
twenty-year-old groupie, only now he can't do that anymore
because he's so sick, so he's just totally in her power, and all
he can do is torture her from like a totally weaker position,
and she's like laughing in his face. My family is sick, man,
they're *sick*. You think your fuckin' father is crazy? What if
like everywhere he went total strangers like worshipped him
as a *god*? Wait till his *health* starts to go. Can you imagine
what that's like? Like seriously, what does that *feel* like, to
be looking ahead like five years and not knowing whether
you're still gonna *be* here? You can totally see why people
are religious, man. I mean how much better would it be to
think you're gonna be *some*where, you know? Instead of
absolutely nowhere. Like *gone*, forever. (*Pause*) That is so

fuckin' scary. I am so fuckin' scared right now. (*Pause*)
I gotta call my girlfriend. You have totally fucked me up, by
the way! How emblematic of your personality is it that you
walk into a room for *ten minutes* and break the *exact item*
calculated to wreak the maximum possible amount of havoc,
no matter where you are? You're a total troublemaker,
Warren. I should totally ban you from my house. I am so
keyed up. I can't shut up. I wish Valerie was here. Maybe
I should call that girl Natalie and see if she'll come over and
give me a blowjob. She really likes me, man. She told my
sister I had beautiful eyes. (*Pause*) I do have totally amazing
eyes. They're a completely amazing, unique shape. Like
most people with my kind of eyes aren't shaped like this at
all. My eyes are like totally intense and direct. Like if I look
people in the eye, like nine out of ten people can't even hold
my *gaze*. Did you do any of that coke?

WARREN. Not yet.

DENNIS. I don't even want to look at it, man. I'm so freaked
out. I totally feel like donating it to *charity* or something...
That is so not funny... I wonder if anybody told his family.

WARREN. I'm sure they did.

DENNIS. I wonder if they'll have a funeral.

WARREN. I'm sure they will.

DENNIS. That's gonna be one big casket. I wonder if
anybody'll show up.

WARREN. Why wouldn't they?

DENNIS. Because nobody *liked* the guy! I called like six
people, and I was so freaked out, and nobody cared at all.
They were all like, 'Wow. That's amazing. Is the coke all
right?' Now, I don't know if that means they're all like
totally callous and unfeeling or whether the guy was just a
totally reprehensible human being.

WARREN. Well, he didn't really leave me with any lastingly
warm impression. I mean, I'm sorry he's dead, but I read the
newspaper this morning, too, you know?

DENNIS. Well, all I know is if *I* had a fuckin' funeral, there
wouldn't be room to *sit*. Someday I'm gonna make a movie
about all of us, man. Like if you made that guy Donald Saulk
a character in a movie, with all that shit in his apartment,
how heavy would that be? And most people would like find
some bad fuckin' actor to like do some caricature sitcom
imitation of this guy and totally miss all the intense subtleties
and qualities of his personality, and if it was me I would just
go in there and use the real *guy*, and it would be so much
heavier, and so much funnier. Don't you think?

WARREN. I don't know.

DENNIS. But don't you think I would be like an amazing
director?

WARREN. I have no idea, man.

Pause.

DENNIS. What do you mean you have no idea?

WARREN. I mean I have no idea.

Pause.

DENNIS. Well I totally would be. I would totally –

WARREN. But you've never *done* it.

DENNIS. What do you mean?

WARREN. I mean you don't know anything *about* it. You just
like movies. And have an interest in people's personalities.

DENNIS. No I don't 'just like movies'. I totally –

WARREN (*on the second 'I'*). I like them too. But I don't
necessarily think you'd be a good movie director, because
I have no idea if you have the slightest talent for it
whatsoever. I'm sorry.

DENNIS. You are really pissing me off.

WARREN. I don't really give a shit, man. Why did you sell my
fuckin' toy collection for nine hundred dollars?

DENNIS. Is that what you're mad about? With poor Stuey moldering in the ground?

WARREN. I don't give a fuck about Stuey, and neither do you. I didn't even *know* him.

DENNIS. So call the guy up and get it back and dig your own fuckin' grave, you little asshole! I am totally sick of you and your moronic fuckin' self-imposed *dilemma*! I've been dealing drugs for five years and I never once dropped any of it on the fucking *floor*! Because I am not an *imbecile*! I cannot believe that you do that, and then you have the nerve to give me shit because I undersold your little *toy* box!

Pause.

WARREN. Why do you have to talk to me that way, man?

DENNIS. Why do I talk to you what way?

WARREN. Why do you have to call me an asshole every five seconds? I don't like it.

DENNIS. What do you mean? We call each other shit all the time. Don't start with me, Warren, because all I've been doing for the last two days is like totally try to help you!

WARREN. I know you're doing *something*, man. But I can barely tell if you're even on my side.

DENNIS. What are you *talking* about? I'm on your side, I'm totally on your side.

WARREN. Then why are you always like, reminding me that I haven't done well with girls for a really long time, man?

DENNIS. Because –

WARREN. And like constantly insulting me and like *teasing* me and like telling me how incompetent I am and what a fuck-up I am, like this running motif like *every time* we hang out?

DENNIS. Because you *are* a fuck-up. So am I! So is everyone we *know*. What is the big deal?

WARREN. And how come every time I said I liked a girl you immediately say she's got a fat ass or like has no tits or she's got a horse face or whatever. You know? Jessica Goldman is the first girl I ever had a chance with who was like clearly good-looking enough that you weren't able to make me feel like a second-rate asshole for wanting to go out with her.

DENNIS. You are really making me mad. That's what you're mad about? Because of that time I said that girl Susan had a horse face? That's just the way I talk, man. We all talk that way, it doesn't mean anything. You can't like suddenly turn around and act all fuckin' hurt and sensitive about that shit, that's the way we *are* with each other. Besides, that girl Susan *did* have a horse face, and everybody else could *see* it. I'm just the only one who *says* it. And when you're with a really good-looking girl I fuckin' say *that*. So don't give me this shit from the back *benches* of the fuckin' *peanut* gallery because it's total bullshit, and I am already so *sick* of you after hanging out with you for less than twenty-four hours in a row that I'm like two seconds away from beating the fucking shit out of you, you little fuckin' asshole! (*Pause*) What do you *mean* I'm not on your *side*?

WARREN. I'm sure you love me, man, and you're totally like my personal hero, but I really don't get the feeling that you are.

A moment. DENNIS steps back. His face twists into a strange shape and then he breaks out with a surprising choking sob. He starts crying. This goes on for a moment. WARREN watches him coldly.

What are you crying about?

DENNIS. What do you *think* I'm crying about?!

WARREN. I assume you feel bad about something you think has happened to you.

DENNIS. *No...* It's because you said I was your hero.

WARREN. Oh.

DENNIS *goes to the kitchenette and blows his nose with a paper towel.*

Pause.

DENNIS. So what are you saying? You want to like, stop being friends with me?

WARREN. I don't know, man. I'm not like, breaking *up* with you... I'm not your *girl*friend.

DENNIS. So what are you saying?

WARREN. I don't know.

Silence.

DENNIS. Well... I can't really...

Silence.

WARREN. Let's just drop it.

DENNIS. All right.

Silence.

WARREN. Can I have that money?

DENNIS *gives* WARREN *the nine hundred dollars.*

Well... I'm only eighteen hundred short.

DENNIS. Well – I'll start moving what's left of this shit today and see how much we can scrape up.

WARREN. It doesn't matter.

Silence.

DENNIS. You wanna smoke pot?

WARREN. All right.

DENNIS *goes to his bedside table and takes out a small plastic bag of pot.*

Where did you get that?

DENNIS. I got it from Stuey last night. Christian sold him some. I'd still like to find out where Christian got it. It fuckin' pisses me off that these ragamuffins are like running around copping drugs that I don't know about. I was gonna get some of that heroin from Stuey till it killed him. I hope it's understood in the community that this coke is really good and that Stuey just overdid it.

WARREN. I'm sure it is.

DENNIS *starts rolling a joint.*

It is sort of amazing that one of us actually died. You know? (*Pause*) Like my dad is always saying, 'Do you know how *bad* you guys would have to fuck up before anything really serious ever happened to you? You and all your friends who went to that fuckin' school where they think it's gonna cripple you for *life* if they teach you how to *spell*? (*Pause*) Do you know what happens to other kids who do the kind of shit you guys do? They *die*, man. And the only difference between you and them is my money...' (*Pause*) But the fact is, he's just so freaked out of his mind that he did so well, and it all blew up in his face anyway... Like he did this great enterprising thing for himself and his family, and made a fortune in this incredibly tough racket, and got a house on the park without any help from anyone, and he never felt bad for anyone who couldn't do the same thing. But when he was at the height of his powers, he totally lost control of his own daughter, and she ended up getting beaten to death by some guy from the world next door to us. And there was nothing he could do about it. (*Pause*) So... for the last nine years he's been trying to literally *pound* his life back into shape. But it's not really going too well, because he's totally by himself. (*Pause*) You know?

DENNIS. I guess. (*Pause*) I can't *believe* you don't think I'm on your *side*.

Pause. WARREN *looks at him as if from a very great distance.*

WARREN. All right, all right. You're on my side.

DENNIS *lights up*.

DENNIS. So? What are you gonna do?

WARREN. I don't know, man. I guess I'll just go home.

DENNIS *smokes pot*. WARREN *sits there*.

The lights fade out.

The End.

THE WAVERLY GALLERY

*This play is dedicated to
my grandmother and my mother*

The Waverly Gallery was first produced by the Williamstown
Theatre Festival (Michael Ritchie, Producer) on 11 August
1999. The cast was as follows:

GLADYS GREEN	Eileen Heckart
ELLEN FINE	Maureen Anderman
DANIEL REED	Josh Hamilton
HOWARD FINE	Mark Blum
DON BOWMAN	Anthony Arkin
ALAN GEORGE	Stephen Mendillo
Director	Scott Ellis

The Waverly Gallery was produced by Anita Waxman,
Elizabeth Williams, Randall L. Wreghitt, Peggy Lieber, and
Eric Lieber, in association with Second Stage Theater, at the
Promenade Theater, New York City, on 27 March 2000. The
cast was as follows:

GLADYS GREEN	Eileen Heckart
ELLEN FINE	Maureen Anderman
DANIEL REED	Josh Hamilton
HOWARD FINE	Mark Blum
DON BOWMAN	Anthony Arkin
GLADYS GREEN	Scotty Bloch
(*matinee performances*)	

Director	Scott Ellis
Set Designer	Derek McLane
Costume Designer	Michael Krass
Lighting Designer	Kenneth Posner
Sound Designer	Bruce Ellman
Original Music	Jason Robert Brown
Casting	Amy Christopher
Production Stage Manager	Lloyd Davis, Jr.

The Waverly Gallery was revived at the John Golden Theatre, New York City, on 25 October 2018. It was produced by Scott Rudin, Eli Bush, John Gore Organization, Len Blavatnik, Columbia Live Stage, Stephanie P. McClelland, James L. Nederlander, Universal Theatrical Group, Eric Falkenstein, Suzanne Grant, Benjamin Lowy, Peter May, Al Nocciolino, Tulchin Bartner Productions, Patty Baker, Bob Boyett, Wendy Federman, Barbara H. Freitag, Heni Koenigsberg, David Mirvish, True Love Productions, Roxanne Seeman and Jamie deRoy, Jason Blum, and The Shubert Organization; with executive producers Joey Parnes, Sue Wagner, and John Johnson. The cast was as follows:

GLADYS GREEN	Elaine May
ELLEN FINE	Joan Allen
DANIEL REED	Lucas Hedges
HOWARD FINE	David Cromer
DON BOWMAN	Michael Cera

Director	Lila Neugebauer
Set Designer	David Zinn
Costume Designer	Ann Roth
Lighting Designer	Brian MacDevitt
Sound Designer	Leon Rothenberg
Original Music	Gabriel Kahan
Casting	Caparelliotis Casting
Production Stage Manager	Charles Means

Characters

GLADYS GREEN, *a former lawyer and Greenwich Village*
activist, runs a small art gallery, eighties
ELLEN FINE, *her daughter, a psychiatrist, fifties*
DANIEL REED, *Ellen's son, a speechwriter, twenties*
HOWARD FINE, *Ellen's husband, Daniel's stepfather,*
a psychiatrist, fifties
DON BOWMAN, *a painter and waiter from Lynn,*
Massachusetts, thirties

Place

The play takes place in New York City, in Greenwich Village
and on the Upper West Side of Manhattan.

Time

Between 1989 and 1991.

ACT ONE

Scene One

A tiny gallery in Greenwich Village in the fall of 1989.
GLADYS GREEN *and her grandson* DANIEL REED *sit on
either side of* GLADYS' *desk, eating sandwiches.* GLADYS *is
eighty-five, extremely energetic and very hard of hearing. She
wears a hearing aid that doesn't do her much good. She is an
extraordinarily garrulous, immensely charming and absolutely
relentless talker who covers her deep and secret embarrassment
at her deafness with even more talking. She lives for company
and conversation and perhaps because of her advancing years
demands the full attention of her interlocutors with a cheerful
and unremitting zeal that can be very wearing after a few
minutes.* DANIEL *is a very bright, occasionally shy,
occasionally sarcastic young man with a sense of humor
sometimes described as dry. He is at present giving* GLADYS
his more or less friendly attention.

GLADYS. I never knew anything was the matter. Your mother
never told me anything. And then one day your father calls
me on the phone and says he's coming by to say goodbye and
that he's moving out. And I said, 'I don't understand! What
happened?' But he wouldn't tell me, and neither would your
mother. I called her and I said, 'What is the matter?' But she
just said that your father had left her and that's all I ever knew
about it. We always liked Mark, everybody did, but we felt so
bad for him, you know... His mother was a little kooky, you
know? She was charming as hell, but she never knew what to
do with him. I *liked* her, but she was a nut, she was
meshugge. Do you know what that word means?

DANIEL. Yes, I know what it means.

GLADYS. What?

DANIEL. I SAID I KNOW WHAT IT MEANS.

GLADYS. It means kooky, you know: a little nutty – And you
know your father never had a real father of his own. But
your father and your grandfather, Herb – my husband –
were very close. He put your father through medical school,
you know –

DANIEL. Yes, I know…

GLADYS. And he said to your father that he would pay for his
medical school whether he married Ellen or not. And he also
paid for Mark to be in treatment, you know, with a
psychiatrist –

DANIEL. Yeah, I know.

GLADYS. And Mark loved that doctor, but he died too. And
your poor father just stood there by the window, crying.
I never saw anything like it. He was absolutely heartbroken.
Because you know he never had a father of his own, not
really. But we always liked Mark. He's a hell of a nice guy,
he really is. His mother was witty as hell, but she was a
kook, a nut, she was nutty. She had a little magazine, I think,
that she used to publish. She was a rather good artist too, and
she had a play on Broadway, and she had a very good sense
of humor. Oh, she was very charming. But she just didn't
know what to do with him. And your mother and father, you
know, they were married in that same apartment, in the one,
you know, the one in the back, the one you live in. They
were married there, did you know that?

DANIEL. Yeah, I did.

GLADYS. What, honey?

DANIEL. YES, I KNEW THAT. I KNEW THAT.

GLADYS. We were very happy in that apartment. You know
I built that apartment, when Herb and I – that's Herb, your
grandfather, my husband – when we bought the building
after we came back from Germany. You know we lived in
Germany for two years, before the War, because Herb was
studying in a laboratory there –

DANIEL. I know!

GLADYS. Well it's a beautiful apartment. Are you happy there, sweet?

DANIEL. Yes, very happy. I love it.

GLADYS. You love it. Well, that's wonderful. And have you got it all… fixed up the way you like it, honey?

DANIEL. Yes, I just got it painted!

GLADYS. Oh, I haven't seen what you did with it.

DANIEL. Yes you have. You've seen it since then.

GLADYS. What?

DANIEL. YOU'VE SEEN IT.

GLADYS. No, I don't think so.

DANIEL. You've seen it a few times. You don't remember.

GLADYS. Well, maybe I don't remember. But we were very happy there. Do you have a lot of parties?

DANIEL. Once in a while.

GLADYS. You do. Well that's wonderful.

DANIEL. No, once in a while! Not very often!

GLADYS. Well why not? You should have parties, we had parties all the time. We had a New Year's Eve party every year –

DANIEL. Well I'm not as much of a social b–

GLADYS. What?

DANIEL. I'm not as much of a social butterfly as you are!

She laughs and gives him a friendly slap on the wrist.

GLADYS. Well why not? Are you shy?

DANIEL. Yeah, I'm a little shy!

GLADYS. You're not shy, are you? Ellen is shy. Your mother is very shy –

DANIEL. Well, she gets it from you!

GLADYS (*laughs again*). From *me*? I was never shy, I love to talk to people! I was never shy! I never understood how your mother can be so shy. She's so beautiful, and she's such a good mother, and she's a damn good doctor. Do you know that, honey?

DANIEL. Yes, I know.

GLADYS. Well your grandfather – that's Herb, your grandfather, my husband – was a doctor too, you know. And he and I were very active in politics at that time. I was with the American Labor Party – Do you know what that is, honey?

DANIEL. Yeah, basically.

GLADYS. And Emily Bradshaw said that I should run on the ticket for City Council. Did you know that, honey?

DANIEL. Yes!

GLADYS. What?

DANIEL. I said I knew that! Hold on – (*Leans in to adjust her hearing aid.*)

| GLADYS. No! Don't fiddle with it! You're gonna break it! What? This damn thing is such a nuisance – What? | DANIEL. Just wait a minute… Hold on. Stop talking – Stop talking for a second! (*Adjusts the hearing aid.*) |

DANIEL (*in a normal voice*). Can you hear me?

She doesn't hear. He adjusts the hearing aid again.

(*Softly.*) Can you hear me?

GLADYS. I can hear you, yes.

He sits back down. She starts to touch the hearing aid.

DANIEL. No, don't touch it! If you can hear me, leave it alone.

She obediently puts her hands on the table.

GLADYS. I won't touch it.

DANIEL. Okay.

She laughs and touches his cheek.

GLADYS. So are you working hard, honey? Are you working too hard?

DANIEL. Not really.

GLADYS. Are you still... writing for the newspaper?

DANIEL. No, I don't write for a newspaper.

GLADYS. What?

DANIEL. I don't write for the newspaper.

GLADYS. You don't. What do you do?

DANIEL. I write speeches for the Environmental Protection Agency.

GLADYS. Who reads them?

DANIEL. No – I write for a politician, for the local head of the Environmental Protection Agency. It's a government agency –

GLADYS. And do they get – do you get criticisms, critiques of them, do people see them? Who publishes them?

DANIEL. No, they don't get published, somebody gives them... Somebody –

GLADYS. Do you enjoy your work?

DANIEL. Yes, I do.

GLADYS. Well that's wonderful. That's absolutely marvelous. But if you ever need any money, you know you can always ask me, and you don't have to pay it back, in case you ever need some spare cash, and we don't have to say anything to your mother.

DANIEL. No, that's all right. Thank you, but I'm all right.

GLADYS. Well I'd *enjoy* giving it to you! Everybody needs money.

DANIEL. That's true.

GLADYS. What?

DANIEL. I SAID THAT'S TRUE.

GLADYS. Well sure it's true. We always had plenty of money, my father always had plenty of money, and then my brother Harold. But he was a real bastard, you know? Nobody ever liked him. He just didn't know how to get along with people. But if you were ever in trouble, ever in real trouble, he would always lend you money. That's important…

DANIEL. Sure…!

GLADYS. Sure. Some people just – they don't know how to get along with people. They just don't know how. They're very troubled. Your father was so charming and so bright – you know he's very smart – but he was very troubled at that time. He couldn't help it. And Ellen was just crazy about him. But she never told me anything. I never knew anything.

DANIEL. I know.

DANIEL gets up abruptly and comes downstage, addressing the audience directly. Behind him GLADYS slowly cleans up the sandwiches.

(*To the audience.*) I want to tell you what happened to my grandmother, Gladys Green, near the end of her life. I lived in her building – where I still live – in Greenwich Village, during the last couple of years when she was there. I live in the back apartment. She was in the front, just down the hall. My grandfather – Herb, her husband – died before I was born, and after that she lived with a man named Ronald, but then he died too, and after that she was by herself. For twenty-eight years she ran a tiny gallery on Waverly Place, around the corner from where we lived. And without being too depressing about it, she didn't always have the best stuff in there. But some of it was pretty good. Most days you could see her in there, watching television or looking out the window. I used to drop by once in a while, but usually if I was walking past the gallery, I'd just duck down behind the cars across the street so she wouldn't see me go by. Until her eyesight got really bad. Then you could just walk right past the window. It's not that I didn't like her. I did. It's just that once you went in there, it was kind of tough getting out again. So I was pretty stingy with the visits.

The last person to have a show there was named Don Bowman, from Massachusetts. He came to the city with an expensive car and no money. He took his pictures into every gallery he could find, until he found my grandmother in the Waverly Gallery off Washington Square.

DANIEL *exits*.

Scene Two

In the little gallery, GLADYS *is looking at* DON BOWMAN*'s portfolio.* DON *is in his mid-thirties, and speaks with a working-class Boston-area accent. He is a little peculiar – and always slightly out of step with those around him, a careful, hardworking and detail-fixated person who devotes a lot of his mental energy to very slowly and carefully arriving at the wrong conclusion.*

GLADYS. You know, these are very good. You're a very good artist.

DON. Yeah, that's my sister. That's her actual wheelchair... and that's her in her bedroom. You can't see it, but –

GLADYS. These are absolutely marvelous.

DON. – behind the bureau there's a ramp for her wheelchair, but the bureau interferes with the angle. That's her cat.

GLADYS. And are you – you know, are you showing them around in the art galleries?

DON. That's my mother...

GLADYS. Another gallery?

DON (*not loud enough*). No, that's my *mother*.

GLADYS *doesn't hear him.*

GLADYS. Uh-huh. Well, this show here has been up for a long time – the paintings are by a very talented artist whom I have known for many years. He lives in Europe now with a man – with his partner. And I told him when he left that I can't keep the pictures up for more than a few weeks, and he said, 'That's okay, keep 'em up as long as you want!' (*Laughs*.) But I'm in a jam! Because I don't know what to do with them. I need someone to take them down. I can't do it myself.

DON. Well –

GLADYS. Are you over at – over at the school?

DON (*laughs*). No, no, I'm not at –

GLADYS. Well what's the matter? Don't you think it's a good school?

DON. No, I –

GLADYS. Are you a New Yorker?

DON. No, I'm from New England.

GLADYS. From New England, well it's very pretty up there. My daughter went to medical school in Boston. She lives up by the park –

DON. Yeah, I'm from just outside of Boston. My mother still lives there. I don't really know anybody in New York. My sister lives in New Jersey –

GLADYS. And my grandson is a – he's – you know, he writes – articles – for the newspaper. You should show him some of your pictures, maybe he'll – you know, maybe he'll write 'em up for you.

DON. What paper does he write for?

She doesn't hear.

What paper does he write for?

She doesn't hear.

Does he –

GLADYS. Would you like to put some of your – your pictures up in here? We can put up a few and see what happens.

DON. Oh – Yes…! Of course! That would be wonderful.

GLADYS. It's not a big place, but it's cute. You know? A lot of students come in here. They look around, and we talk, and a lot of them want to show me their work. There are a lot of good artists around, but they don't have anyone to help them. It's not a fancy place, but it's all right.

DON. No, I really like it. It has a lot of character.

GLADYS. I used to have a lot of shows in here, but I have a bad – foot, and I can't walk so well, so I don't come in as much as I used to. I've been on this corner for quite a few years now. I live right around the corner, and my grandson has the apartment in the back. I live in the front.

DON. Uh-huh…

GLADYS. I just walk over from my apartment, and I bring a little – sandwich. I have a little – television, that I like to watch sometimes. Something's wrong with it so I don't watch it anymore. But I come in and I read the paper, and I always keep that door locked, because you never know who the hell is going to come in these days. This whole neighborhood is changing. This one's sellin' drugs, and that one's tryin' to – get your money – and that one's boppin' people on the head. They have all kinds of signals, they have red hats and blue hats, and you can't tell one from the other, and there are a lot of people now from *South Korea*. They're very well dressed, they've got a lot of money, but that government they have doesn't let them – They don't want to live *there*. They want to come *here*. And the man who runs the hotel likes to have the gallery in the building because people stop by and look in. But he's redoing the whole place –

DON. Yeah, I saw the hotel was under construc–

GLADYS. Now if you want to put two or three pictures up, you'll have to hang them yourself –

DON. That's no problem –

GLADYS. And if you sell anything, the gallery takes fifty percent of the – of the sale. That's half and half. Now, I don't know what kind of prices you want to charge –

DON. All right. Now if I could –

GLADYS. What?

DON (*louder*). I was just wondering if I could store the rest of the stuff somewhere around here –

GLADYS. Well sure, you can keep them in the back –

DON. – because I been drivin' back and forth to New Jersey and I don't like to have the pictures rattlin' around in the car every day. I work as a waiter up in Lynn, in Massachusetts, and my plan was to come down here and stay with my sister, but she's in a wheelchair, and her house is pretty small, and I didn't realize it's almost a two-hour drive each way, so –

GLADYS. Don't you have an apartment?

DON. No, I –

GLADYS. Well you can't sleep on the street!

DON. Well, last night I was too tired to drive all the way back, so I did actually sleep in the car, but –

GLADYS. In the car!

DON. Well the front seat reclines all the way back, so it wasn't really too bad –

GLADYS. Well I'll tell you what. You can buy yourself a little… cot. And I have a room in the back here, where I keep the pictures. Why don't you get yourself a little – you know, a little fold-out cot, and you can stay in the back there until you get yourself settled in. I only use the place in the day – I live right around the corner – Here, would you like to see it?

DON. Well… um…

GLADYS. I don't know if you'll be very comfortable – but it's better than sleeping on the street! Somebody's liable to come along and bop you on the head! This whole neighborhood is changing. There's always some racket outside. They're always setting things off or blowing somethin' up… This used to be a beautiful neighborhood. Now you don't know which one is on drugs and which one is *crazy*…

DON *follows her as she makes her slow way toward the back.*

DON. Well – if I could really – I mean, if you don't mind, that would be incredibly convenient –

GLADYS. Well why should I mind? I like helping young people. All they want is a little chance. But they don't have anyone to help them.

DON. I mean, eventually it would be great to have a whole show here…

GLADYS *stops walking so she can talk some more.*

GLADYS. I don't come in very often. I never ran this place to make money. I'm a lawyer for many years, but I don't practice anymore. It just gives me something to do, you know? And I enjoy it. I really do. I've had some rather good artists in here… But if you want, we can take down all these pictures, because the artist is in – in Europe. I'm very angry at him because he left for Europe and he left me all these pictures! I don't know what to do with them. You have to change the show after a while because people walk by and they want to see something new. Do you have enough pictures to put up in here?

DON. Oh I've got more pictures than you want…

She doesn't hear. Pause.

I say, I've probably got more pictures than you want.

GLADYS. Well why shouldn't I want them? I think they show a lot of talent. You're a very talented artist.

DON. Thank you…!

Scene Three

DANIEL *enters as the lights crossfade from the gallery to*
ELLEN *and* HOWARD's *kitchen across the stage. As* DON
exits the gallery, ELLEN *and* HOWARD FINE *enter and sit at
the kitchen table.* ELLEN *is an Upper West Side psychiatrist
and mother, shy with strangers, devoted to her family, but easily
frazzled – especially by her mother, and particularly when she
is frightened.* HOWARD *is a genial, loving, generous man, also
a psychiatrist, who prides himself on being straightforward and
practical – occasionally to the point of insensitivity.*

(*NOTE: When the family speaks to* GLADYS *they must always
speak very loudly and clearly to be heard – but not too loud or
her hearing aid whistles. Unless you are right next to her, she
cannot really hear a normal tone of voice, even when the
hearing aid is functioning properly.*)

GLADYS. Hello, honey. (*Grabs* DANIEL's *face and kisses it.*)
   How are you, honey? All right?

DANIEL. Yes, I'm fine thanks.

GLADYS. What?

DANIEL. I said I'm fine!

GLADYS. Good. I'm glad.

DANIEL. Why don't you come in and have some dinner!

GLADYS. What?

DANIEL. I said come eat dinner!

   DANIEL *and* GLADYS *cross toward* ELLEN *and*
   HOWARD, *who are at the table, mid-meal.*

GLADYS. All right, honey, what are we having?

DANIEL. I'm not sure. I think we're having meat loaf!

GLADYS. We're not having chicken, are we?

DANIEL. No – we're having meat loaf.

GLADYS. I've had chicken three times already this week.

DANIEL (*louder*). We're not having chicken! We're having MEAT LOAF. MEAT LOAF.

GLADYS (*still not hearing*). Well, that's all right. Your mother is a wonderful cook.

DANIEL *sits* GLADYS *at one end of the table, then sits between her and* ELLEN. HOWARD *is at the other end.*

That whole neighborhood is changing. (*To* DANIEL.) Honey? Do you think the Village has changed much in the last five years?

DANIEL. Yes! It's been changing for a lot longer than that!

GLADYS. The whole place is changing. And there are a lot of people now from South Korea.

ELLEN. What is this South *Korea* thing?

GLADYS. They're everywhere you look! They're very well dressed, and they have a lot of money. They come in the gallery all the time. The whole neighborhood is changing.

DANIEL. I guess a lot of the NYU students are Asian but I don't really know...

DANIEL. Sure!

GLADYS. That bank around the corner used to be a very friendly bank. I knew the manager for many years, and it was always a very friendly place. Now, the whole place is black. The whole bank. It's all – *black*. And we *wanted* that. We fought for that, for many years. But you go in there and they won't talk to you. I went in and stood there for half an hour and nobody would even talk to me. And there are so many *people* now. That whole neighborhood is changing. Don't you think so, honey?

DANIEL. Yes!

HOWARD (*to* GLADYS, *shouting, very loud*). YES IT'S TOO BAD! IT WAS ONCE A LOVELY NEIGHBORHOOD.

ELLEN. Don't shout please…

GLADYS. Oh it was a beautiful neighborhood. We were very happy there. Do you have a lot of friends up in – in the country – up – up in – where you go?

ELLEN. Vermont.

GLADYS. What?

ELLEN. We go to Vermont.

GLADYS. And you have a lot of friends there?

ELLEN. No. Not many. A few.

GLADYS. But the people up there know you? And they come around? Do you entertain much up there?

HOWARD. NO WE DON'T LIKE TO HAVE TOO MANY PEOPLE UP THERE, GLADYS!

ELLEN. Howard don't *shout*, it makes it *worse*.

GLADYS. I didn't hear.

DANIEL. He said –

HOWARD (*barely lower*). I SAID, WE GO THERE BECAUSE WE WANT TO GET *AWAY* FROM PEOPLE.

GLADYS. Oh, he's teasing.

HOWARD. NO, WE'RE VERY UNFRIENDLY. WE DON'T LIKE TO SEE TOO MANY PEOPLE.

GLADYS (*to* DANIEL). He's teasing you.

HOWARD. WHEN YOU HAD – LISTEN: WHEN YOU HAD THE HOUSE ON FIRE ISLAND ALL THOSE YEARS, YOU LIKED TO ENTERTAIN ALL THE TIME –

GLADYS. Well sure, everybody likes to have parties –

HOWARD. BUT WE DON'T ENJOY THAT THE WAY YOU DID! WE LOVE THE COUNTRY AND WE LIKE THE SCENERY, BUT WE DON'T LIKE HAVING A LOT OF PEOPLE UP THERE BECAUSE WE SEE TOO MANY PEOPLE HERE IN THE CITY.

GLADYS. Well sure, everybody likes to see people – We used to have people all the time when we went to Fire Island.

HOWARD. RIGHT!

GLADYS. We had a beautiful house there and we entertained quite a lot.

HOWARD. RIGHT! WE DON'T LIKE THAT!

GLADYS. Well it's a beautiful place. (*To* DANIEL.) Honey, do you want some of these – potatoes?

DANIEL (*very loud*). NO THANK YOU.

ELLEN. Danny, you don't have to shout – There she goes.

GLADYS *is fiddling with her hearing aid.*

Don't touch your hearing aid –

GLADYS. It's whistling –

ELLEN (*getting up*). Just a minute – Don't touch it – (*Comes around and adjusts the hearing aid.*)

ELLEN. Don't hold it with your – all you have to do is – All you have to do is touch it with your finger – Don't grab the knob – Howard, it's too *small* for her, she can't get her finger on it – J–

GLADYS. There's a terrible whistling. Can you hear that? Does anybody hear that whistling?

HOWARD. Honey, why don't you do it *for* her?

ELLEN *patiently adjusts the hearing aid.*

GLADYS (*laughs nervously*). What a crazy business!

HOWARD. Daniel, pass me the potatoes.

DANIEL *passes the potatoes.*

ELLEN (*in a normal voice*). Can you hear me?

HOWARD (*takes potatoes*). Thank you.

ELLEN *readjusts the hearing aid.*

ELLEN (*in a normal voice*). Can you hear me?

GLADYS. Yes. Perfect. (*Immediately starts to touch the hearing aid.*)

ELLEN. No don't touch it anymore – !   DANIEL. Leave it alone if you can hear!

GLADYS. Up! I won't go near it!

They resume eating.

You know, Ellen, that one in the gallery, that young artist, has got a sister somewhere who's in a wheelchair, and a mother in – you know, where you go – in the country –

HOWARD. NO, GLADYS, WE GO TO VERMONT! HE'S FROM MASSACHUSETTS!

ELLEN. Howard, don't *shout* at her!   DANIEL. You don't have to shout!

GLADYS. Oh, he's from Massachusetts? I didn't know that.

ELLEN. Yes you did. But you forgot.

GLADYS. What?

HOWARD. SOMETIMES YOUR MEMORY ISN'T SO GOOD.

GLADYS (*hearing but ignoring this comment*). Ellen, this dinner is absolutely delicious.

ELLEN. Thank you.

GLADYS. Absolutely marvelous. (*Pushing a dish of broccoli.*) Does anybody want any of this? Honey? Do you want any of this – vegetable? It's very good.

DANIEL. No, I've got some of my own right here, thanks!

GLADYS. Do you want some:

DANIEL. NO I HAVE SOME. THANK YOU!

GLADYS *offers* DANIEL *some soda.*

GLADYS. Would you like some of this drink?

DANIEL. NO THANKS!

ELLEN. Volume.

DANIEL. Sorry. Sorry.

GLADYS. It has a very good – flavor. Go ahead and try some. I can't drink all of this.

DANIEL. No thank you.

ELLEN (*under her breath*). 'Can you cook?'

GLADYS. This dinner is absolutely delicious.

ELLEN. No one could accuse her of being unappreciative.

HOWARD (*to* DANIEL). Are you still seeing that same horrible girl?

GLADYS. Do you know how to cook, honey?

DANIEL (*to* HOWARD). Um – I don't really know. I –

GLADYS (*to* DANIEL). Did you ever learn to cook?

DANIEL. A little bit!

GLADYS *cheers and claps her hands.*

GLADYS. You do? Well good for you! Are you a good cook?

HOWARD (*to* DANIEL). Is that not a suitable subject for conversation?

DANIEL (*to* HOWARD). Um – (*Turns to* GLADYS.) I can only cook a little bit! I can't *really* cook –

GLADYS. Well who taught you how?

DANIEL. I taught myself!

HOWARD. Dan? Is that not a suitable subject for conversation?

GLADYS. And do you ever have friends over and – you know – cook 'em up something to eat?

DANIEL (*to* HOWARD). No, it doesn't matter. I don't care. She's driving me crazy, that's all.

GLADYS. What's the matter, honey?

DANIEL. Nothing!

HOWARD. Why do you go out with all these crazy girls?

DANIEL. I don't know.

GLADYS. I never learned how to cook. I never used to cook anything.

HOWARD. Well as you know, I hate to butt in, but there are several perfectly nice young ladies at the Institute I'd be happy to fix you up with if you're interested?

GLADYS. We had a woman who used to come in and cook for us... Ellen, do you remember Fanny?... Ellen? Do you remember Fanny?

DANIEL. I don't know – I don't really want to –

ELLEN (*quiet*). Yes.

HOWARD. Well, it's just a suggestion... It's too bad you're shy about that sort of thing.

GLADYS. You don't remember her.
ELLEN. Of course I remember her.

DANIEL. Yeah, well... I... I just... I don't know I'm not really –

GLADYS. She was a marvelous cook. She used to cook everything. I never learned how. I never liked to cook.

HOWARD. It's fine, sweetheart. Just let me know if you're interested.

ELLEN. Interested in what?

HOWARD. I offered to fix him up with one of the young single women at the Institute.

GLADYS. Ellen, I want to bring – that young artist, the one who's having a show – the – the one –

ELLEN. Oh...!

DANIEL. Don!

HOWARD. There's a very nice young lady in my program who mentioned to

GLADYS. Don. Should I ask him to come up here next week?

me that she'd like to meet somebody, and I –

Ellen? You know what I think I'll do?

Ellen? You know what I think I'll do?

ELLEN. Howard – I can't listen to six different people talking to me at the same time – !

HOWARD (*to* ELLEN). Sorry.

GLADYS....I'm gonna bring that young artist up with me next week so you can meet him.

ELLEN. Please don't! I don't need anybody new to cook for!

GLADYS. What:

ELLEN. DON'T bring him up next week, I don't want to cook DINNER for everybody! We'll meet him on Saturday. DON'T invite him for dinner!

GLADYS. Don't invite him. Well, that's fine. I don't need to invite him, I don't need to invite anybody. I thought you might want to meet him. He's a very interesting guy.

ELLEN. We will meet him on Saturday.

GLADYS. What?

ELLEN. We will meet him on SATURDAY.

GLADYS. He's from the same place, you know, where you go up – on the weekend –

ELLEN. She's getting worse.

DANIEL. Oh, she's definitely getting worse, Mom.

GLADYS. What's the matter, honey?

DANIEL. Nothing! Everything's fine! Do you want some more?

GLADYS. Oh! No! I couldn't eat another thing.

ELLEN. 'You got any coffee lying around?'

GLADYS. Ellen, is there any coffee lying around?

ELLEN. Not yet! I'm just about to make some!

GLADYS. Does anybody else want any? Honey, do you like coffee?

DANIEL. Yes I do.

GLADYS. Are you a coffee lover?

DANIEL. Yes I am. I'm a coffee lover.

GLADYS. Where's the dog?

ELLEN. I'm going to blow my brains out.

DANIEL. The dog is in the other room!

GLADYS. What's the matter? Is she hiding?

DANIEL. She's waiting for food.

GLADYS. What's the matter? Didn't anybody feed her?

ELLEN. No, we're going to let her starve!

HOWARD. Honey, please before we all go insane.

GLADYS. Shouldn't somebody give her something?

ELLEN. DON'T GIVE HER ANYTHING, SHE'S NOT SUPPOSED TO BEG!

GLADYS. Ohhhhhh, the poor thing, she must be hungry.

ELLEN. Please don't feed her   DANIEL. She's fine! She was
  anything! She's not   just fed! She just ate a little
  supposed to beg!   while ago!

GLADYS. That dog is just the sweetest little animal. Do you take her up with you when you go away to – when you go up to –

DANIEL, HOWARD *and* ELLEN. Vermont!

GLADYS. Is that where it is?

DANIEL (*getting up*). I have to take a break.

GLADYS. Where you going, hon?

DANIEL. In the living room!

GLADYS. What?

DANIEL (*learns in, speaks softly*). In the living room.

GLADYS. Does anybody want any coffee?

ELLEN. I'm just *making* it! Give me five minutes to make it…!

DANIEL. I'll make it.

ELLEN *walks out*.

GLADYS. What's the matter? What's wrong with Ellen?

DANIEL. Nothing!

HOWARD. She's just tired!

DANIEL *laughs*.

GLADYS. Ohhhhhhhh, poor Ellen. Is she working too hard?
I think she works too hard. Your mother works harder than
anyone I know. She's always working.

HOWARD. Gladys, millions of people work very hard, every
day, all day long!

DANIEL. What are you trying to do, improve her character?

HOWARD (*shrugs*). Sure!

GLADYS. You got any coffee lyin' around?

DANIEL. I'm just about to make it! (*Goes around the corner to
make coffee*.)

GLADYS. You know, I told that young artist that he should get
himself… should get himself a little – cot, and put it in the
back room –

ELLEN (*off*). Howard, will you *say* something to her about
that?

HOWARD. Honey, what do	GLADYS. – so he won't have
you want me to say?	to drive all that way every
	day. He doesn't know a

ELLEN (*off*). Tell her she can't let him *do* that until we at least *meet* him – soul in the city, and I said, 'Well you can't stay with *me*, there's no room in that apartment – '

What's the matter?

HOWARD. Why don't *you* tell her?

ELLEN (*off*). Because I've told her five times already –

DANIEL *reappears, eating ice cream out of the carton.*

GLADYS. What's the matter, honey?

DANIEL. Nothing!

GLADYS. This young artist is about the same age as you are – and I think he's very talented. He works like hell on those pictures and he has a very charming personality.

HOWARD. LISTEN: WE WANT TO MEET HIM BEFORE YOU LET HIM MOVE IN THE BACK OF THE GALLERY.

GLADYS. Well you *will* meet him. What's the matter?

HOWARD. BECAUSE, GLADYS –

GLADYS. His mother doesn't live in the city. And I don't think she wants him to be here. I think she's a real nutcase.

HOWARD. Gladys –

GLADYS. I think she's kooky.

HOWARD. – GLADYS – LISTEN TO ME.

GLADYS. Yes.

HOWARD. WE DON'T WANT YOU TO AGREE –

ELLEN (*off*). Don't *shout*!

HOWARD. Honey, I can't *help* it!

ELLEN (*off*). It's too *loud* for her, Howard!

HOWARD (*slightly lower*). Gladys, don't tell him he can stay there until we meet him and make sure everything's all right!

GLADYS. I already told him if he wants –

HOWARD. No, Gladys! Listen to me! I'm sure he's very nice, but it's not appropriate to have him stay there until we make sure there's nothing peculiar about him.

GLADYS. Well why should he have to lug that car around when nobody's in that room all day long –

HOWARD (*on 'nobody's'*). It's not appropriate to have a stranger sleeping in the back of the gallery if you don't know anything about him.

GLADYS. But he's not living with *me*. I don't want that, I'm not lookin' for that anymore…!

HOWARD. I understand that. And I'm also sure he's perfectly harmless. But until we meet him, you still have to tell him he's going to have to make some other arrangement.

ELLEN (*off*). How is she going to do that? She can't even remember his *name*.

HOWARD. Then *you* tell her,	GLADYS. What's the matter?
because I –	What's wrong?
(*To* GLADYS.) Nothing!	
Just do what you're told.	
You know how to do that.	

GLADYS. I always do what I'm told!

HOWARD. Right! Except when you don't want to!

GLADYS. Well what's wrong with that?

Everyone laughs.

HOWARD. Just wait until we meet him! And don't argue!

GLADYS. All right, who's arguing?

DANIEL (*eating ice cream*). Mom, do you want any ice cream?

ELLEN (*off*). No thank you.

DANIEL. Well, I'm going to finish it…

ELLEN (*off*). Be my guest.

GLADYS *hums to herself because no one is talking to her.*

HOWARD. Is this girl you're seeing also involved in politics?

DANIEL. I'm not actually seeing her, she can't make up her mind whether or not I'm seeing her...

HOWARD. Is she involved in politics?

DANIEL. No, she's involved in torture. She comes over and she tortures me and then she goes away and looks around for somebody to torture her – which she actually seems to prefer – but she has extremely high standards, so if she can't find anyone sufficiently diabolical, she comes back and tortures me some more.

HOWARD. Jesus Christ. She sounds delightful.

DANIEL. Oh, she's great.

ELLEN *enters and goes over to* GLADYS.

ELLEN (*softly*). Why don't you go sit in the living room and I'll bring you some coffee?

GLADYS. Ellen? Can I do something in here? Do you want me to do the dishes?

ELLEN. No thanks. There's nothing to do.

GLADYS *hums to herself again under the following:*

DANIEL. Anyway, it doesn't matter because she's going to Turkey next week anyway.

ELLEN. Turkey! What's she doing in Turkey?

DANIEL. I don't know. Traveling around. Lecturing at a torture symposium, I don't know.

ELLEN. Well, maybe she'll   HOWARD. Good! Maybe
stay there!   she'll emigrate!

GLADYS. Ellen, can I help clean off the table?

ELLEN. No thank you. It's almost done. (*Goes around the corner.*)

HOWARD. Is this girl in analysis?

DANIEL. Yes. Unfortunately her analyst recently committed suicide.

HOWARD. He did? No...

DANIEL. Yes. That's the third psychoanalyst who's tried to treat her and ended up killing himself: She's cutting a swath of terror through the New York Psychoanalytic Institute. I'm surprised you guys haven't seen anything about it in the *Psychoanalytic Quarterly*.

HOWARD (*laughing*). Come on...!

DANIEL (*laughing*). It's true – They say she has no superego. They're dropping like flies.

They laugh. GLADYS *smiles.*

GLADYS. What's he laughing at, honey? What's he laughing at? What's everybody laughing at?

DANIEL. Nothing, nothing, it's not important.

He starts reading a section of the newspaper. HOWARD *eats a cookie.* GLADYS *resumes humming to herself.*

Scene Four

The gallery. HOWARD *is talking to* DON. DANIEL *is looking at the pictures.*

DON. Oh yeah, she's a terrific lady. Only I don't think that hearing aid of hers is very powerful because I often have to repeat myself when I'm talkin' to her. But she is extremely sharp. You can see that right away –

HOWARD. Yes she is, in her own inimitable fashion –

DON. But I can see where it's already kind of frustrating – because you know, like, the other day: I was movin' my car – That's my car right out front there – the maroon one, the Lincoln – and when I come back, Gladys says to me there was a couple in here and they want to buy a picture...!

HOWARD. Oh – !

DON. So I'm thinkin', 'Terrific!' I been in New York City two weeks, I got my pictures up in a gallery in Greenwich Village, and I just sold my first picture!

HOWARD. Congratulations!

DON. Wait – that's not the end of it. Because it turns out she didn't get a *name*.

HOWARD (*smiles to* DANIEL). Jesus Christ...

DON. I *think*, because she couldn't *hear* them. And I almost tear the place apart lookin' for a scrap of paper or something 'n case she wrote it down, and don't you know it: No name, no paper, and I'm still waitin' for 'em. They sure haven't been back yet.

HOWARD. I'm afraid that's more her memory than her hearing aid...

DON. Well, she remembers stuff, but plenty of times I'll say something to her and I can tell, kinda *tell* she didn't really hear me, but she doesn't want to let on. So I think it's the hearing aid problem more than anything else... They make some pretty good ones now. I don't know what kind she's got

now, but boy, it'd be great if somebody could get her
a better one. Because God only knows how many pictures
I really sold, if you see what I mean. But I'm not complaining.
She's a great lady, but she's just kinda stubborn.

ELLEN *comes in from the street.*

HOWARD. Yes she is. (*To* ELLEN.) Hello there.

ELLEN. Hello. (*Sits.*) Blurf. What a day.

DON. Everything all right?

ELLEN. Oh, fine. Howard, I made her show me how she does
her insulin, and she's been – she sticks the needle *through*
the gauze pad, and then she pulls plunger *up* – so all she does
is fill the syringe with blood, and then she throws it away.
So –

HOWARD. For Christ's   DANIEL. I'm amazed she can
    sake…   even *see* that needle.

ELLEN. – for all I know she hasn't taken it for *days*. *Weeks*, for
all I know.

HOWARD. Well, maybe we should –

ELLEN. I'm going to have Florence do it when she comes in
the mornings, but she's only there twice a week. We're
gonna have to get someone to come in the rest of the time.
It doesn't seem to be *killing* her, but…

DON. What's wrong, she has diabetes?

ELLEN. Yes, very mild – she takes *this* much insulin in the
mornings. (*Indicates tiny amount.*) But you still have to do it
every day. I'm gonna talk to Dr Wagner again… (*Pause*)
That *sign* of hers outside is really crummy looking. It's half
off, I'm gonna call my cousin Bill.

DANIEL. Hey, did you see the renovations they're doing in the
hotel?

HOWARD. Oh yes…

ELLEN. Yes, he's really jazzing it up. I looked inside. They've got a new floor and an iron – gate – or trellis or something. It actually looks rather nice.

DANIEL. Yeah, the whole lobby was like *rubble* for about six months, but now it looks pretty good –

HOWARD (*to* DON). The hotel this gallery is a part of used to be the seediest, most God-awful place –

ELLEN. That's not true. When I was growing up it was very nice. It was a nice, rather quaint, residential Greenwich Village hotel...

DON. Is there somethin' wrong with the guy who runs it? Gladys...

ELLEN. Oh –

HOWARD. No, that's just –

ELLEN. – He snubbed her, or she thinks he snubbed her, or maybe he said hello and she didn't *hear* him... I don't know. Anyway...

HOWARD. Anyway, that was it. *Criminal*.

ELLEN. Well I don't know. Maybe he *was* rude to her. I think he's a little peculiar.

DON. Yeah, *I* met that guy, the owner – Mr Georgio? Georgianni?

ELLEN. George. Alan George.

DON. I thought he was Italian.

ELLEN. I don't think so...

DON. 'Georgio.' That sounds Italian.

ELLEN....unless he changed   DANIEL. I thought he was
his name or something.   Jewish. He's Jewish, that
                                                guy.

HOWARD. They probably changed it at Ellis Island, like everyone else. Right?

DON. Are you all Jewish?

Pause.

ELLEN. Well – yes…

HOWARD (*to* DANIEL).
You're Jewish. You're
Jewish. You're *Jewish*.

DANIEL. I'm half-Jewish:
But since my mother's
Jewish, that means I'm
Jewish – by ancient
Jewish law.

ELLEN. We're not very religious.

HOWARD. What do you mean we're not very religious? We're not religious at *all*. Except *I* was raised –

DANIEL. We're liberal Upper West Side atheistic Jewish intellectuals – and we really like German choral music.

ELLEN *and* HOWARD *laugh.*

DON. My family's not very religious either. Well, I suppose my father was, in a way, but not really… He used to drag me kickin' and screamin' to church every Sunday, but my mother always stayed at home…

Silence.

HOWARD. Actually, it's very interesting: Gladys' father was from Russia, where he was a bookmaker for the Czar –

ELLEN. Book*binder*,
Howard. He wasn't –

DANIEL. He was a
book*binder*. It wasn't like
he was the Czar's *bookie*.

HOWARD. Yes, excuse me, bookbinder for the Czar. And he came here in the teens, I think, or possibly earlier –

ELLEN. Oh, I think earlier, Howard –

HOWARD. And he founded a very successful publishing business by carting Jewish religious books around the Lower East Side in a wheelbarrow –

DON. Really.

HOWARD. Until Gladys' nephew took it over from *his* father and proceeded to run it into the ground. Right? Schmuck!

DON. No, I didn't know that –

ELLEN. And my mother –   HOWARD. And Gladys
                              thinks it's all bullshit.

ELLEN. Yes, my whole childhood I was raised to think that
anybody who was religious *at all* was some kind of *moron*.

HOWARD. Gladys is very broad-minded.

ELLEN. Well, she was always –

HOWARD. Right? Like a good communist.

ELLEN. Well, she *was* a communist. I spent my whole
childhood listening to her and my father and their friends
argue *politics* all night long. My father would sit there and
play devil's advocate to all my mother's friends, they'd have
screaming fights until two in the morning and then she'd get
up at the crack of dawn to go stand on a milk carton in
Washington Square and campaign for low-income housing.
She was very impressive in her own maddening way. But
those discussions used to drive me *crazy*...

HOWARD. Really? I always thought you enjoyed them...

ELLEN. Ha ha.

HOWARD (*to* DON). But I'll tell you, if you ever wanted
anything done in New York, you called Gladys.

ELLEN. Oh yes.

DANIEL. Oh yeah.

HOWARD. An apartment, a *job*, a lawyer...

ELLEN. A moving company –

DANIEL. She used to –

HOWARD (*simultaneously with* DANIEL, *to* DON). When
I was divorced from my first wife, I called Gladys and I told
her I needed an apartment, and in *twenty-four hours* she
found me a wonderful little apartment on Eighty-sixth Street,
right across the park from where my children were living,

with a separate office space so I could see patients – and half
a block from the park so I could walk my dog.

DON. Really.

HOWARD....It was amazing!

ELLEN (*to* HOWARD *and* DON). She was very good at that...

DANIEL (*to* DON). When I was a little kid she was always
going off on these trips around the world – She took me to
the Yucatán when I was ten so I could see the pyramids –

HOWARD....And by the time she got off the boat she'd know
everybody on board, she'd know everything about them...

ELLEN. Right, and then she'd bring them all back to New York
and invite them over so I could cook dinner for them.

HOWARD (*to* ELLEN). A lot's changed in twenty years, kid!

ELLEN. And then she'd take *Zique* with her. (*Pronounced like
'Zeke'*.)

DANIEL. She used to have this psychotic Dalmatian –

ELLEN. Zique!

HOWARD. Which is spelled –

ELLEN. Z-I-Q-U-E, for some   HOWARD (*on* ELLEN*'s 'Q'*).
reason.   Z-I-Q-U-E.

DANIEL. – who used to hide under the table when anybody
came into the room.

ELLEN. And who she used to take on these cruises where they
didn't allow dogs –

DANIEL. And she'd say –

ELLEN. 'Oh, they don't allow dogs on that boat but I just take
her anyway – '

DANIEL *and* ELLEN. ' – *They* don't mind.'

HOWARD (*to* DON). This was the craziest fuckin' dog you
ever met.

ELLEN (*to* HOWARD). Right, because *you* told her to get her.

HOWARD. I didn't tell her to get *Zique*.

ELLEN. You did too!   DANIEL. Yes you did!

HOWARD (*to* DON). I told Gladys I thought she should get
    a *dog* –

ELLEN. Boy, was she mad at you.

HOWARD. – because at the time, we were worried about her
    being in the gallery by herself with all the crazies running
    around…

ELLEN (*to* HOWARD). Right, and she got very offended…

HOWARD. Right, she got very offended…

ELLEN.… because you called her a little old lady…

HOWARD. Because I told her I didn't think it was such a great
    idea for a little old lady to sit by herself in the window all
    day long, when you've got –

ELLEN. And was she mad!

HOWARD. What can I say? I was my usual tactful self.

ELLEN.… And this was fifteen *years* ago.

DANIEL. Yeah, so you said she should get an *attack* dog.

HOWARD. I didn't say an *attack* dog. Come on!

ELLEN. Yes you did,   DANIEL. Yes you did!
Howard.   You said she should get
                             a German shepherd!

HOWARD (*to* DANIEL, *on 'German'*). I told her to get a *dog*,
    in case some lunatic walks in, she should have a dog who's
    gonna bark at them and scare them away. (*To* DON.) Right?
    So she goes to the pound –

DANIEL (*to* DON). And she   HOWARD. – and she comes
comes back with –   back with this skinny little
                                    cadaverous Dalmatian –

DANIEL. Who *shakes*!

HOWARD. – who *shakes*, and hides under the table every time
you come into the room!

ELLEN, DANIEL and HOWARD are all laughing.

DON. That's funny…

HOWARD. …so I said, 'Gladys, what the hell are you doing?
That dog wouldn't scare *any*body!'

ELLEN. …She was very fond of her.

HOWARD. Listen, it was a wonderful thing for her.

ELLEN. Zique wasn't so bad. She just shook.

DANIEL. Unbelievable.

Silence.

HOWARD (*to* DON). Well… you don't seem too dangerous.

DON. Oh… Thank you.

Pause.

HOWARD. So –   DON. Now all you gotta do is
                            tell that to Mr Georgio.

ELLEN. Oh no don't worry about him. I don't think he ever
comes *in* here.

DON. Oh, he was sure in here the other *day*. And I don't think
he was too happy about my bein' here…

Pause. ELLEN *and* HOWARD *look at each other and then
back at* DON.

ELLEN. Oh really?

HOWARD. Really?

Pause. DON *is a bit taken aback.*

DON. Well, yeah –

DANIEL. Why? What did he   ELLEN. Did he say anything
say?   to you?

DON. Oh no, he just –

ELLEN. I didn't think he ever came *in* here...

DON. No, he's been in here a couple of times. He –

ELLEN. My mother always thought he was rather strange.

HOWARD. What did he say?

DON. I don't remember exactly. I didn't talk to him for very long...

ELLEN. Well, I don't see why he should mind...

DANIEL. Yeah, what does he care?

HOWARD. Listen: He's probably just being a pain in the ass.

DON. Oh, I think he's probably worried somebody's gonna see me in here late at night and think I'm tryin' to rob the place.

DANIEL. Rob it of what?

HOWARD. No – That's crazy.

DANIEL. What would you steal?

DON. No, I could see his point. Somebody could come in at night and try to steal my pictures off the walls.

Pause.

DANIEL. What do mean, like, Art Thieves?

HOWARD. No...

DON. It could happen.

DANIEL. I don't think so.

HOWARD. It's highly unlikely.

ELLEN. I'll give him a call on Monday. But I don't see why he should have any objection –

DON. Yeah, he probably had a bee in his bonnet about something else... He said he was gonna talk to Gladys, so he probably straightened it out with her.

DANIEL (*a joke:*). Oh yes. I'm sure she cleared everything right up.

HOWARD. At any rate, I don't think we have to worry about that now...

ELLEN. I'll give him a call... I hope that's not going to be a problem.

HOWARD. I don't think so, honey. (*To* DON.) Listen: I think we'd like to buy one of your pictures.

DON. Oh – ! That's great. Wow. That's – okay, fantastic.

HOWARD. My oldest son is having a birthday next week, and his wife is expecting a baby, and I think one of these would make a terrific birthday gift.

DON. Great. Uh –

HOWARD (*pointing*). I like this one. Do you like this one, sweetheart?

ELLEN (*looking*). Ooh, yes.

DON. Oh yeah, that's a little wharf in my home town. I tried really hard to get in all the details. This guy here runs a bait and tackle store. And these birds – the birds come and sit on top of this guy's sign all day long. Drives him nuts, 'cause – well, you know, 'cause they deface the sign. So he's always out there cleaning it off. I didn't put that in. I tried to be faithful to what's actually there, otherwise...

HOWARD. Sold. Sold. Now, I notice you don't have any prices on these... How about... Is three hundred dollars... fair?   DON. Oh, well, I, uh...

DON (*disappointed*). Oh. Sure. Absolutely. That's great... You know, you're Gladys' family... Three hundred – that's more than fair. That's one of my favorites. And that's – a nice – uh – frame you're getting, too –

HOWARD. And listen: You don't have to worry about Gladys forgetting our names! Right?

DON. Right. Right.

ELLEN (*cheerfully*). I remember when she *got* this place.

Scene Five

As DANIEL *comes forward and addresses the audience,*
ELLEN*'s kitchen lights up.* ELLEN *talks on the phone silently,*
slowly turning her back to us.

DANIEL (*to the audience*). My mother called Mr George, who
said he had no problem with Don staying in the gallery. So
Don moved into the little room in the back – which was
basically a closet – he moved his car around, he walked my
grandmother back and forth from the house, and sometimes
he cooked her lunch. Late at night if you looked past the
drug dealers on the corner, you could usually see Don
through the gallery window, hovering over his pictures,
touching them up with a little brush.

My mother hired a nurse's aide named Marva to come in the
mornings when Florence wasn't there, to give Gladys
breakfast and help with her insulin. She hated it. She said
there were these *women* in the house and they wouldn't go
away. Mom took her to the eye doctor and the ear doctor.
Paid her bills, paid her taxes. I dropped by her apartment to
say hello once in a while. I let her take me to dinner once a
month at the restaurant next door. They were really nice to
her there, so she really liked that. She rang my doorbell, a
lot. Sometimes I was nice to her. Sometimes I yelled at her.
And she went to the gallery, almost every day. Until winter
came and she stopped going to the gallery for the time being
because she couldn't stand the cold. So she stayed in her
apartment with those *women* and we waited for the spring.

Then in January, Mr George called my mother and told her
he was taking away the gallery and turning it into a breakfast
café for his hotel.

DANIEL *turns and enters the kitchen.*

ELLEN. Anyway –

DANIEL. What did he say?

ELLEN. He says he's turning the gallery into a café and connecting it to the rest of the hotel, and he wants her to be out by the end of May.

DANIEL. The end of *May*? He's got to be kidding.

ELLEN. I *knew* something like this would happen… I mean, I obviously didn't know it would happen but I was afraid something like this would happen.

DANIEL. Well – I mean, can't we – Can he do that: Doesn't he have to –

ELLEN. Well, honey, she doesn't even have a lease.

DANIEL. She doesn't have a *lease*?

ELLEN. No, she always said she –

DANIEL. She's been in there for twenty-eight years and she doesn't have a lease?

ELLEN. No. And you know, I asked him if it was because Don's been in there for so long and he said, 'Oh no, it's got nothing to do with that.' But maybe he thinks she's peculiar, sitting there all day long… And then Don's in there at night… I don't know, maybe it's no good for his new… I don't really know. He obviously has – he's having plans drawn up, so… (*Pause*) It's just – if he kicks her out I don't know what she's going to *do*.

Pause.

DANIEL. How can she not have a lease?

ELLEN. I don't know. She used to say she didn't want a lease because then he could raise the rent.

DANIEL. What?

ELLEN. I don't *know*. Nobody ever used that space. It's not even attached to the rest of the hotel. But he wants to knock a wall down and put in a kitchen and use it as a breakfast café for the hotel.

DANIEL. Well, can't she… (*Pause*) I mean, what if we say no? What can he –

ELLEN. Well I thought of that, honey, but if she has no lease there's really not much we can do about it. We could refuse to get out, but then he could start sending in process servers and people to harass her and I don't want that…

DANIEL. No…

ELLEN.…She wouldn't know what was going on.

DANIEL. Serve somebody right if he sent them in there after her – they'd run out screaming.

ELLEN (*short laugh*). Right.

GLADYS (*off*). Ellen? Ellen?

DANIEL. What is she gonna *do*?

ELLEN. I don't know.

GLADYS (*off*). Hello? Hello? Ellen? Where are you? Where'd you go?

ELLEN *goes out*.

ELLEN (*off*). I'm just in the kitchen! I'm just ta– I'm just talking to Danny about something!   GLADYS (*off*). Where were you, honey? What's the matter?

GLADYS (*off*). What's the matter? Is he crying?

DANIEL (*to himself*). Am I what?

ELLEN (*off*). No! Why would he be crying?

GLADYS (*off*). I don't know. I thought somebody was crying.

ELLEN (*off*). You were probably having a dream! Why don't you sit here and in a few minutes I'll bring you something to drink!

GLADYS (*off*). All right. I'll stay here.

ELLEN *enters*.

ELLEN. You don't look like you're crying.

DANIEL. Mom, this is really bad.

ELLEN. Well, I can ask Arthur if he knows some kind of fancy legal maneuver, but I'm pretty sure there's nothing to be done.

DANIEL. Yeah, because maybe – Don't they have to give notice, or something?

ELLEN. He's giving us five months.

DANIEL. Five months.

ELLEN. She doesn't even go there in the winter. I don't think she's been in there since November. She just sits all day long in that tiny little apartment. *You're* busy, and I can't have her up here more than once or twice a week or I go out of my mind. She complained to me all last winter how she's lonely, she's lonely – well she is very lonely. She won't *read* – or she *can't* read – And Florence, who's a *saint*, says she can't even figure out how to work the television… What's she going to *do* all day long? (*Pause*) And I feel bad for *you*. I only get it twice a week, but you're on the front lines –

DANIEL. Listen – I'm not –

ELLEN. You can't spend your life running around taking care of her. Karl says he went in yesterday and she was asleep on the sofa…

DANIEL. Yeah I know. You told me.

ELLEN. And she had left the coffee pot lying on its side on the burner and the entire apartment was filled with smoke.

DANIEL. I know. You *told* me.

ELLEN. I'm afraid one of these days she's going to burn the whole house down.

Silence.

He's got some fuckin' nerve kicking her out of that gallery for his – fuckin' hotel expansions.

DANIEL. I know…

Pause.

ELLEN. I mean, eventually she's going to have to move in here, but I'm dreading that day. Because when she does, *I'm* going to have to move *out*.

DANIEL. Well –

ELLEN (*her voice suddenly catches*). Do you know what she said to me last week? (*Pause*) She wants to get a job in a *law* firm. Did I know anybody who she could work for as a *lawyer*. (*Pause*) And now Don's on her shit list because he wants to visit his mother again –

DANIEL. Yeah I know, she gave me a whole long monologue about that recently –

ELLEN *sees something and walks out.*

ELLEN (*off*). PLEASE DON'T FEED THE DOG!

GLADYS (*off*). But she's so hungry – !

ELLEN (*off*). I'M GOING TO FEED HER *DINNER* IN A FEW MINUTES! DON'T *FEED* HER, SHE'S NOT SUPPOSED TO BEG!

GLADYS (*off*). Well what are you so angry about?

DANIEL. Mom…!

ELLEN *stalks in with a plate of crackers and cheese. She clatters it down on the table.*

ELLEN. Howard thinks we should get her a cat.

DANIEL. A cat?

ELLEN. Well, you don't have to walk a cat, and you can leave its food out all day long, and it shits in a cat box, and she's so fond of Daisy, so maybe it's not such a terrible idea. She can feed it all day long until it explodes. She'll love it.

DANIEL. Yeah, but what happens if she opens her door at night and it runs out? How's she gonna get it back?

ELLEN. I don't know... That's probably a good point. (*Looks offstage.*) Here she comes... I'm not going to tell her now.

DANIEL. No...

ELLEN. I'm not up to it...

DANIEL. Well, we can wait a little while till we figure out what to do.

GLADYS *enters*.

GLADYS. What's the matter, Ellen? Ellen? What's the matter?

ELLEN (*loud but not too loud*). I really wish you wouldn't feed the dog scraps. We don't want her to beg.

GLADYS. I want to talk to you about that young – artist – you know – he wants to put up a show –

ELLEN. No he *is* putting up a show.

GLADYS. But now he says he's leaving! He's going back to – to where he lives, and he's leaving me all his pictures! He says he's just packing off and leaving them there! And –

ELLEN. What?... No he's not. No he's not.

DANIEL. He's just going –

ELLEN. He's not leaving. Stop talking a minute. Stop talking.

GLADYS. I never know where he *is*! One day he shows up, one day he's going *away* – I never –

ELLEN. *Listen* to me! He is just going home for the weekend! He will be back on Monday!

GLADYS. Who told you that?

DANIEL *and* ELLEN. HE DID!

GLADYS *winces in pain and touches her hearing aid*.

GLADYS. What?

DANIEL. *He* did.

ELLEN. He has to go home for a few days to see his mother and to make a little money. He's not leaving you the pictures. He's only going for the weekend.

GLADYS. No.

DANIEL. Yes! He's going
home to make some money   ELLEN (*to* DANIEL). What
and to see his mother...   are we gonna tell *him*?
He wants to see his
mother!

GLADYS. Well what's she buggin' him for? *I* can't put up that show myself! I don't know what to do!

DANIEL. You don't have to do anything! He's going to be back in THREE DAYS!

GLADYS. Three days? Why didn't he tell me that?

ELLEN. He did tell you. You just forgot.

GLADYS. I think he's very sneaky.

DANIEL. Fine. He's sneaky. But he'll be back in three days.

ELLEN (*to* DANIEL). I'm going to call Arthur. Although I'm sure he'll say there's nothing to be done –

Offstage the front door opens.

GLADYS. Has anybody fed the dog?

ELLEN. – but I might as well –

HOWARD *comes in, in a suit, carrying a soft briefcase.*

HOWARD. Hello, dear. (*Kisses* DANIEL.) How are you?

DANIEL. Hi.

GLADYS. Hello!

HOWARD (*kisses* GLADYS). HELLO GLADYS!

He crosses away from GLADYS *and kisses* ELLEN.

Hello, dear.

ELLEN. Mr George is taking back the gallery.

HOWARD. He's what?

ELLEN. He's building a café for the hotel and he wants her to be out in May.

HOWARD. Oh, fuck.

GLADYS. Did anybody feed the dog?

HOWARD. Have you told her?

ELLEN. No, I have to get up my nerve. And I also think I should call Arthur and see what he thinks –

HOWARD. Oh, *shit*.

GLADYS (*to* DANIEL). Honey?

DANIEL (*trying to listen to* HOWARD *and* ELLEN). Just a minute...!

ELLEN. Although I'm fairly sure there's nothing she can do about it. She doesn't have a lease, I don't think there's anything written down, and he wants to put in the café *this summer.*	GLADYS. Did anybody give the dog her supper?
	DANIEL. Not yet. We'll feed her in a few minutes!
	GLADYS. What?
HOWARD. When did he call?	
	DANIEL. We'll feed her in a few minutes.
ELLEN. Ten minutes ago.	

GLADYS. Do you think the Village has changed lately?

DANIEL. Yes!

GLADYS (*applauds*). Well! Somebody agrees with me!

DANIEL. Uh-huh!

HOWARD. All right. Why don't you go call Arthur?	GLADYS. I sit in that window all day long, and it never used to be so crowded before.
	DANIEL (*to* GLADYS).
ELLEN. I don't even know if he's still in the office. He's probably gone by now.	Uh-huh.

HOWARD. Why don't you call him anyway? Call him at home.

ELLEN. Well, I don't want to bother him at home. I can –

HOWARD. Honey – !

DANIEL. Mom, for Christ's sake, call him at home! He won't mind.

HOWARD. Your mother is very pushy.

GLADYS. What's the matter, honey?

DANIEL. Nothing!

ELLEN. Maybe he's still at the office. (*Exits.*)

GLADYS. Where's Ellen going?

DANIEL. Nowhere!

GLADYS. The man who runs that hotel is changing the whole place. I saw him on the street, and his daughter was looking for him and he walked right by her and he wouldn't even talk to her! She was crying. She was. And he's got a lot of people from Europe in there now.

DANIEL. Uh-huh!

HOWARD. Dan, I was thinking that she likes Daisy so much, it might be a nice thing for her if we got her a little cat.

GLADYS (*to* DANIEL). Honey, do you know how to cook?

DANIEL (*trying to answer* HOWARD). A little!

GLADYS. Your mother is a wonderful cook. I never learned how to cook anything!

HOWARD. Dan…?

DANIEL. Yeah, I know, but I told Mom I don't know what she's going to do if she opens the door and it runs out. She couldn't get it back, she can't chase it up the stairs, or if it gets out on the street – (*To* GLADYS.) Yes!

GLADYS. Are you still writing for the newspaper, honey?

Honey? Are you still writing for that newspaper?

GLADYS. Are you working hard?

DANIEL. So-so!

GLADYS. So-so. Well that's good.

HOWARD. Well – it's just a thought. Maybe we could put up a gate…

ELLEN *enters. During the following,* GLADYS *hums to herself.*

ELLEN. He's not there. I left him a –

DANIEL. Did you call him at home?

ELLEN. No, I left a message for him at the office. I don't want to bother him at home –

HOWARD. Honey, for Christ's sake…!

ELLEN. I will call him in the morning! Theyre not kicking her out *tomorrow*!

GLADYS. Kicking who out?

They turn to her, startled that she heard this.

Silence.

ELLEN. Nobody. We're talking about somebody you don't know.

GLADYS. Oh.

GLADYS *resumes humming*.

ELLEN. I don't know what to tell her. We're going to have to move her in here and then I'm going to slit my wrists.

GLADYS *spots the dog, offstage*.

GLADYS. Look at the dog. She's crying.

DANIEL. No she's not!

GLADYS. She wants to come in here. Nobody's talking to her.

Pause.

ELLEN. I'm going to start dinner.

ELLEN *exits*.

144

ACT TWO

Scene One

ELLEN*'s living room.* GLADYS *sits.* ELLEN *stands nearby.*
DANIEL *stands downstage, holding an unopened bottle of beer.*
He addresses the audience.

DANIEL. Now came the time to tell Gladys they were taking
away her gallery. We avoided it for as long as we could
because we had no idea what to do with her afterwards.
She was starting to lose some words. She couldn't really
remember anybody's name except Ellen's, and she didn't
recognize anyone outside the immediate family anymore.
My father came to New York for a visit and she knew she was
glad to see him, but she didn't quite know who he was. Long
monologues that used to be part of her regular repertoire
dropped out of her conversation for good. I stopped going out
to dinner with her because it got to be too much of an ordeal.
She rang my doorbell so much I stopped answering it all the
time. Instead I'd just go to the door and look through the
peephole to make sure she was okay, and then I'd watch this
weird little convex image of her turn around in the hallway
and go back into her apartment.

Every day I came home from work, knowing she'd been alone
all afternoon, and I listened at her door, hoping she'd be asleep
so I wouldn't have to go in, knowing that if I didn't, she'd be
alone all night until Marva showed up in the morning.

But as soon as it got warmer she started going to the gallery
again. She sat there and talked to Don and anybody else who
wandered in, and it really seemed to cheer her up. One time
she got hysterical about something when she was alone in
the gallery, and the cops came by and this one young cop
told me, 'She shouldn't be left alone like that: It's not safe.'
Sometimes people talked as if we weren't facing the true
degree of her decline – and maybe we weren't. But I don't

know what we were supposed to do. She didn't want to live
with Mom any more than Mom wanted to live with her.
Mom never even talked about putting her in a nursing home.
And I thought it was better for her to be at risk alone in the
gallery than to be locked in her apartment all day long.

He opens the beer and goes into the living room to join
ELLEN *and* GLADYS.

(*NOTE: While* GLADYS *now has a lot of trouble finding the
right words, she still knows exactly what she is trying to say,
and still addresses herself directly to the others with the
same dogged persistence. In other words, she is not lost in
her own world, nor disconnected from the others, nor is she
talking to herself. She at all times pressures them for
answers, and when they ignore or placate her it drives her
even harder to get a real response from them.*)

GLADYS. I want to sell that – there are two – places, and
I want to sell one of them, and find another place. Because
I can't stay there all day long, and there's a woman there
who comes in every day. She's a very good-looking black
woman, and I went to the bathroom and she was standing
there, standing up, peeing like a man, into the – *cup*.

ELLEN. Have you heard this one yet?

DANIEL. Yeah, you told me.

GLADYS. She was making a pass! And she wouldn't go away!
Just *looking* at me! With the door wide open. And the one in
the gallery, I told him to go around to the – places, on
Madison Avenue, and go in and bring them an – invi–
invitation, because he's opening a show –

ELLEN. All right. I'm going to tell her.

DANIEL. All right.

GLADYS. Those pictures have been up for a few weeks now
and he hasn't even had the show yet, and I said to him –

ELLEN. LISTEN: MR GEORGE IS TAKING AWAY THE
GALLERY. HE WANTS TO TAKE THE GALLERY BACK
FOR THE HOTEL, SO YOU'RE GOING TO HAVE TO

MOVE OUT OF THE GALLERY IN TWO MONTHS,
AFTER DON OPENS HIS SHOW.

Pause.

GLADYS. Well *good* then. I'll give it up and that'll be that for
that, and I'll get a job being a lawyer.

ELLEN. You don't have to worry about that right now. You
have another two months before you have to move out, and
there's plenty –

GLADYS. Because I can't run that place by myself! So I'll sell
it and get myself set up in an – an – a house – an office. (*To*
DANIEL.) Maybe you can take that place in the front for
me, honey, and you can use it for the newspaper.

DANIEL. No, I don't need another place, that's your apartment.
You don't have to move out of your apartment, only the
gallery!

GLADYS. As soon as my – foot – gets better, I'm gonna start
lookin' around for a town – so I can move to another town.

ELLEN. Jesus Christ, she's really – it's word salad.

GLADYS. Because I can't manage by myself! And there's one
woman who comes in and sits there – Hm! (*Demonstrates.*)
And she doesn't say a word all day long. And I want
someone to get *rid* of her.

ELLEN. We can't get rid of her –

GLADYS. They want me to cook for them, and throw a party,
and entertain them, but I can't *do* that anymore. I'm sick!

ELLEN. They're there to cook for *you*! They are helping me
take care of you, because otherwise I have to come down
every day and do your insulin myself. They are there to
make things easier for *me*.

GLADYS. Well they *should* help you! You have your own
family –

ELLEN. We can talk about that later. I just wanted to tell you
that Mr George is taking back the gallery, but we don't have
to do anything for a couple of months!

GLADYS. Well who's gonna take care of all those pictures?
I'll have to talk with that man, I know his daughter –

ELLEN. Don will take care of the pictures, he'll take the
pictures with him.

GLADYS. Well – I've had that – the – the place –

ELLEN. Gallery.

GLADYS. – gallery, for many years and nobody comes in
there. So I'll sell it. You can have the place in the front, and
I'll get a job in an office. (*To* DANIEL.) Do they have any
jobs in your office, honey?

Silence.

ELLEN. We can talk about that later. You'll have one last
opening with Don's show, and we can worry about your
apartment later.

GLADYS. I think that's very sensible. Worry about it later.
Good!

DANIEL *and* ELLEN *look at each other – i.e., it can't be
this easy.*

Scene Two

The gallery. DON*'s opening. On the desk is a big platter of
cheese and crackers, plastic cups and paper napkins and a
bottle of wine.* GLADYS *sits behind the desk.* DON *and*
DANIEL *stand together, across the room from her; each has
a plastic cup of wine.* DON *is eating Chinese.*

Everyone is in a good mood, especially GLADYS *and* DON.

DON. But every time I try to tell her I'm just goin' back home
for a few days to see my mother, she goes haywire. It's that
darn hearing aid.

DANIEL. You've got to be kidding. It's not her hearing aid.

DON. No, I'm tellin' you, it's not a good model. And this stuff about my mother is just plain ridiculous.

DANIEL. Yeah, well, it's been really great that you've been in here, it's been great for her –

GLADYS. Your mother was here before, sweet. I don't know what happened to her. Is she coming down?

DANIEL. She went to do some errands. She'll be back later.

GLADYS. She came in and then she just went – she – I don't know what happened to her. Do you want some of this – bottle – want some of this – liquor?

DON. Yeah, she was in before with your stepfather. They came in few hours ago –

DANIEL. Yeah, I know, I saw them at the house.

DANIEL (*to* GLADYS). No thank you! I have some!

DON. Well, I'm really excited. I put an ad in this art newsletter newspaper. I been bustin' my back on these pictures, and I don't mind tellin' you I'm pretty excited. You know, I think the problem before was that I didn't really have an 'opening.' People would look in, but I was workin' on the pictures –

GLADYS. So what's new, honey? Are you working hard? Is everything kablooey in the back of the –

DANIEL. No, everything's fine!

DON. You know – I was workin' on the pictures literally day and night, and then with the cold weather she didn't come in too much, but now it's all set and the weather's good. I don't know if you noticed the new sign –

DANIEL. Yeah, my cousin Bill made it: He put it up in the winter, didn't he?

DON. Oh yeah, yeah, right. You been in since then, haven't you?

GLADYS. I want to sell that place in the – the business in the – When my – toe – I want to get rid

DANIEL. Yeah, a lot. I was here when the cops came... of that place, it's too dark for me in the winter. And now there's a little *girl* –

DON. Yeah, what the heck was that all about?

DANIEL. I don't know. She thought somebody was – (*To* GLADYS.) What?

GLADYS. What's the matter, honey?

DANIEL. NOTHING. I DIDN'T HEAR WHAT YOU SAID.

GLADYS. What did I say?

DANIEL. I don't know.

GLADYS. Well, me neither.

GLADYS *laughs*. DANIEL *laughs too*.

DON (*points to a picture*). I notice a lot of the people who look through the window were payin' attention to this one...

DANIEL (*to* GLADYS). I'M JUST GOING TO LOOK AT THE PICTURES.

GLADYS. Well don't you have to – fix them up in – to get them the way you want it?

DANIEL. UM – NO! I'M GOING TO LOOK AT SOME OF THE PICTURES! THE PAINTINGS!

DON. This is my favorite. That's my mother. You see this macramé over here? She did that by hand, like when I was a kid, and I was always intrigued by that. And one day, she was gonna throw it out –

GLADYS (*picks up a piece of cheese*). Does anybody want some of this – stuff!

DANIEL. NO THANK YOU!

GLADYS. It's delicious!

DON. – and I said, 'Why don't you just put it on the wall?' So I put it up for her, made a little frame for it, and then I figured, you know, thread *fades*...

DANIEL. Uh-huh…

DON. So I figured it's not gonna last forever, so I featured it in the picture. I painted the whole room, separately – and then I painted my mother while she was *in* the room. Everything you see is really there in real life. I tried to get the details right because that's what you remember when you think about something, so I tried like hell to get them the way they are.

DANIEL. It's great…

GLADYS. Honey? Do you want some? This – cook– cookie is absolutely delicious. Anybody want to try some?

DANIEL. NO THANKS! IN A MINUTE!

GLADYS *starts humming.*

DON. Anyway, I don't know if you like that one…

DANIEL. Did you – Did you mean to write three thousand dollars? These pictures are three thousand dollars apiece?

DON. No, that one's three thousand, those over there are two, because that's a smaller canvas, and the rest of these are three.

DANIEL. Gee, I hope you can sell them.

DON. Well, first they gotta come in, right? (*Squints out the picture window.*) That couple's been by about five times now.

DANIEL. I didn't know what time to come by.

DON. Well, we been open for about four and a half, five hours – Since about eleven o'clock this morning. Not too many people came in yet, but it's so beautiful outside today. I tried to get my sister to come in, but it's a big ordeal for her to travel. She's pretty much a stay-at-home. And I don't get on too good with my brother-in-law. He takes good care of her, but he's – I don't know. He's always gotta be tellin' everybody what to do. He's one of those guys.

DANIEL. When I was ten I broke my wrist outside on the hotel awning. Gladys was having a big opening for somebody and I went outside and I was playing tag with some kids, and I whipped around and ran right into the awning pole – and I cracked a bone in my wrist.

DON. Oh yeah?

DANIEL (*turning toward the desk*). And then another time I was in here, and she used to have a coffeemaker on the floor by the desk over there, and –

GLADYS. How are you, honey?

DANIEL. FINE THANKS.

GLADYS. You havin' a good time? Did you look at the pictures?

DANIEL. YES! I'M LOOKING AT THEM NOW! (*To* DON.) And I kicked over the boiling water and it went all over my leg. Burned the shit out of me. I got all these blisters on my ankle…

Pause.

DON. Well, I'm pretty excited. I mean I don't usually get too excited, but this whole thing is kind of like a dream come true for me. You know, where I come from, in my town, you tell 'em you paint pictures and they look at you like you got a screw loose or something.

DANIEL. Yeah, it's nice. This was a nice gallery.

DON. Well, you know, Dan – I hope this isn't too presumptuous or anything, but I was thinkin', you know you must know some of the people in the art department at your newspaper, and I was wondering if it wouldn't be to much trouble to put a bug in their ear and see if they could send somebody down to check out the show.

Pause.

DANIEL. Well, um, Don – the thing is, I don't, uh, I don't actually work for a newspaper.

DON. Because even a small blurb can make a big difference to a new show if it's in *The New York Times*. (*Pause*) What?

DANIEL. I don't work for *The New York Times*.

DON. Oh. Really? What paper do you work for?

DANIEL. No – I don't work for a newspaper. I work for the Environmental Protection Agency... They don't have an art department.

DON. Didn't I hear Gladys ask you if you were still workin' at *The New York Times*?

DANIEL. Yeah, I know, I know, but I can't keep telling her –

And you said Yes!

DANIEL. Don, I – I really don't work for *The New York Times*. I don't even have a subscription.

DON. Oh. Huh. Well. I'm sorry. I – Phooey. Oh well. So don't know anyone who... no, huh?

DANIEL. Sorry. I wish I –

GLADYS. Did you look at the pictures, honey?

DANIEL. YEAH, I THINK THEY'RE TERRIFIC.

GLADYS. Would you like me to buy one for you? I think one of these little ones would look just – in your place – in the – do you have pictures up in there?

DANIEL. Yeah, I have a lot!

GLADYS. I've never seen that one. That place in there.

DANIEL. What do you mean? You've seen it a million times!

GLADYS. I've never been in there.

DANIEL. Sure you have. You were in there last week!

GLADYS. Which one do you like, honey? Tell me which – tell me the – the show you like, and I'll fix it up for you. I want to buy it for you.

DANIEL (*unsure if he wants a picture*). Well – LET ME LOOK SOME MORE AND I'LL LET YOU KNOW!

GLADYS. Your mother bought two of them –

DANIEL. I KNOW! (*To* DON.) Oh, did she buy another two, or…

DON. No, no, from when they were in here in the fall.

DANIEL. Oh yeah, they got 'em for my stepbrother.

DON. Did his wife have the baby?

DANIEL. Yeah, a girl. She had her last month.

DON. I've never been married.

Brief silence.

ELLEN *comes in.*

ELLEN. Hello.

DON. Welcome back.

GLADYS. Look, Ellen's here!

ELLEN (*a joke, to* DANIEL *and* DON). Did you recognize me?

DANIEL. Yup.

ELLEN. Any customers?

DON. Not yet, but I think people are really out enjoying the weather today. A lot of people are lookin' in, but I think they'll probably come in more after the weekend.

ELLEN. I'm going to take her home, she must be exhausted.

DON. Yeah, she's been talkin' a mile a minute since we got here this morning.

ELLEN (*to* DANIEL). Where's your young lady friend? Didn't you say she might –

DANIEL. Yeah, she had something to do.

ELLEN. Is that situation any better?

DANIEL. Well, yesterday it was.

ELLEN. Oh dear… Not easy.

DANIEL. That's right.

ELLEN. Well, I'm gonna take her home – (*Goes to* GLADYS.) HELLO. WOULD YOU LIKE TO GO HOME?

GLADYS. Sure, are we going to New York?

ELLEN looks at DANIEL, surprised and distressed by this new low.

ELLEN (*to* GLADYS). No – We're *in* New York. I said do you want to go home, to your apartment?

No response. ELLEN *looks at* DANIEL *again, worried, and then back at* GLADYS.

IT'S ALMOST TIME FOR DINNER. WHY DON'T YOU LET ME TAKE YOU HOME.

GLADYS. I had no idea it was so late! Are you tired, honey?

ELLEN. No, it's not late, but it's time to go home!

GLADYS. All right, let me find my purse –

ELLEN. Your purse is on the back of the chair!

GLADYS. Wait – I don't have my keys –

ELLEN. I have your keys, I have them right here.

GLADYS (*looks through her bag*). Wait a minute, let me make sure I've got everything. I don't know where I put my – (*Dumps her purse out on the desk.*)

ELLEN. There she goes.

GLADYS looks through her stuff.

DANIEL. Mom, I'm gonna go talk to Mr George.

ELLEN. Well, honey, I already talked to him –

DANIEL. Well let me just try. I'm gonna call him and go see him and see if he can – I mean, she's not gonna be able to –

ELLEN. Well good then, go talk to him. There's certainly nothing to *lose*...

DANIEL. Yeah, because this is just awful – I mean – I –

DON. What are you gonna try to get him to let us stay open?

DANIEL. Well, I thought I'd go see if I can get another year out of him, because what difference would it make? And she can't – She's got to have something to *do*.

ELLEN (*sighs*). Well, good luck.

DANIEL. Yeah, I know, but –

ELLEN (*to* GLADYS). WHAT ARE YOU LOOKING FOR? (*Pause*) WHAT ARE YOU LOOKING FOR?

GLADYS. I'm looking for my keys! I can't find them!

ELLEN (*shows keys*). Your keys are right here! I have them in my hand.

GLADYS. Oh! Where'd you find them?

ELLEN. You gave them to me this morning! COME ON. IT'S TIME TO GO HOME.

As ELLEN *helps* GLADYS *with her belongings, and helps her up:*

DON. Well, this is just great. I want to thank all of you, because this has been just tremendous for me. I know things are gonna work out now for me, because I really believe that if you want something bad enough, you can have it as long as you don't quit trying. I mean – Greenwich Village – New York City gallery. I've been waiting for this day my whole life.

Scene Three

ELLEN*'s living room.* GLADYS *sits in a rocker.* ELLEN *sits on the sofa looking through a mail-order catalogue.* DANIEL *and* HOWARD *stand nearby.*

DANIEL. It was *the* most depressing thing I ever saw. Nobody comes in all day long, she's behind the desk – oblivious, like she's hosting a party, and he's standing around eating *cheese* in this empty gallery and he says to us, 'I've been waiting for this day *my whole life.*' It was just –

HOWARD. Jesus Christ.

DANIEL. It was the most depressing thing I ever saw –

HOWARD. Jesus Christ. That *is* really depressing... Oy. I'm gonna call my folks. (*Takes a step.*) Dan, I called my folks last night and my mother picked up, and she was very upset, crying – and she said, 'I can't stand it anymore, he's terrible, he's driving me crazy, he won't listen to anybody, he's so awful...' So I said, 'Listen, he's ninety-three years old. He's a little difficult. Put him on the phone.' He gets on the phone, I say, 'Listen, Dad, what's the matter? Mom seems very upset.' He says, '*I'll* tell you what's the matter – I knew this marriage was a mistake sixty-three years ago. I'm leaving, I'm getting a divorce, and I'm moving to China.' So what do you think of that?

DANIEL. Wow.

HOWARD (*moving to exit*). So things are good all over with the old folks, right? If you don't lose your marbles and one of you doesn't die young, you get old together and torture each other to death.

DANIEL. Great.

HOWARD. See if I can calm him down... So fucking crazy...

He exits. GLADYS *looks at the dog, offstage.*

GLADYS. Look at the dog. Ellen. Look at the dog. She's showing off. Isn't that sweet? That is the sweetest little animal. Look, she knows we're talking about her. She's showing off.

DANIEL. She doesn't know we're talking about her, she's a dog!

GLADYS. I had a beautiful little dog. Did you ever meet my dog, honey?

DANIEL. Sure!

GLADYS. Do you remember her?

DANIEL. Of course I remember her.

GLADYS. What?

DANIEL. I said I REMEMBER HER.

GLADYS. You do? She was the sweetest little thing. Ellen, do you remember that little dog I had?

ELLEN *doesn't answer. She turns the page of her catalogue.*

This one is a little devil. Always sniffin' around somewhere. Look, she has a – a paw. She's scared you're gonna put her out in the street. She's trying to sing to you. Look at her. Don't you think I should give her something?

ELLEN. NO!

GLADYS. All right. (*To* DANIEL.) Do you know how to cook?

DANIEL (*sighs*). A little bit.

GLADYS. You do! That's wonderful. I never cooked much. In that place, I have a little – fire, and I make myself a little sandwich. Does Ellen like to cook?

ELLEN *puts down the catalogue.*

Ellen? Do you know how to cook?

Pause. ELLEN *is really shocked.*

ELLEN. I've been cooking you dinner here every Wednesday for twenty *years*...!

GLADYS (*laughs*). Well where did you learn how to fix it up? Who told you?

ELLEN. I think she's gotten worse.

DANIEL. Oh, Mom.

GLADYS. You know, that one – the one in the back – he says he's leaving because his mother doesn't want him to be here –

ELLEN (*on 'want'*). No, it's got nothing to do with his mother –

GLADYS. What?

ELLEN. He's leaving because the hotel is taking back the gallery!

GLADYS. Yes, I know that…

ELLEN. He has to go back because he doesn't have a job and you have to get out of the gallery.

GLADYS. Well, what am I going to *do* all day long?

Silence.

I can't stay cooped up in that place all day long by myself! I'll go crazy!

ELLEN. We can talk about that later.

GLADYS. I think I'm going to look around and set myself up in a… in a… in a…

ELLEN. See? She forgets a lot of words…

GLADYS. In a little – you know, maybe I can get some work as a lawyer in an office. I still have a – paper – a – passport – and I can do a little of it – I don't need much, but I have to get out and do *some*thing –

ELLEN. Let's just get the gallery settled first and then we can worry about that later.

GLADYS. I think I'll go talk to that one who runs the hotel. I know his daughter –

ELLEN. There's nothing to talk to him about – (*To* DANIEL.)
By the way, did you ever call Mr George? Or did you
decide –

DANIEL. Yeah, no, I'm gonna try to go see him this week, but
I don't know if it'll do any –

GLADYS. What?

ELLEN. There is nothing to talk to him about –

DANIEL. THERE'S PROBABLY NOTHING WE CAN DO.
YOU DON'T HAVE A LEASE.

GLADYS. Well maybe you and I can set something up in that
place in the back. Would you like that, honey?

DANIEL. Let's worry about one thing at a time!

GLADYS. One thing at a time. You know, I think that's very
smart. We'll do it one – word – at a time.

DANIEL. Good!

GLADYS. Good. (*Pause*) Look at the dog... Ohhhhhh, look at
the poor thing, she's hungry –

GLADYS *picks up a plate of crackers.*

ELLEN. DON'T *FEED* HER! SHE'S ALREADY EATEN!
She's getting too FAT! DON'T *FEED* HER!

GLADYS. Well why are you so angry?

ELLEN *gets up and grabs the plate.*

ELLEN. I TOLD YOU *TEN THOUSAND TIMES* NOT TO
FEED HER! SHE'S TOO FAT AND SHE'S ALREADY
EATEN!

DANIEL. Mom! She can't help it!

ELLEN (*starts to cry*). Well I can't help it either, I can't *stand* it!

ELLEN *runs into the other room.*

GLADYS (*bursts into tears*). Why is she angry at me? What did
I do?

DANIEL. She's not angry, she's just tired. She doesn't want you to feed the dog.

GLADYS. Well I'm not going to stay here if nobody wants me I'll go home! (*Still crying, she gets up with great difficulty.*) I don't know why she's always so angry at me! What did I do? Why is she yelling at me? I don't understand!

DANIEL (*calling*). Mom...!

GLADYS. I'm going home, I'm going to kill myself.

DANIEL. DON'T KILL YOURSELF.

GLADYS (*looks for her purse*). Well I can't stay cooped up in that apartment all day long! No one ever comes in there!

DANIEL. PLEASE SIT DOWN. IT'S ALL RIGHT, WE'LL FIND YOU SOMETHING ELSE TO DO –

GLADYS. I can't stand it in there and I don't want to come here if nobody wants me here. I'll go home and kill myself. Where's my purse? I lost my purse!

DANIEL. IT'S ON THE ARM OF YOUR CHAIR –

GLADYS. Why is Ellen so angry at me?

ELLEN *comes back in and stands there.*

DANIEL. Will you tell her you're not mad at her!

GLADYS. I can't find my keys! I lost my keys! I won't be able to get back in! What am I going to do? I won't have anywhere to sleep! I'll be sleeping on the street!

ELLEN (*comes forward, softly*). Your keys are in your bag. But you don't have to leave. Do you want some coffee?

GLADYS. I don't want to stay if you're going to yell at me! I don't know what I did!

ELLEN. I'm not yelling at you, everything's fine.

HOWARD *enters.*

GLADYS. I want to get another – place – He won't take the pictures down, he says he's going *home*!

The doorbell rings.

GLADYS. And if he leaves the pictures up I can't *do* it by myself –

ELLEN. Hold on a minute, sit down, I have to get the door. Howard will you get the *door*?

I don't understand. What's the matter?

DANIEL. I'll get it!

ELLEN. I have to get the doorbell! Just wait one second!

GLADYS. I can't find my money –

DANIEL (*going*). Mom, I'm *getting* it!

ELLEN. You don't need any money. That's Don and he's going to take you home in a taxi.

GLADYS. Does he know the way?

ELLEN. Yes, he knows the way –

GLADYS. But I haven't got my keys!

ELLEN (*looking through* GLADYS' *bag*). I'm just finding them, they're in your bag.

HOWARD. ELLEN IS FINDING THEM!

DANIEL brings DON in.

DANIEL. Hi, we're having a little scene here.

DON. Oh, that's all right.

GLADYS. I don't understand anything. I can't go home without my keys!

ELLEN (*waving the keys*). Here they are. They're right here. Don't cry. Your keys are right here. Stop crying.

The keys are on an elastic bracelet. ELLEN *puts them on* GLADYS' *wrist.*

GLADYS. What?

ELLEN. There's nothing to cry about.

GLADYS. What's wrong with crying?

HOWARD. NOTHING.

ELLEN. Sit down and take your time. Look, Don's here now, and he's going to take you home in a taxi. I'll call you in the morning when you're feeling better.

HOWARD (*to* DON). Hello.

DON. Hi there.

HOWARD. Just another evening at the Fine house.

GLADYS. I can't breathe.

DON. Yeah...

ELLEN. Because you're in a panic.

GLADYS. I am in a panic. I can't breathe... I'm dizzy...

ELLEN. Just sit down. Nothing's wrong with you, you're just upset.

GLADYS (*sitting*). All right, I'll sit down. (*Bursts into tears again.*)

ELLEN. Come on, don't cry...

GLADYS (*getting up again*). I don't want to go out on the street!

ELLEN. Nobody's going on the street. You're going to settle down and then Don is going to take you home in a taxi and I'll talk to you tomorrow.

GLADYS. Where's my bag?

ELLEN. It's right here.

GLADYS. I had a coat when I came in.

HOWARD (*to* DON). Was the traffic bad coming up? Did you take a taxi, or did you drive your car?

ELLEN. No you didn't. It's very warm out. You didn't bring a coat.

GLADYS. I didn't?

DON. No, I took a taxi because you can't get a

parking space down there if
you wait too late…

ELLEN. No.

HOWARD. All right. We'll
refund you.

GLADYS. Well now I upset
you.

DON. Oh, that's all right.
you don't have to.

ELLEN. I'm not upset, you
are.

HOWARD. Don't be
ridiculous. We'll pay for it.

GLADYS. Yes. I am upset.
I'm sorry, honey. I'm all
mixed up.

DON. Well, uh…

ELLEN. It's all right.

GLADYS (*to* DON). Hello. We're having a – (*Makes a fist.*)
a punch-up. (*Laughs.*)

ELLEN. 'Ha ha ha.'

DON. Hello, Gladys!

GLADYS. What did he say?

ELLEN. He said hello. Now, do you have everything?

GLADYS. Yes. Where are my keys?

ELLEN. Around your wrist.

GLADYS (*rattling them*). Oh here they are. (*Laughs.*) They're
right here.

Silence.

What's everyone so upset about?

HOWARD. WE'RE UPSET BECAUSE IT'S A SHAME
ABOUT THE GALLERY.

GLADYS. Well I'm upset too!

HOWARD. IT WAS A WONDERFUL PLACE FOR YOU BUT
IT'S BEEN VERY DIFFICULT FOR YOU TO MANAGE
LATELY!

ELLEN. Don't shout, Howard.

HOWARD. BUT IT WAS A WONDERFUL PLACE AND YOU HAD A LOT OF GOOD YEARS THERE.

GLADYS. Yes I did.

HOWARD. LISTEN, IT'S NO FUN TO GET OLD.

GLADYS. What?

HOWARD. I SAID IT'S NO FUN GETTING OLD!

GLADYS. Well why do you always say that to me? Nobody wants to hear that – !

HOWARD (*surprised*). I'M SORRY. I GUESS I'M NOT SO TACTFUL. I won't say it anymore.

GLADYS. 'You're old! You're getting old!' That's not a helpful thing to say.

HOWARD. I – I'm sorry. Sometimes I'm not so smart.

GLADYS. Sure you're smart! This whole family's smart! (*To* DON.) Do you have money for a taxi?

DON. Yep, right here.

GLADYS. I'm very angry at you.

DON. I just got here.

HOWARD. That doesn't matter!

DANIEL (*kissing her*). Bye, Grandma.

GLADYS. Goodbye, honey. When will I see you?

DANIEL. I'll see you tomorrow.

GLADYS. Do you want a ride with us? Are you going to the city?

DANIEL. No – We're *in* the city. I'm going home on my bicycle.

GLADYS. But if you came with us, you could ride in a taxicab.

DANIEL. I want to take my bike, I like riding it!

GLADYS. All right. (*To* ELLEN.) He says he wants to ride his bicycle.

ELLEN. Yes, I heard him. I'm standing right here. (*Kisses* GLADYS.)

GLADYS. Goodbye, honey.

ELLEN. I'll call you tomorrow.

GLADYS (*to* DON). What are *you* upset about?

DON. I'm not upset.

HOWARD. Gladys, *you're* upset!

GLADYS. I am upset. I'm all – mixed up. (*Starts to cry again*.) I don't want to stay in that place with those women! They don't talk to you and I don't know what to say to them! They sit there all day long and they never say two words to anybody!

ELLEN. We can talk about it tomorrow.

GLADYS. I don't understand what happened! Herb and I had a *good* life! We had a good life...!

HOWARD. Yes you did.

GLADYS. I don't understand what happened to me...

ELLEN. Don't cry. We'll figure something out tomorrow.

GLADYS. Tomorrow. All right. I'm very upset.

GLADYS *and* DON *go out*.

HOWARD. Goodnight, Don.

DON (*off*). So long...

ELLEN *closes the door. Pause*.

ELLEN. I know everybody has to get *old*...

She stops talking. They all stand by the door for a moment.

Scene Four

DANIEL *comes forward.*

DANIEL (*to the audience*). I did go to see Mr George. I asked
him for another year. Just one more year before he took away
the gallery, because after that it wouldn't make any
difference anymore. And I thought it would make a great
difference now.

He was very sympathetic. He said he had an aunt who was
going through the same thing. But he told me the same thing
he told my mother on the phone. The café was scheduled to
open *that* summer, and there was absolutely nothing he could
do about it.

Then he asked if we'd given any thought to putting Gladys in
a home. I got kind of angry and I said we didn't really want to
do that. She didn't like old people. She liked to be where the
action was. She thought she was running a gallery. He said this
is really the time her family should be taking care of her.
(*Pause*) There were no more attempts to dissuade him.

I kept thinking there must be something we could do, only
I just couldn't think of what it was. I had a dream where I put
her on a bus from Vermont to New York, and I wanted to get
her settled and get off, but as she hobbled down the aisle
I was afraid she'd be knocked over by the bus's motion, and
it occurred to me that she'd never know where to change
buses, that it was impossible to put her on a bus by herself
because she'd never make it. But I couldn't go with her and
was all too late. Her mind was smashed to pieces, and the
person she used to be hadn't really been around for a long
time... But the pieces were still *her* pieces. (*Pause*) I guess
we all wanted to get out of it.

*As a clock chimes twelve, the lights rise on the hallway
between* GLADYS' *and* DANIEL's *apartments.* GLADYS,
wearing an old housecoat, slowly walks to DANIEL's *door
and rings the bell, a loud horrible electric buzzer of
a doorbell. Pause. She rings it again. Pause. She turns
around and starts to walk slowly back to her door.*

DANIEL, *half-asleep, opens his door, putting on a bathrobe.*

DANIEL. HELLO...!

GLADYS (*turning*). Hello? Hello?

DANIEL. HELLO. WHAT'S THE MATTER?

GLADYS. Ohhhhh, I'm sorry, sweetie, did I wake you?

DANIEL. YES!

GLADYS. Ohhhhh, I'm sorry. I tried to ring your doorbell
yesterday and nobody was there. I didn't know where you
were. I was worried. You weren't home.

DANIEL. So *what*?

GLADYS. Well I didn't know   DANIEL. I'm here *now* – and
where you. were. Where is   Mom is asleep – You
your mother? I tried to call   probably –
her but she's not home.

GLADYS. What, honey?

DANIEL (*slowly and distinctly*). You probably misdialed. Mom
is probably asleep. It's after midnight.

GLADYS. Oh, do you want to come in and sit down?

DANIEL. NO. I WANT TO GO BACK TO SLEEP. IT'S VERY
LATE.

GLADYS. Oh. All right. I'm awfully sorry I woke you, honey.

DANIEL. That's okay.

GLADYS. Are you like me? Can you go right back to sleep?

DANIEL. YES.

GLADYS. All right, honey, I'm sorry.

DANIEL. IT'S ALL RIGHT.

*He goes back inside. She goes very slowly inside her
apartment. Muffled and distant, the church bells chime three
o'clock.* GLADYS *comes back out, fully dressed, carrying
her purse. She rings* DANIEL's *bell.*

Pause. She rings again. DANIEL *jerks open the door, hair rumpled, in his underwear.*

GLADYS. What's the matter, honey, is the house burning down?

DANIEL. What?

GLADYS. Is the house burning down?

DANIEL. No.

GLADYS. Where did your mother go, honey? Is she in your apartment?

DANIEL. No!

GLADYS. Well why didn't
    she say goodbye to me!
    She was here before and
    then she ran out and she
    didn't say goodbye! I don't   DANIEL. What? Mom wasn't
    know where she went! Why   here!
    did she leave like that? What   No – No – Listen a –
    did I do to her?   *Listen* a minute!

DANIEL. She hasn't been here for hours! She was here last night – LAST NIGHT!

GLADYS. But why didn't she say goodbye?!

DANIEL. She *did* say goodbye. She said goodbye last night! And now it's after midnight and she's home asleep!

GLADYS. No!

DANIEL. YES! SHE WAS HERE BEFORE AND SHE SAID GOODBYE AND NOW IT'S AFTER MIDNIGHT!

GLADYS. Well why did she run out like that? I thought we were going to the country!

DANIEL. NO! YOU'RE MIXED UP! NOBODY'S GOING TO THE COUNTRY!

GLADYS. *They* don't have to invite me! I'll just stay here by myself!

DANIEL. THEY'RE NOT IN THE COUNTRY!

GLADYS. But where are they?

DANIEL. AT HOME IN BED!

GLADYS. Why? What time is it?

DANIEL. IT IS THREE O'CLOCK IN THE MORNING!

GLADYS (*hand to mouth, shocked*). I had no idea it was so late.

DANIEL. WELL, IT IS.

GLADYS (*bursts into tears*). But why didn't your mother tell me she was leaving!

DANIEL. SHE *DID* TELL YOU! SHE *DID* TELL YOU!

GLADYS. NO! SHE NEVER TOLD ME ANYTHING – !

DANIEL. YES SHE *DID*!

GLADYS. NO!

DANIEL. YOU NEVER BELIEVE *ANY*BODY!

GLADYS. BUT SHE NEVER TOLD ME SHE WAS LEAVING!

   DANIEL *actually slams his own head into his front door.*
   GLADYS *gasps and takes a step back.*

DANIEL. MOM IS ASLEEP! HOWARD IS ASLEEP! IT IS THREE O'CLOCK IN THE MORNING! (*Pause. Slightly calmer.*) THEY WERE HERE LAST NIGHT. THEY SAID GOODBYE, AND YOU'RE GOING UP THERE FOR DINNER ON WEDNESDAY!

GLADYS. You're very angry.

DANIEL. No, but I'M TRYING TO GET SOME SLEEP!

GLADYS. What's the matter, honey? Are you having trouble sleeping?

   DANIEL *starts to answer. He half-laughs.*

   I thought Ellen was mad at me.

DANIEL. NO. NOBODY'S MAD AT ANYBODY.

GLADYS. Well that's all I care about. Do you want to come inside for a minute?

DANIEL. NO, I WANT TO GO BACK TO SLEEP. IT'S VERY LATE AT NIGHT. YOU SHOULD TRY TO SLEEP ALSO! AND I'LL SEE YOU LATER.

GLADYS. All right, honey. I'm sorry.

DANIEL. It's all right!

GLADYS *turns around and walks slowly to her door.*
DANIEL *turns and goes inside his apartment as she goes inside hers. Pause. The distant clock chimes five.*

GLADYS (*off*). Help! Help! Somebody help me!

GLADYS *comes out from her apartment, and goes toward vestibule door.*

Help! Help! Somebody stole my dog! Help! Help!

DANIEL *opens his door and runs out, tying his bathrobe around him.*

Honey help me, somebody stole my dog! They ran out into the street and –

DANIEL. Grandma –

GLADYS. – I can't find her anywhere! I think somebody stole her!

DANIEL. Grandma, you don't have a dog –

GLADYS. What are you talking about! She's gone!

DANIEL. Nobody stole your dog. She died a long time ago. You're having a bad dream.

GLADYS. But they were just in here –

DANIEL. Who was in here?

GLADYS. Billy and Pearl –
They were in here two

minutes ago and they ran out, and the dog ran out, and I can't *find* her!	DANIEL. No! Listen to me – PLEASE LISTEN TO ME!

GLADYS. I'm listening.

DANIEL. You are having a dream. The dog died many years ago. Billy and Pearl are in Fairfield, in Connecticut. They've been there for fifteen years, they weren't here. You've been having a bad dream.

GLADYS. Do you want to go upstairs and check?

DANIEL. No. It's five o'clock in the morning, nobody is here but you and me, there's no dog. There is no dog.

GLADYS. Are you sure?

DANIEL. Yes.

GLADYS (*doubtful*). Well, all right…

DANIEL. Come into your apartment. Did you eat anything yesterday?

He takes her into her apartment as they talk. The lights go up in her living room.

Sometimes when you don't eat you get a little confused.
I want you to eat something –

GLADYS. But I'm not hungry. I have to fix something for the people to eat for dinner – I can't –

DANIEL. No, nobody is coming for dinner. It's very early in the morning and I want you to eat something. Sit down here. Sit down. SIT DOWN.

GLADYS. But they'll be looking for me – !

DANIEL. NO! NOBODY'S LOOKING FOR YOU! SIT DOWN!

She sits in a chair. He exits.

GLADYS. Maybe you should check upstairs. I think something happened to them. There were – three of them, and they came in and they – (*Stares at the empty chair.*) Where –

DANIEL *enters with a bowl of yoghurt. He puts it in front of her.*

Is he going to get coffee? Oh, no, I couldn't eat anything, I'm not hungry!

DANIEL. Just eat this – please!

GLADYS. But I'm not hungry!

DANIEL. IF YOU DON'T EAT THIS I'M GOING TO KILL MYSELF!

GLADYS. But I *can't* – !

DANIEL. PLEASE PLEASE PLEASE PLEASE PLEASE PLEASE EAT THIS! *PLEASE!*

He's screaming so much she starts eating.

GLADYS. This is delicious.

DANIEL. Good.

GLADYS. It's very good. (*Eats.*) So what's new with you, honey? Are you working hard?

DANIEL *laughs.*

Are you still working for the – the television?

DANIEL. Yes!

GLADYS. For the magazine? And people call you and you bring them here and fix up what you want them to do for you?

DANIEL. Yes.

GLADYS. What are you doing now?

DANIEL. Um, I'm –

GLADYS (*twists around*). Where did he go?

Pause.

DANIEL. Who?

GLADYS (*points at an empty chair*). Didn't you see him?

DANIEL (*very rattled*). Who? There's nobody there.

GLADYS. He was sitting right there, just a minute ago. Your –
Herb! Your *brother*. Where did he go?

Pause.

DANIEL. He – he's not here.

GLADYS. What?

DANIEL *looks at her for a long moment.*

DANIEL. He'll be back later.

GLADYS. Do you want me to give him a message for you?

DANIEL. Um –

GLADYS' *voice has now dropped to a normal level we
haven't heard before. She seems calmer and more self-
possessed, more like her old self must have been once. She
seems to have momentarily crossed over to another place
altogether. She speaks as if* DANIEL *is just one of three or
four people in the room with whom she is talking.*

GLADYS. I used to work for Herb in that lab, you know, when
Herb and I were living in Germany. We used to play tennis
and go dancing – and it was really rather nice. But that was
when the Nazis were marchin' around all over the place,
so after a while we decided to get the hell out of there and
come home.

DANIEL. Can you understand me?

GLADYS *looks right at him, but it's impossible to tell who
or what she is really seeing or hearing.*

GLADYS. What?

DANIEL. Can you understand what I'm saying?

GLADYS. I don't know. I never knew what I was doing...!

DANIEL *gets up and goes to the phone.* GLADYS *does not
notice.*

But when we got to that train station, they were all there to stamp your ticket, and he takes my ticket and he looks at me and he says, 'Bist du judische?' Do you know what that means? It means 'Are you Jewish?' And I looked at him and I said, 'Ich spreche kein Deutsche' – 'I don't speak German.' (*Pause*) But when I took Ellen down South to visit Herb at that army base, it was so damn hot down there, all you could do is sit on the porch and fan yourself! There was no one to talk to. Everyone needs someone to talk to, otherwise you'd just go nutty. I love to talk to people.

DANIEL *dials the phone*.

I'm havin' a good time!

DANIEL *starts crying suddenly and keeps dialing*.

Everybody likes to have a good time. What's wrong with that? (*Eats*.)

DANIEL (*on the phone*).
Mom. Hi, it's me, I'm sorry to wake you – Well I don't know. She's completely out of her mind. She's hallucinating I don't know what, and she's literally talking nonstop. I haven't slept in three days, she wakes me five times a night, and she never, never stops ringing my – doorbell. And I can't take it anymore. I'm really sorry. (*Starts crying again*.) Can you come get her?… Okay. Yeah. All right. I'm really sorry. (*Hangs up*.)

GLADYS. We never did what anybody told us! We used to sneak out of the house all the time! We'd go up to Harlem to hear music, we'd go out dancing… We had a marvelous time. We really did. Now, I used to play a lot of tennis, but I was never very good at it. I just played it for fun, you know. But Jean was a wonderful tennis player, oh, she was marvelous. And you know Ellen was a wonderful tennis player when she was a teenager. Oh, everybody likes to do those things. Nobody likes

> sittin' around in a stuffy old
> house with a lot of boring
> people. You know?

DANIEL *sits on the sofa.*

GLADYS. But Ellen's always been shy, poor thing. We were so
happy when she married Mark because he's had a rough
time, he really has. You can't spend all your time running
around, nobody'll know what you're talking about!

DANIEL *shuts his eyes.*

But Mark is very charming, he works very hard, he's a hell
of a nice guy, and he's a damn good doctor. (*To* DANIEL.)
You're a good doctor.

The lights fade out. The distant clock chimes eight times.

Scene Five

The lights come up on DANIEL, *asleep on the sofa.* GLADYS
is offstage. We can just hear her talking steadily in her sleep.

GLADYS (*murmurs indistinctly offstage*)....There were the
four of us. My sisters, Harriet and Jean, and there was Harold,
of course. He was the youngest. And we had a big old house
out in Brooklyn. Of course this was a long time ago...

ELLEN *uses her key to come into the apartment.*
DANIEL *wakes up with a start.*

ELLEN. Hello.

DANIEL. Oh – Hi.

ELLEN. Did you get any sleep?

DANIEL. Not really. I was afraid she would wander outside...
She finally went to sleep an hour ago... Except she's been
talking in her sleep nonstop... Man, she sure does like to talk.

ELLEN. Oh dear. I'm sorry, Danny. I feel just terrible. We'll take her for a few days and let you get some sleep.

DANIEL (*yawning*). Yeah, I could really use it...

ELLEN *walks around the room.*

ELLEN. I really think we're going to have to move her in with us after the summer. She can't stay here anymore. And if we can rent this place out as an office, we could get a couple of thousand bucks for it and use the money to hire somebody around the clock, because this is really no good... Anyway, why don't you go in your apartment and get some sleep.

DANIEL. Yeah, all right.

Pause.

ELLEN. How are things with you and that girl? You said she...

DANIEL. Um, yeah, she started dating one of my friends.

ELLEN. Oh dear.

DANIEL. She says that my feelings for her are not her issue.

ELLEN. Not her what?

DANIEL. I don't know. I don't really want to talk about it.

ELLEN. Okay...

DANIEL. I guess I'll give her one more try and then give up.

GLADYS (*murmurs offstage*)....We were very lucky. Our parents gave us a wonderful education... We went to museums and concerts and galleries... I never liked school very much, I was always sneakin' off to the library to read plays... (*Trails off.*)

DANIEL. She spent the whole night talking about Herb and Harold and her sisters...

ELLEN. It's all *in* there, I guess. It's just... it's just all – jumbled up... (*Pause*) I *wish* – she would just die peacefully in her sleep, but Dr Wagner says there's nothing wrong with her physically. She could go on like this for another ten years...

DANIEL. Great.

GLADYS (*murmurs offstage*)....Well, we were very anxious, naturally, because nobody ever explained it to us and we just didn't know what to do...

ELLEN. I wonder what she *thinks*. If she thinks anything.

DANIEL. I don't know...

ELLEN. Well... when I get senile just put a bullet through my head.

There is a startled pause.

DANIEL. You won't get senile.

Silence. DON *lets himself into the apartment with a key.*

DON. Oh – Good morning.

ELLEN. Good morning.

DON. Anything the matter?

ELLEN. No, nothing. She had a bad night, so I'm gonna take her uptown for a few days...

DON. Oh. Oh.

ELLEN. How are you?

DON. Uh... well, not so good to tell you the honest truth – uh –

ELLEN. Why? What's the m–

DON. – somebody smashed the windows in my car last night.

ELLEN *and* DANIEL. What?

DON. Somebody smashed all   DANIEL. What is going *on*?
my windows –

                       ELLEN (*with* DANIEL). I *saw*
                       a bunch of windows
                       smashed up –

DON. Yeah! I just went to move my car and three of the windows were smashed in. I asked the doorman in front of the building on the corner if he saw what happened and he said the night guy told him some kids came by last night in a limousine or somethin' and –

ELLEN. Oh my God…

DON. – and one of 'em jumped out of the car and – You want to get this? He smashed in the windows of a buncha cars with one of those – with a giant-sized bottle of champagne.

ELLEN. Are you serious?

DON. Yeah! The guy just went up and down the street smashin' in windows, jumps back in the limousine and drives away down the street.

DANIEL. Jesus Christ.

DON. Do you believe that? I mean, what the hell is *that*?

ELLEN. Did anybody *see* them?

DON. Yeah somebody saw 'em, the night doorman saw the whole thing! He's the one who told the day guy about it. And I asked him, I said, 'Why the heck didn't the guy *do* something? What, the guy just stands there and watches 'em breakin' everybody's windows?'

DANIEL. Those cars get smashed all the time.

DON. I don't even know if I'm covered for vandalism. I know I'm covered for theft… I… You know, Ellen, I don't want to let you down or anything, but I guess I've had it. I'm pretty optimistic by nature, but I gotta admit I'm very, very discouraged by this city. I mean, I surrender. You know? I gotta go home. I can't – I can't even afford this. You been great to me, but…

Silence.

ELLEN. I wouldn't think you could *break* a car window with a bottle.

DON. I guess those giant-sized bottles are made of pretty thick glass. Who knows? Anyway, I figured I'd tell Gladys I can't go to the gallery today. Cops said I should come in and file

a report, but what the hell are *they* gonna do? They should talk
to the friggin' night doorman, is what they should do. But...

Pause.

ELLEN. Well – you have keys to the gallery, right? So...

DON. Yeah, I'll pack the stuff up tomorrow morning. I might
have to make two trips, but I'll let you know what I'm gonna
do. Hope nobody hikes the car while it's sittin' there with no
windows. I, uh – I'm feeling very depressed.

ELLEN. Well, I'm sorry. That's very unpleasant.

DANIEL. Yeah...

DON. I'll say it's unpleasant. (*Pause*) All right, so... Where's
she gonna be, your house?

ELLEN. Yeah, for a few days at least, if you want to –

DON. Okay, I'll swing by later and say goodbye to her,
probably tomorrow... I'd sure like to get my hands on
whoever it was... I don't know if they were white or black or
what, but... They probably were *white*. I was always worried
about these crazy drug guys. Just goes to show you...

ELLEN. Well – That is really revolting.

DON. Well – *I* don't live here.

ELLEN. Okay, Don, see you later.

DANIEL. So long.

DON. Yeah, so long. (*Exits.*)

ELLEN. That is really charming...

GLADYS (*off*). Ohhhhhhhhhh! Ellen? Ellen? Where's Ellen?

They listen closely, thinking she's awake. Pause.

(*Off, still asleep.*) I don't know when they're going to get
there... We never did it that way before...

ELLEN *heads into* GLADYS' *bedroom.*

Scene Six

DANIEL *comes forward. Behind him,* HOWARD *enters, carrying boxes. Under* DANIEL's *speech,* ELLEN *enters with* GLADYS, *who is dressed in a coat.* ELLEN *sits her down and puts her sneakers on for her as* HOWARD *moves boxes.* (*They are moving* GLADYS *out.*)

DANIEL (*to the audience*). After the summer was over, Mom and Howard moved Gladys out of her apartment and up to their building. When I went by the hotel in the fall, I saw that Mr George had not yet begun construction in the gallery. It was exactly as Gladys had left it when we moved her out. Even her desk was still there... A year and a half later, he still hadn't begun construction, and when he finally did, the restaurant didn't actually open until two summers had gone by. And it wasn't a breakfast café, it was just a regular restaurant. It wasn't even attached to the rest of the hotel.

Pause. It seems like he has more to say, but he just stands there for a moment.

HOWARD. Dan.

DANIEL (*turns*). Yeah...

HOWARD. Can you give me a hand with the door, dear?

DANIEL *opens the door for* HOWARD, *who goes out carrying a box.*

Thank you.

ELLEN *kneels in front of* GLADYS, *takes off her slippers and puts on her shoes for her.*

ELLEN (*to* GLADYS). OKAY, WE'RE GOING TO GO NOW.

GLADYS. Are we going to New York?

ELLEN. Yes. Come on. It's time to go.

GLADYS. Who's gonna keep an eye on the – Honey, who's gonna keep an eye on the basement?

ELLEN. WE'LL TAKE CARE OF THE APARTMENT. YOU DON'T HAVE TO WORRY ABOUT THAT ANYMORE.

GLADYS. Well he's worried because he doesn't have a place to stay in the summertime! Are you going to go back for the summer?

ELLEN. NO, IT'S OCTOBER NOW. WE'RE NOT GOING ANYWHERE.

GLADYS. There are two – places in the back. Have you seen those little places? I want to get out when the weather gets better and find myself a little job, because –

ELLEN. COME ON OUT TO THE CAR.

GLADYS. What's the matter? Where am I going?

ELLEN. We're all going uptown together!

GLADYS (*beginning to panic*). But where are you taking me? I can't go outside, I don't have any money!

ELLEN. You don't need any money. Howard and I are going uptown to MY house in the CAR.

GLADYS. No! I don't want to   ELLEN. It's all right, it's
go! Why are you throwing   time to –
me out?

ELLEN. We're not throwing you out, we're all going together.

GLADYS (*crying*). But I don't want to go anywhere, I want to go to New York, I want to get a job!

ELLEN (*walking her toward the door*). We are going to New York! We're all going there now and we're going to have some dinner!

GLADYS. I don't *want* to go outside – I don't have any – *shoulder* – I don't have any *weapons* – Why are you trying to kill me?

ELLEN. Nobody is killing you. Howard will take you out to the car and I'll be right there and then we're going for a short trip in the car to my house, and we'll all be together the whole time. The car is right outside.

GLADYS. Are you going to Brooklyn? Is everybody going to Brooklyn?

HOWARD (*gently takes her arm*). WE'RE GOING UPTOWN TO OUR HOUSE. IT'S A VERY SHORT TRIP.

GLADYS (*crying again*). I don't want to go, I don't understand where you're taking me! I don't want to go by myself!

HOWARD. We'll be with you the whole time. Keep walking.

GLADYS. Keep walking. I don't even know where I'm going! What did I ever do to you?

HOWARD. You didn't do anything and nothing bad is going to happen.

GLADYS. I don't want to go! Where's Ellen? I don't understand why I have to go! I want to paint that place and sell it to the real estate and nobody ever *listens to me*! Wait – wait – I don't have my keys!

HOWARD. YOUR KEYS ARE IN YOUR BAG!

ELLEN. They're around her wrist.

HOWARD. YOU DON'T NEED ANY KEYS –

ELLEN (*stepping up to her*). Your keys are around your wrist. HERE. HERE. BUT YOU DON'T NEED THEM BECAUSE YOU'RE GOING TO STAY WITH US FROM NOW ON.

GLADYS. I don't want to go with you, I want to find my own apartment and I want to get a *job*!

ELLEN. WE CAN TALK ABOUT THAT LATER.

GLADYS. I don't understand where you're taking me!

HOWARD. You'll see where you are when you get there!

HOWARD *takes* GLADYS *out*.

GLADYS (*off*). No! No! I don't want to go with you! I don't want to go!

ELLEN *shuts the door. Silence*.

ELLEN. Oy. All right. (*Pause*) Do you have the lamp?

DANIEL. Yeah, you gave it to me this morning.

ELLEN. Okay. And you don't want the... bureau, no, that's for Annie...

Silence. ELLEN looks around the room.

ELLEN. This place looks really dismal.

DANIEL. Are you gonna fix it up before you try to rent it? or...

ELLEN. Oh yes, we have to, the whole ceiling looks like it's about to come down. (*Pause*) I don't know. I feel so awful. I feel so dismal and hopeless. I don't know what's going to happen to her but I wish it would just happen. (*Pause*) I know she always drove me crazy, but she was never a bad person. She was very loving. And she always wished me well.

DANIEL. I love you, Mom.

ELLEN. I love you too, sweetheart.

ELLEN starts crying. They put their arms around each other.

I came down here in the spring one time, and I caught up with her as she was on her way to the gallery... And she was crawling along at a snail's pace, and her ankles looked so skinny, they were like *tooth*picks – and she just looked like this skinny old lady on the street, she looked as though a wind could blow her over. (*Pause*) She doesn't understand what's happening to her and neither do I...

DANIEL. Mom, I love you so much I can't even tell you. I don't know what I'd do...

After a moment, she pulls away.

ELLEN. All right. I don't want to leave poor Howard with her alone in the car.

DANIEL. All right, I'll see you for dinner tomorrow.

ELLEN. All right, sweetheart. Ay yai yai. Maybe we'll all survive.

She kisses him. Pause.

I think this really did me in. (*Pause*) Let me know if you change your mind about the bureau.

DANIEL. Okay, Mom, I'll see you tomorrow.

ELLEN. Goodbye, sweetheart.

She goes out. DANIEL *comes forward.*

DANIEL (*to the audience*). Gladys moved in with Mom and Howard, where she just got worse and worse. For the last two months of her life all she did was moan, whether she was awake or asleep. A friend of mine said the whole thing was just unanswerable, and I guess it was. After she moved uptown, I would see her when I went to visit, but I was out of it now.

My mother never got out. With the help of Howard, Florence and Marva, she stood by Gladys for the next two years. She took care of her and dressed her and cleaned her up and fed her and watched her fall apart, day in and day out with nothing to stop it and no relief in sight.

One night Mom called me up and told me she thought Gladys was dying. I rode my bike uptown and went into the back room where Gladys lived now. By that time she was just this tiny, eighty-seven-year-old body, lying in the back of her daughter's apartment, hanging on with almost nothing, but struggling anyway for one more breath.

She finally died around two in the morning. And after that, it was a lot easier to remember what she was like before. But I never want to forget what happened to her. I want to remember every detail, because it really happened to her, and it seems like somebody should remember it.

It's not true that if you try hard enough you'll prevail in the end. Because so many people try so hard, and they don't prevail. But they keep trying. They keep struggling. And they love each other so much; it makes you think it must be worth a lot to be alive.

He exits as the lights fade out.

The End.

LOBBY HERO

Author's Note
Kenneth Lonergan

This new edition of *Lobby Hero* contains some very minor cuts and adjustments – just a few lines, really – plus one more significant deletion of a speech I always had my doubts about. I don't like to make changes to a play long after it's basically finished, because I know I'm not as connected to it as I was before. It's true that after a while, your perspective on a play usually becomes much clearer. It's easier to describe to other people (like actors and directors). But one reason you can see the play more clearly is because you are further away from it. You may be able to analyze its parts more consistently and with greater precision, but you are less fit to adjust them, because you are no longer inside the machine with your hands on all the ropes – knowing exactly where each one is and understanding instinctively how it connects to all the rest. It's like the difference between talking to someone who is in love and being in love yourself. Your understanding is engaged in the first case and your emotional life in the second. But you can't write a play without both, and you can't make it any better twenty years later without both. At least, I can't.

That said, if the same few little problems continue to bug me over time, if they are little enough and grating enough, I'll take a chance and try to fix them. The recent Broadway production of *Lobby Hero* gave me a chance to see whether these small cuts and changes would work onstage, and I think they do. The truth is these alterations are so minor that I hesitate even to point them out. But since people familiar with the play might notice the adjustments in this edition, I thought it was worth mentioning.

April 2018

Lobby Hero was first produced by Playwrights Horizons, Inc. (Tim Sanford, Artistic Director; Leslie Marcus, Managing Director; William Russo, General Manager) and opened in New York City on 13 March 2001. The cast was as follows:

JEFF	Glenn Fitzgerald
WILLIAM	Dion Graham
BILL	Tate Donovan
DAWN	Heather Burns

Director	Mark Brokaw
Set Designer	Allen Moyer
Costume Designer	Michael Krass
Lighting Designer	Mark McCullough
Sound Designer	Janet Kalas
Production Manager	Christopher Boll
Stage Manager	James FitzSimmon

The Playwrights Horizons production was subsequently presented by Jenny Wiener, Jon Steingart and Hal Luftig at the John Houseman Theater, New York City, on 8 May 2001.

Lobby Hero received its UK premiere at the Donmar
Warehouse, London, on 4 April 2002. The cast was as follows:

JEFF	David Tennant
WILLIAM	Gary McDonald
BILL	Dominic Rowan
DAWN	Charlotte Randle
Director	Mark Brokaw
Designer	Robert Jones
Lighting Designer	Rick Fisher
Sound *Designer*	Fergus O'Hare

Lobby Hero was revived by Second Stage Theater (Carole
Rothman, Founder and Artistic Director; Casey Reitz,
Executive Director; Christopher Burney, Artistic Producer) and
opened at the Hayes Theater, New York, on 26 March 2018.
The cast was as follows:

JEFF	Michael Cera
WILLIAM	Brian Tyree Henry
BILL	Chris Evans
DAWN	Bel Powley
Director	Trip Cullman
Set Designer	David Rockwell
Costume Designer	Paloma Young
Lighting Designer	Japhy Weideman
Sound Designer	Darron L West
Dialect Coach	Kate Wilson
Production Stage Manager	Barclay Stiff
Stage Manager	Kelly Levy

Casting   Telsey + Company
                                   Adam Caldwell
                                   William Cantler
                                   Karyn Casl
Production Manager   Bethany Weinstein Stewert
General Manager   Seth Shepsle

Characters

JEFF, *a uniformed security guard, late twenties*
WILLIAM, *his captain, late twenties*
BILL, *a uniformed policeman, around thirty*
DAWN, *his rookie partner, early twenties*

Place

The play takes place in the spacious lobby of a middle-income
high-rise apartment building in Manhattan and in the street
outside.

Time

Mid-November, 2000.

ACT ONE

Scene One

The spacious, impersonal lobby of a middle-income high-rise apartment building in Manhattan, and the street immediately outside the glass lobby doors. It is very late at night in mid-November. We hear the periodic sound of cars going by. JEFF, a uniformed security guard in his late twenties, is at his station reading a paperback novel.

WILLIAM, his uniformed supervisor, black, and also in his late twenties, enters onto the street, then into the lobby.

JEFF. Hey, William.

WILLIAM. How's it going there, Jeff?

JEFF. Oh, just fine thanks.

WILLIAM. Any problems tonight?

JEFF. No, none to speak of.

WILLIAM. None 'to speak of?'

JEFF. No problems.

WILLIAM. You want to tell me what the police were doing here?

JEFF. Oh...

WILLIAM. That was a policeman I just saw coming out the building, wasn't it?

JEFF. Oh – Yeah. But –

WILLIAM. You want to tell me what he was doing here?

JEFF. Oh – he was just making a social call, that's all.

WILLIAM. On you?

JEFF. What?

WILLIAM. A social call on you?

JEFF (*laughs*). No, on one of the tenants.

WILLIAM. Can I see your book?

JEFF. Sure.

>   WILLIAM *looks at the sign-in book at* JEFF*'s station.*

>   It was just what's-his-name. That one you're –

WILLIAM (*on 'that'*). Who, Bill?

JEFF. Yeah.

WILLIAM. Is that why you didn't write it down?

JEFF. Um –

WILLIAM. Do you know you're supposed to write it down?

JEFF. Um, yeah.

WILLIAM. Do you know that whenever the police come to the premises you're supposed to make an entry? That's what this Special Remarks is for, right here.

JEFF. Yeah, I –

WILLIAM. Did you know that?

JEFF. Yes.

WILLIAM. Then how come there's no entry?

JEFF. Because he was here on a social visit, that's why.

WILLIAM. Then how come there's no entry on the sign-in sheet?

JEFF. Because I'm a fuck-up?

WILLIAM. See? No record in the Special Remarks and nobody signed it in the book. No record. No entry.

JEFF. Do you make the cops sign the book?

WILLIAM. Yes. Or I sign it for them. Yes. And that's what you do too. That's what everybody does, who works under me. Now –

>   JEFF *starts to speak.*

No no no, look, if you stick to the rules, then you never have to have a discussion about whether or not you were justified *not* sticking to the rules, you understand? Now next time the cops come, if it's official business, make a special entry. If it's a social visit and you don't wish to offend, then enter the visit yourself. Okay?

JEFF. Okay.

WILLIAM. Now write it down. And estimate when they arrived and when they left. (*As* JEFF *does so*.) See, man, it's sloppy. It's sloppy. Every time I come in here, man, you're always laughing and telling jokes and putting on the charm, and you're sloppy on the job. Look at this. Look at this. (*Opens the drawers of* JEFF's *station*.) Look at this mess in here, man. It's – Look at this shit. You got gum wrappers, sandwich bags, pornographic magazines – This is a disgusting mess. Now I want you to clean this shit up, man. Tonight. After you're through with your shift. Because I don't want you cleaning up this refuse while you're on duty, man. That's on your own time.

JEFF. Hey William, gimme a break.

WILLIAM. No, man –

JEFF. I am like the most conscientious guy in this whole building. The rest of these guys are like a bunch of crack addicts and degenerates –

WILLIAM. Not for long they're not.

JEFF. Not for long? They're a bunch of –

WILLIAM (*on 'They're'*). Any man on my command who can't straighten out and fly right is gonna get busted, man. I'm giving you guys fair warning, and that means you too, Jeff, man. You're a good man, okay? But you're always making jokes.

JEFF *starts to protest*.

No, listen. Every time I turn around I'm hearing one joke after another and it makes me question how serious a person you are.

JEFF. How else am I supposed to stay awake?

WILLIAM *is not amused.*

I'm just kidding.

WILLIAM. I'm glad to hear that, Jeff, because if I ever catch
you or anybody else ever sleeping on a shift I will fire your
ass on the spot, just like I did last week with Louie Moore,
over on Fifty-eighth Street. He was two years away from
retirement, I found him asleep on his shift, and I stood him
up and I ripped the badge right off his shirt and I'll do the
same thing to you. Do you understand me?

JEFF. Yes, yes, I understand. That certainly was terrific how
you fired that skinny old man right before he was supposed
to retire.

WILLIAM. He wasn't doing his job, man. Nobody's paying
him to take a nap. Now I'm gonna ask you again. What was
that cop doing here?

JEFF. I *told* you why he was here.

WILLIAM. Because if he was here asking to see me, Jeff,
I want you to tell me. Even if he told you not to. I want you
to tell me. Do you understand?

JEFF. What? He didn't ask about you.

WILLIAM. Okay.

JEFF. Why would he be looking for you? Or shouldn't I ask.

WILLIAM. It's none of your business, man.

JEFF. Okay. I'm not askin'.

WILLIAM. See? Always gotta be invading somebody's private
business.

JEFF. Hey, get off my *back*, all right?

WILLIAM. Excuse me?

JEFF. I said get off my back. I didn't *do* anything to you. And
this is not even my shit in here, it's Manuel's.

He slaps the drawer closed.

WILLIAM. All right. I'm sorry. I got a call – my fuckin' brother got picked up by the cops – I don't even want to *tell* you what for – and I just want to be prepared if the police come around asking about his whereabouts.

JEFF. Oh. (*Beat.*) Okay. I'm sorry.

WILLIAM. That's all right.

JEFF. Well – They really weren't here to see you.

WILLIAM. All right. It just seemed like a strange coincidence.

JEFF. Well, I mean – is your brother all right?

WILLIAM. I don't know. I haven't spoken to him.

JEFF. I didn't even know you had a brother.

WILLIAM. Well, I do.

JEFF. What did they bust him for?

WILLIAM *shakes his head.*

Okay, skip it.

WILLIAM. My brother's fucked up. He's always been a fuck-up. Always been selfish. Always been wild and selfish: You know the type. Living like a free spirit or what have you, while everybody else is trying to work. You know the type? I mean – I don't know, man. Sometimes you just have to wash your hands of a person. Because you just get no recompense. You know what I mean there, Jeff? You must know what I mean. You've seen something of the world. I've never seen anything of the world. I've been working for security firms since I was sixteen years old. Do you know I'm the youngest captain in the history of this firm? But I'm square, man. You know? I'm square. I'm no fun.

JEFF. That's very true.

WILLIAM. And I will bust your ass, all you guys, if you mess up on my shifts, because I don't *let* people mess up on my shifts. That's how I got to *be* the youngest captain in the

history of this fucking no-account security firm. I can't
believe some of the people they hire, man. Can you?
I mean – Did you happen to see that article in *The New York
Times* about security companies in New York City? Guys
with long prison records, rapists, murderers, anybody at all
who can sign his name they stick a gun on his waist and set
him up to protect somebody. You want to explain that
insanity to me? I personally got rid of three guys they had
working for this company, man, because these guys were just
out-and-out criminals. You can't just hire anybody who looks
like he can manhandle a person, you know?

JEFF. Sure.

WILLIAM. Anyway, I'm just rambling.

JEFF. Ramble away, man. This is the highlight of my night.

WILLIAM. So how's it going with you anyway, Jeff?
Everything all right?

JEFF. Yeah, pretty good. I been looking for apartments.

WILLIAM. Oh yeah? How's that going?

JEFF. Pretty good. I saw this one place today that was actually
really pretty nice, but it was a little out of my range. I still
owe my brother a lot of money.

WILLIAM. Maybe he'll forgive the debt.

JEFF. I don't want him to forgive the debt. I wanna pay him
back every cent I owe him – with interest. The hell with that.
I'd rather live in that room for the next five years if it meant
I couldn't pay him back. I'm a reformed character, man.
I don't take nothin' off of nobody, no thank you, no more.

WILLIAM. I can see I've been a very positive influence on you,
Jeff.

JEFF. You have, man, you're a positive inspiration.

Silence.

Hey, you know, I got that book you told me about… *The Six
Habits of Self-Motivated People*?

WILLIAM. Oh yeah? Did you read it?

JEFF. Well, I *tried* to read it…

WILLIAM. All right, you know what?

JEFF. – I just couldn't get past the first two habits.

WILLIAM. Yeah, all right –

JEFF. – I guess I wasn't really that motivated.

WILLIAM. – All right, never mind.

JEFF. No, seriously. I did try to read it. I just don't usually respond to that kind of stuff. I mean I'm sure it has good stuff in it… It just kind of seemed like bullshit to me.

WILLIAM. Well, you have to have an open mind.

JEFF. Yeah, I guess…

WILLIAM. And you have to be willing to address some of your own shortcomings. Otherwise you're just wasting your time.

JEFF. Well, see, I don't have any shortcomings. So that's probably why I couldn't get into it…

  WILLIAM *is not amused.*

  I do have a terrific sense of humor though. That's one thing you can definitely say about me.

WILLIAM. Yeah. Keep laughing, Jeff.

JEFF. I'm just kidding. Maybe it was good. To tell you the truth I couldn't really focus on it too well. I'm having trouble concentrating on anything I read lately.

WILLIAM. Oh yeah? Why is that?

JEFF. I don't know. I guess I have a lot on my mind these days.

WILLIAM. Like what?

JEFF. Well, my best friend from when I was a kid, my friend Scott, is getting married in a few days, so I've been roped into arranging this bachelor party we're supposed to give him. So that's distracting…

WILLIAM. From what?

JEFF. What?

WILLIAM. Distracting from what? All you do is sit here. You
have no interests –

JEFF. I have interests –

WILLIAM. No family –

JEFF. I have a family –

WILLIAM. But you have no wife, no children –

JEFF. Oh, well –

WILLIAM. That's what *I* mean by a family – Somebody you're
responsible for.

JEFF. Well –

WILLIAM. – You have no ambition, as far as I can see –

JEFF. I don't tell you everything about myself.

WILLIAM. Okay, good. I'm glad to hear it. But that's why I try
to get you to improve your mind a little bit and apply
yourself to something. Aim a little higher. But I can see it's
a hopeless cause.

JEFF. You just don't want to admit –

WILLIAM (*without stopping*). You're probably intended to be
just one of those guys who drifts through life doing one job
or another, no plan, no specific intentions of any kind… And
one day you're gonna wake up in a lobby just like this one,
except everybody's gonna be calling you 'Pops.' And then
you're gonna look back and remember: 'I should have
listened to that guy William. He's the only one that ever took
the time to try to encourage me to cultivate my potential. My
whole family was content to see me fritter my life away, but
that William, man, he really tried to get me to focus my
energies a little bit. And doddering useless old unemployed
Pops doorman that I am, I have to admit he could have been
a positive influence on me if I hadn't been such a callous,

careless kind of joke-telling, sit-on-my-ass-my-whole-life type of person when I was younger.' But I guess that's all right, because you're not really trying to climb any higher anyway. You see what I mean?

JEFF. I just wish to hell you'd stop trying to butter me up all the time. You know it's embarrassing for both of us the way you're always coming in here trying to kiss my ass.

WILLIAM. Okay. Keep laughing, Jeff. 'Cause the joker laughs last. And the joker's gonna laugh last at you.

JEFF. What do you mean, like the Joker from *Batman*?

WILLIAM. No –

JEFF. What the fuck are you talking about?

WILLIAM. I just mean – Like, you know, like the generic joker. Like the laughing figure of Fate, or whatever you want to call it.

JEFF (*a joke:*). Oh, sure, *that* joker. Everyone's terrified of him.

WILLIAM. Go ahead and laugh, Jeff. The joker laughs last.

JEFF. I have interests…

WILLIAM. I'm glad to hear it.

JEFF. …Just 'cause I don't tell *you* about it doesn't mean I don't have them.

WILLIAM. All right, good.

JEFF. – Anyway you work here too, man! So what are you getting on *my* ass   WILLIAM. Oh no I don't! about it for? What do you mean, 'No you don't'? *You're* working the graveyard shift!

WILLIAM. *I'm* working the graveyard shift cause that's the shift everybody messes up, okay? I told Joe Collier I was gonna weed out the bad apples in this company and that's exactly what I'm gonna do. That's what I'm doing on the graveyard shift, Jeff. I'm not just sitting here getting old before my time...

JEFF. I'm not getting old	WILLIAM....I'm working
before my time –	my way through the
Oh good for you!	ranks...

WILLIAM....and by the time I'm through I'm gonna clean this place up and move up into management, and if they don't want to move me up the way that I deserve, I'm gonna go off on my own and set myself up to compete with these bums, because I know I could do a better job than them with my eyes closed.

JEFF. Okay, good for you. I was in the Goddamn *Navy* for three years...

WILLIAM. All right, don't lose your temper...

JEFF. No, man, why you gotta come in here and be ragging on me all the time?

WILLIAM. Oh, oh, you can dish it out but you can't take it.

JEFF. I can take it, but there's a *limit*. There's a *level*. I been busting my ass all year tryin' to get my shit together.

WILLIAM. All right –

JEFF. – You of all people should be *encouraging* me. I just had a little bad luck, that's all. Anybody could have a little bad luck.

WILLIAM. Didn't you tell me you got kicked out of the Navy for being on guard duty smoking marijuana?

JEFF. Yeah, but it was bad luck that I got *caught*. The rest of my friends are still sailin' the ocean blue gettin' stoned out of their minds. I get high *one time* and suddenly I'm out on my ass?

WILLIAM. All I'm sayin' is if you hadn't been smoking that stuff in the first place you wouldn't have to be relying on any kind of luck – good, bad, or otherwise. Personally, I believe in giving people a second chance. And I like you. I don't know why I like you, but I do. I regard you as a project. I think you have a lot of potential.

JEFF. No you don't.

WILLIAM. Yes I do, Jeff. Because every human being walking around on this earth has potential, Jeff, including you.

JEFF. Oh Jesus Christ.

WILLIAM. Go ahead and laugh. You probably have more potential than the rest of these guys put together.

Pause.

JEFF. You think?

WILLIAM. Yes I do. If you really applied yourself…? Who knows what you might be good at down the road? You can't measure that potential. It's never been measured.

JEFF. Well, thanks, William. I take that as encouragement.

WILLIAM. That's how it's meant. But you can't just –

JEFF. I always thought I had a lot of potential. I guess I just lost my way a little bit.

WILLIAM. That happens to a lot of people, Jeff. But you can't just –

JEFF. I know. And I'm not blaming anybody else – seriously. But I really had a rough time the last couple of years.

WILLIAM *starts to speak.*

I'm not sayin' it's all bad luck. I know you gotta take some responsibility for yourself –

WILLIAM. That's right.

JEFF. I know, I know. But do you know from the time I came home from the Navy my old man wouldn't even talk to me? I only went into the Navy to get him off my back in the first place. Then I get kicked out –

WILLIAM. Why wouldn't he talk to you?

JEFF. Because he was ashamed of me, that's why. 'Cause he was this big Navy guy, 'cause he saved all these guys' lives on his ship when he was in Korea. Big deal.

WILLIAM. Really.

JEFF. Yeah. It's actually a really amazing story. Ship hits an old mine at two o'clock in the morning, twenty-three guys trapped below decks. Everybody jumps overboard except my old man. He finds a blowtorch, goes below decks in the pitch dark, the ship is goin' like *this* – (*Makes a steep incline with his hand.*) these guys are screamin' for their lives, there's water comin' up to his elbows… Two minutes before the ship goes down he cuts open the bulkhead, everybody gets out. Twenty-three guys he saved, not one of 'em drowned.

WILLIAM. That's very impressive.

JEFF. Yeah: I know it is impressive, because my whole *life* I gotta hear this fuckin' story. Several times a year as you can probably imagine, over and over and over again. Every year when I was a kid they had this big get-together in New Jersey; they send flowers, cards, whiskey, cigars, all these old guys and their wives and kids and grandkids who they never woulda had all cryin' and kissin' my old man and makin' speeches about what a great guy he is. And I'm like, Yeah, that's because you only gotta see the guy *once a year*, for like three and a half hours at a time. Any of you morons tried living with this guy for two days you'd throw him in the fucking ocean and drown him yourself. Asshole. Maybe if *my* ship woulda blown up I woulda got a better start in life. Anyway, so naturally when I got kicked out the guy won't even talk to me. And I don't mean for a few days. I mean he never talked to me again. He don't want my *mother* talking to me, I got nowhere to live, I bum around like a… *bum*. I gotta move in with Marty, which is totally humiliating. My old man dies, thank God –

WILLIAM. All right…

JEFF. – I can't get a job, I try to work up a little stake playing poker, I turn around I got the Goddamn loan sharks comin'

after me, I gotta borrow five thousand dollars from my
brother to keep me from getting my legs broken. I date this
girl, it turns out she used to be a prostitute. So okay,
nobody's perfect. Then it turns out she's *still* a prostitute,
only now she only does it 'on the side,' whatever the hell
that means. I break up with her, I'm scared I'm gonna get
AIDS, I can't meet anybody –

WILLIAM. Yeah, I get the idea.

JEFF. And *then*, William, *then*, I come to you, William, and with
your beautiful generosity, you give me this job, you take a
little interest in me, and look at me now: I'm payin' my own
rent to Marty, buyin' my own groceries. I'm lookin' around for
my own place, which'll be the first time I had my own home
in six years. My own little living room where I can sit and
watch TV; a nice little kitchen I can cook my own meals in...
Invite a girl over for dinner and be the *only one there with her*.
And I'm a healthy happy member of the workforce for nine
months straight come Friday. And I'll tell you something else,
man, my spirit is okay. I don't have a broken spirit. I just want
to stick it out here for at least a year, so I can really get that
under my belt – just for my own – just psychologically.

WILLIAM. No, I think that's smart –

JEFF. Yeah, that's what I told myself. At least one year, right?
Day shift, night shift, I don't care. And William, I owe it all
to you. So see? You really helped somebody. Now that might
just be your good character, but it's my good luck.

WILLIAM. Glad to be of service, Jeff. You're doin' all right.

JEFF. Thanks, man. I gotta tell you, I feel pretty good.

WILLIAM. All right, man. I should get going on my rounds.

WILLIAM *doesn't move*.

JEFF. Hey, have you seen that little cop – what's that big-shot
cop's name?

WILLIAM. Who, Bill?

JEFF. Yeah, Bill. Have you seen his new partner?

WILLIAM. Yes.

JEFF. Can I share something with you? Sometimes I have this fantasy I'm being tied up and interrogated by all these lady cops – Like they have me handcuffed to a chair, and I'm naked, and they're walking around in nothing but their hats and gun belts...

WILLIAM (*not interested*). You know what, Jeff?

JEFF....and the way they get me to talk is by taking turns – you know, doing stuff to me – like, sexually arousing me, see, but only up to a certain point, till I can't take it anymore and I have to tell 'em what they want to know, so I can get some relief.

Pause.

WILLIAM. What in the world makes you think I'd be interested in that, man?

JEFF. I don't know. You think that little cop would be interested? Maybe she'd find it titillating. You know: sexy.

WILLIAM. I have no idea. But if I were you I'd just forget about the whole thing because she'll just end up making you feel small.

JEFF. Why would you say that?

WILLIAM. Because whatever you do, you're just an imitation cop and she's a real cop. And if you get involved with some lady policewoman it is a sure bet you're gonna end up feeling outranked and outclassed.

JEFF. I always feel that way. My last girlfriend was a tollbooth collector, and *she* intimidated the shit out of me. At least if I was going out with a cop, I'd feel, you know, somewhat safe.

WILLIAM. Go ahead and laugh, man. You know what's gonna happen to you?

JEFF. Yeah, I know, the Joker's gonna get me.

Silence.

What's the matter, man? You worried about your brother?

WILLIAM. Yeah, I'm pretty worried.

JEFF. So but, what did he do?

> WILLIAM *does not respond.*

> What's the matter? You can tell me.

WILLIAM. It's not a question of that, Jeff...

JEFF. I'm not gonna say anything... Maybe I could be helpful. Maybe I could give you some special insight into the workings of the fuck-up mind.

WILLIAM. I'm sure you could.

JEFF. That's okay. I don't wanna... I just want to offer my services as a friendly person, that's all. But if it's too private, I understand. No pressure. I don't take it – you know... I don't take it personally or anything.

WILLIAM. All right... I should get going.

JEFF. Hey, maybe you should run upstairs and see Mrs Heinvald for a few minutes before you take off. She's looking unbelievable.

WILLIAM. No thanks, Jeff.

JEFF. Come on, man, I think a little visit to ol' Mrs Heinvald might be just what you need.

WILLIAM. I don't think my wife would appreciate that too much, man.

JEFF. All right. I hope your brother's all right.

WILLIAM. Thank you. (*Pause*) I'll see you tomorrow.

JEFF. I'll be here.

WILLIAM. I know you will, Jeff.

> WILLIAM *walks out.* JEFF *is left alone in the lobby. He locks the door, goes to his station, picks up his paperback novel and starts reading. He gets bored, looks up, and stares off into the long night ahead.*

Scene Two

Late the next night. JEFF *is in the lobby. Two uniformed police officers,* BILL, *around thirty, and* DAWN, *early twenties, are on the street outside.* JEFF *cannot hear them.*

BILL. Take it easy, will you? Just take it easy.

DAWN. I'm sorry. I guess I'm still a little bit shook up, you know?

BILL. Hey, that is totally natural, I'd be worried if you weren't a little shook up. Okay?

DAWN. Yeah, okay.

BILL. But. Just want you to know, you handled yourself pretty good back there.

DAWN. Yeah? (*Pause*) It was no big deal.

BILL. You kept your head, you took control of the situation, you did exactly what you were supposed to do. Okay? You were great!

DAWN (*delighted*). Shut up.

BILL. I'm serious.

DAWN. So but, is there really gonna be like an inquiry?

BILL. Yeah, but don't worry about that…

DAWN. But what do they usually do? Do they –

BILL. They just – You gotta go down to the Trial Room… they ask you what happened… they ask me what happened… They read your *report*, they read *my* report… Then they say okay, thanks, and that's it. Don't worry about it. Anyway, that guy's gonna be fine… I mean, I personally wouldn'ta hit him quite that *hard*… But that's a judgment call. You know? Plus the fact is, if *I* hit him like that he'd probably be dead right now.

DAWN. Yeah, well, for a minute there I thought he was dead, you know?

BILL. Believe me. That guy is fine. Don't worry about it. Besides, he totally had it comin'.

DAWN. You told me you gotta establish yourself...

BILL. Absolutely. No question about it. I don't think there's an officer in the Division, male or female, wouldn'ta done the exact same thing the exact same way. Only probably not as good.

DAWN. Thanks. (*Pause*) That means a lot, comin' from you.

BILL. What do you mean?

DAWN (*looking at her shoes*). Well you know – I mean – that's all.

BILL. What did I ever do to deserve such high praise?

DAWN. You? Oh, only nothin'.

BILL. Seriously.

DAWN. What did you *do* – ? Come on.

She shakes her head, smiling.

BILL. You like the way I handle myself.

DAWN. Uh, slightly. Yeah.

BILL. But what do you *think* of me? Seriously now. What do you think of *me*?

DAWN. I think you're – I think you're the most dedicated person I ever met.

BILL. Don't butter me up.

DAWN. I think you're the best cop I ever saw.

BILL. No shit?

DAWN. Don't ask me questions if you don't want a straight answer. I don't fuck around. You want to know something all you gotta do is ask me. You want a lot of bullshit you can go talk to Lieutenant Finelli or whatever his fuckin' name is.

BILL. You don't like Bob Finelli?

DAWN. I don't care. He can talk shit if he wants. I don't care.

BILL. So I'm the best cop you ever saw?

DAWN. You heard what I said. You also got a swelled head the size of... somethin' really big, but you're the kind of cop I'd like to be, and that's the truth.

BILL. You're fulla crap.

DAWN. No –

BILL. All those guys've been filling your head with a lotta shit. So don't pay too much attention to any kind of flashy stories you mighta heard about me. You know last month? When I got my commendation – now that's the fifth year in a row I got that commendation. So *what*? I'm finally on the list to get my gold shield, these guys are runnin' around Jerry McAllen's house, sayin' shit about me, callin' me Supercop, and I – Frank Hall. Gives me this T-shirt with a – with one of them photographs, you can get the photograph put on the T-shirt...?

DAWN (*smiling*). Yeah...?

BILL. And he had this T-shirt made with my head on a picture of Superman – underneath it says 'Super Bill.' But that is *bull*shit.

DAWN. I don't think it's bullshit.

BILL. Okay, tough guy.

She is smiling openly, embarrassed.

What are you smilin' like that for?

DAWN (*turning away*). I don't know.

BILL. What are you turnin' away for?

DAWN. I'm not turning away.

BILL. What are you, flirting with me?

DAWN. No.

BILL. You flirting with your partner?

DAWN. No…!

BILL. That's against the law, you know.

DAWN. No it's not. I'm not doin' it, but it's not against the law if I was.

BILL. Any more of this and I'm gonna sue your ass for sexual harassment.

DAWN. Yeah, right, I think it's a little late for that.

Pause. They look at each other.

BILL. All right. I'm gonna go up and see my friend Jim for a few minutes, and then we're gonna get back to work. Then after we sign out, we'll go get ourselves a little drink…? If you want. If not, I totally understand.

Long pause.

DAWN. All right.

BILL. All right, good. (*Pause*) Now straighten up and try to behave yourself – good-looking.

DAWN. I'll try.

They go into the lobby. JEFF *looks up from his book.*

JEFF. Evening, guys.

BILL. I'm just going to 22-J. You don't have to call up.

BILL *moves past him toward the exit to the elevators.*

JEFF. Sorry – Officer? Officer? Could I just get your autograph here?

He gestures to his visitor sign-in book. BILL *misunderstands him.*

BILL (*pleased*). You want my autograph?

JEFF. If you don't mind.

BILL. All right…

BILL *approaches the desk and breaks out his pen.*

So how do you know who I am?

JEFF. I don't know. I've seen you *around*... Who are you?

BILL. You just told me you wanted an autograph.

JEFF. Oh – No, I just meant could you sign in, in my book here. I was just using an amusing form of words.

BILL *looks at him and puts his pen away.* DAWN *is amused.*

BILL (*to* DAWN). I'll be down in a few minutes.

JEFF. Actually – Officer? I'm sorry. If you could just sign in, that'd be –

BILL. Don't worry about it, it's all right.

BILL *exits.* JEFF *signs him in.* DAWN *waits.* JEFF *looks at her. Long pause.*

JEFF. How you doin'?

DAWN. Good.

JEFF. Busy night?

DAWN. Not so busy.

JEFF. Things have really been hoppin' around here, I gotta tell you.

DAWN. Oh yeah?

JEFF. Oh my God, I haven't had a minute to sit down. People comin' *in* the lobby, people goin' *out* of the lobby. Elevator goin' up, elevator goin' down. *Thoughts* flyin' in and out of my head: It's been crazy.

DAWN. Maybe you better just slow it down.

JEFF (*gesturing to the busy lobby around him*). How can I?

DAWN. I don't know.

JEFF. Hey, can I ask you something, Officer?

DAWN. Yeah?

JEFF. Do you know why the New York City cops changed from the light-blue shirts to the dark-blue shirts recently? Like a couple of years ago?

DAWN. No, why?

JEFF. No – I'm not sayin' like, 'Do you know,' and then like I tell you the *answer*. I'm really asking, 'cause I thought you might know.

DAWN. Oh. No. I don't.

JEFF. But remember how a long time ago, like when we were kids, the police uniforms used to be all dark blue? And then around the 1980s I guess, they switched to the dark-blue pants and a light-blue shirt? And then recently they switched 'em back to the dark-blue pants and a dark-blue shirt again? What *I* always wondered was, did they throw out all the old dark-blue pants when they did that? Or did they just throw out the light-blue shirts and then get dark-blue shirts that matched the old dark-blue pants, so they wouldn't have to buy all new pants? Because that would be quite a savings.

DAWN. I have no idea.

JEFF. If you think about it, you could be wearing pants right now that were being worn by some lady cop in 1975, if you think about it. Except I guess the women police officers didn't wear pants back in 1975. I don't mean they didn't wear *pants*, like they were walkin' around in their underwear. I just mean I think they were still wearin' skirts back then, weren't they? I know I'm blathering, I'm just completely in love with you – can I just say that?

DAWN. Okay, take it easy.

JEFF. No, I am, man: I seen you go by a lot over the last few weeks and I just think you are *it*, man; I'd do anything if you would just give me the time of *day*.

DAWN. Okay –

JEFF. And I don't mean any disrespect –

DAWN. Oh of course not.

JEFF. Your generation of lady cops are like *pioneers* as far as I'm concerned. I think you guys are *great*. But I also happen to find most of you extremely sexy, okay?

DAWN. Get outta here.

JEFF. How long have you been a cop?

DAWN. I don't know. How long you been a doorman?

Pause.

JEFF. No, I'm not a doorman. I'm a security officer.

DAWN. Congratulations. Now how about givin' me a break.

JEFF. Sure. Fine. (*Pause*) Givin' the cop a break. (*Pause*) I guess
it's just the gun, and the handcuffs... the big stick.

DAWN. All right already!

JEFF. Hey, look: You're wearin' a uniform and I'm wearin'
a uniform.

DAWN. So?

JEFF. So we both got uniforms. Let's get together.

DAWN. You meet a lot of girls this way?

JEFF. No, hardly any. (*Pause*) What do you work, ten to six?

DAWN. So?

JEFF. Just askin'. I'm on twelve to eight. But I don't mind it. It's
quiet. Plus, like, that's the other thing: Not a lot of people
come in after 1 or 2 a.m., so I always have a newspaper, see,
so what I do is after two I lock the door, and I take the
newspaper, and I sit like this... (*Putting the newspaper in front
of his face.*) so it looks like I'm reading the paper, and I can
just sleep that way. And if somebody's at the door they knock,
and if somebody comes downstairs the elevator dings, and I
just swing around and here I am. (*Demonstrates.*) See?

DAWN. Oh yeah, if I lived here that'd make me feel real safe.

JEFF. They feel safe. They don't know I'm sleeping. But I
actually – See, this is just temporary for me. I've only been
doin' this nine months. And it's a good job, but I couldn't be
a security guard my whole life. You know? I'm way too
restless. Plus I lived all over the world when I was a kid,

'cause my dad was in the Navy, and then I was in the Navy, so I know there's a bigger world out there. I really actually want to get into advertising, is what my dream is.

DAWN. Oh yeah...?

JEFF. I don't mean that to sound too pathetic, like 'How's *this* guy ever gonna get into advertising?' But I often thought that that could be a field that I might be kind of good at. Thinkin' up funny slogans for things...

DAWN. Uh-huh...?

JEFF. ...Thinkin' up different ways to advertise things. Well, I know it's probably a pretty hard field to get into, obviously, so at this point it's pretty much in fantasy land, but... (*Pause*) Must be interesting being a cop.

DAWN. It's interesting.

JEFF. You're a rookie, right? Come on, I can tell you're a rookie.

DAWN. Oh yeah?

JEFF. Boy, you must have a lot of guts. That's all I can say. I mean I know it takes guts just to be a cop in the first place, but to be a woman cop? That takes guts. Hats off to you. I'm not kidding.

DAWN. Yeah, well, I wouldn't know about that.

JEFF. Are there a lot of cops in your family or something?

DAWN. I'm the first.

JEFF. Good for you, man. That's awesome. I'm the first security guard in my family.

DAWN. Oh yeah?

JEFF. Yeah. It's kind of a point of pride with me.

DAWN. Yeah, I could see that.

JEFF. Hey, is it true that a female cop – (*As she starts to bristle.*) Now wait a minute, this is not bullshit; I'm really curious.

DAWN. Yeah…?

JEFF. Is it true that a female cop is likelier to shoot her gun or use her weapon or whatever than a male cop because she can't – you know, because she can't overpower you in any other way?

DAWN. No. That's a myth. They teach you a lot more than shooting, believe me.

JEFF. Really? Like what? (*Stepping back.*) I'm not asking for a demonstration, I'm just asking like what do they teach you. Have you been involved in –

DAWN (*on 'been'*). They teach you a lot of things. Like –

JEFF. Like what?

DAWN. Like you try to control the situation –

JEFF. So like how do you –   DAWN. Like tonight we had
                                     to break up this brawl –

JEFF. Oh yeah? I'm sorry –

DAWN. That's all right. So we get there and these two guys are goin' at it outside this restaurant, right? So Bill – that's my partner –

JEFF (*overlapping*). Uh-huh? Yeah, I know –

DAWN. – he pulls this one guy away, and I go, 'Okay, let's break it up.' So then this big fat guy whips around, he says, 'Why? What are *you* gonna do about it, bitch?' Then he starts *chargin'* me.

JEFF. Really? This is a fantastic story!

DAWN. Oh yeah. But what you do is you just pivot back, like you pivot back and then you bring your nightstick up – you know, not to take their head off, but just to bring 'em down. Except I guess I got a little enthusiastic and I really whacked this guy, and that was it. Boom.

JEFF. What do you mean, boom? What happened to him?

DAWN. Nothin'. He had to go to the hospital.

JEFF. Really? You put him in the hospital?

DAWN. Oh yeah. You shoulda seen him. There was fuckin' blood *every*where. It was superficial of course. But your head can really bleed a lot.

JEFF. So… don't take this the wrong way, but would that qualify as police brutality at all?

DAWN. No. No way! He was totally comin' at me. And this guy was huge. But then, naturally of course two seconds later his wife comes outta the restaurant and she's screamin' 'I'm an attorney, I'm callin' the CCRB, I'm gonna sue you…'

JEFF. Calling the who?

DAWN. The CCRB? The
Civilian Complaint Review
Board? Which – you know –   JEFF. Oh, yeah, okay, yeah.
is definitely their right to
do that. But that could be kinda serious for me, 'cause I'm still on my probation? Like your first six months you're not like a full cop. You're what they call a Probationary Officer. And if you can't handle it or you just screw up, you're just out. You're off the Force. But Bill saw the whole thing and he says it's no problem. So I gotta go through a little song and dance. Big deal.

JEFF. And you didn't have to use your gun.

DAWN. Oh no. Definitely not. He was just some stupid drunk.

JEFF. But are you a pretty good shot?

DAWN. Yeah. I'm okay.

JEFF. That's excellent. (*Pause*) So what's he doin' up there anyway? Investigatin' a crime or somethin'?

DAWN. No, he's just saying hello to a friend.

JEFF. He's a friend of Mrs Heinvald?

Pause.

DAWN. Who?

JEFF. Mrs Heinvald.The lady in 22-J.

DAWN (*confused*). No.Yeah. (*Pause*) 22-J – Yeah. I guess so. (*Pause*) *I* don't know her. *I* don't know who lives there.

JEFF. Well, I don't wanna say nothin', but he's liable to be up there a long time.

DAWN. What's it to you?

JEFF. I didn't say anything. I just don't see why you should have to cool your heels in the lobby eating your heart out while he's upstairs gettin' laid.

Pause.

DAWN. He's not gettin' laid.

JEFF. Oh, come on.

DAWN. Hey, look: First of all – we're in the middle of our shift.

JEFF. Oh my God, excuse me, you're right, it's impossible.

Pause.

DAWN. Who did you say lives in that apartment?

JEFF. Mrs Heinvald. Amy Heinvald. She's an actress or a model or something. She's divorced. She's...

DAWN. Have you seen him here a lot?

JEFF. Sure, I seen him a few times. How long you been working together?

Pause.

DAWN. What makes you think he's... you know.

JEFF. Because the lady he's visiting has a very active social schedule, if you see what I mean.

DAWN. No. I don't.

JEFF. I just mean she –

DAWN. What do you mean?

JEFF. I mean she's got a lot of boyfriends. That's all.

DAWN*'s heart slowly breaks.*

Hey, don't listen to me. I don't know what I'm talking about. Maybe I'm wrong. Maybe your partner is like, her favorite uncle or something.

DAWN. Yeah.

She moves away from him.

JEFF. Hey... how come male cops are so big and fat and female cops are so young and beautiful?

DAWN. Yeah, how come doormen never know when to shut up?

JEFF. I don't know. That's an interesting point. Only I wouldn't be able to comment on it because I'm not a doorman. I'm a security guard.

DAWN. I don't fucking believe this.

JEFF. Hey, the guy is only human. You gotta *see* this lady –

DAWN. Hey, look: I'm not talking about him. I don't even – Look, you wanna know something? I don't even know why I'm *talking* to you. And if my partner wants to take time off his shift to go get laid with Mrs Whatever-She-Is, you know what? More power to him, that's what I say –

JEFF. I agree!

DAWN. Because I seen him do more good for more people than anybody I ever met in my *life*. And if he wants to see that *model* in 22-J, that is his business, not mine –

JEFF. Sure!

DAWN. – and not yours. And I don't need to get *hit* on by the night *doorman* while he's upstairs gettin' his rocks off with some fuckin' whore.

JEFF. Hey lady, I am not a doorman, I'm a security guard. I told you three fuckin' times already – In	DAWN. I don't give a shit what you are, just keep your mouth shut! Good!

fact, I'm a security *specialist*! So –

Just keep your mouth shut! You talk to me, you keep your mouth shut, you understand?

JEFF. What?

DAWN. What?

Pause.

JEFF. How can I talk to you and keep my mouth shut at the same time?

DAWN. Forget it. For*get* about it. For*get* about it.

Pause.

JEFF. I'm not trying to make trouble.

DAWN. Just stop trying to pick me up.

JEFF. I'm not trying to pick you up –

DAWN. Why don't you try speaking to me like I was an officer of the law? Just like, as an experiment.

JEFF. I'm sorry. I'm not usually this attracted to police officers.

DAWN. Well, you're lucky.

She moves away from him. Pause.

JEFF. What's your name?

DAWN. Officer Wilson.

JEFF. Oh come on. What's your name? (*Pause*) Are you a sports fan? Come on. That's a harmless question. What do you like, basketball? A lot of girls like basketball. It's graceful. Well, a lot of sports are very graceful though, actually. What's your feeling about the impending garbage strike? My name's Jeff. Twenty-seven, never been married, never been in debt. Well, I have been in a little bit of debt actually, but that's pretty much all cleared up now. I'm a different person now. Really, I've turned over a whole new leaf –

DAWN. Would you shut *up*?

JEFF. Sure, I'd be glad to. Why don't *you* say something for a few seconds and then I'll say something back and we'll go on like that. I'm a Goddamn security guard for Christ's sake. I'm lonely as shit. There's three other guys in this building and I never see them except on the video screen. I'll shut up. I'd love to hear somebody else talk.

DAWN. I just don't feel like it right this minute.

JEFF. I understand. I'm not trying to make trouble. And don't listen to me. I don't know what he's doin' up there. I don't know anything about it.

DAWN. Hey, what do I care? The fucking guy is married anyway.

JEFF *goes back to his station and picks up his book. Long silence.*

Can you believe this shit?

JEFF (*puts down his book*). Yeah…They probably don't warn you about this kind of thing in the Police Academy.

DAWN (*a bitter joke*). Sure they do. I took a seminar.

JEFF. What happens if there's a major outbreak of crime on your beat under these circumstances?

DAWN. Oh, then I'm supposed to buzz him.

JEFF. Are there a lot of romances between cops?

DAWN. I don't know… Some of them get married.

JEFF. No, but, I mean like illicit, kind of behind-the-scenes in the back of the squad car type romances.

DAWN. *You're* gonna end up in the back of the squad car in a minute.

JEFF. But seriously, is that a pretty widespread problem?

DAWN. I'm sure it's no different than other kinds of jobs.

JEFF. Well, in other kinds of jobs people have affairs all the time.

DAWN. Well.

Pause.

JEFF. Are you in love with that guy?

DAWN. Who.

JEFF. You know. Your partner. (*Pause*) Because if you are,
I would say that you were in love with the wrong guy.

DAWN. I'm not in love with anybody. I just admired him, that's
all. Okay? He made life a little easier for me in the
Department. Okay? I mean, you look up to somebody, you
take them seriously – and then – That's all. Okay?

JEFF. Okay. (*Pause*) I think it's great what you're doing.
(*Pause*) Your family must be proud of you.

DAWN. Oh, they think I'm nuts. (*Pause*) Well, not exactly, I
mean, my mother thinks I'm a little bit nuts, but I happen to
think that she's nuts too, so there's no harm done there, right?

JEFF. You have a lot of brothers? I bet you have a lot of –

DAWN (*on 'bet'*). But I guess generally they're proud... I was
near the top of my class at the Academy... I just... I just
fucked up with *this* prick, that's all. And now I'm *screwed*.
Because I obviously really misjudged him, you know? And
for all I know he's been shootin' his mouth off all over the
department. And it wouldn't have been so hard to avoid the
whole thing in the first place. But these guys... I mean, they
seen so much horrible shit, it's like they don't give a damn
about anything. So you gotta walk around like you don't give
a damn about anything either. But they know you still do.
And they wanna like, stamp it out of you or something. And
like, test you, all the time. And it's always like: 'Hey –
you're not men, you're not women: You're cops. Act like
cops and you'll be treated like cops.' Only then it turns out
they got a pool going as to who's gonna fuck you first, okay?
And that's fine. I can handle it. You *make* them respect you.
But then somebody decent comes along, and goes out of his
way to make life easier for you – and I didn't even *ask* him,

because I didn't expect anything different – I didn't *want* anything different. And then, Oh my God, it's true love – Except when he comes down in that elevator, just watch: because *I'm* gonna be the one who's gonna be supposed to act like I'm a cop! I mean... (*Pause*) And then I got *you*.

JEFF. So far I'm like the nicest guy in the whole story.

DAWN. Yeah...!

JEFF. So why don't you tell me your name?

DAWN. Because maybe I don't feel like it, Jeff.

JEFF. Okay. You don't have to tell me your name. But, uh, do you want to, uh, do you want to go to a basketball game with me tomorrow afternoon? I got tickets to the Knicks game.

DAWN. I don't like basketball.

JEFF. Okay. Well, um, after I'm finished watchin' the basketball game with my *mother*, would you like to go dancing with me? I don't want to get you on the rebound or anything, but I don't know if I'm ever gonna see you again... I know I'll see your *partner* again... Sorry. I'm sorry.

DAWN. I don't care.

JEFF. ...We'll put on our dress uniforms, we'll go dancin', get bombed and come to work.

DAWN *starts crying and turns away.*

DAWN. God damn it...!

JEFF. What's the matter?

DAWN. I can't be cryin' on duty...!

JEFF. Come on... You'll drive around, you'll shoot some perpetrators, you'll feel better.

DAWN. He is a son of a bitch...!

JEFF. You know what? You're damn right. And I'll tell you something else –

Offstage the elevator pings. They both look sharp as BILL *enters.* (*NOTE: He is hatless now.*)

BILL. Okay. You ready?

DAWN. Yeah.

BILL. What's the matter?

DAWN. Nothin'. What do you mean?

BILL. You got a funny look on your face.

DAWN (*shrugs*). I don't know how I look.

   DAWN *looks away.* BILL *looks at* JEFF.

BILL (*to* JEFF). How you doin'?

JEFF. I'm fine. How are you?

BILL. I'm fine too. (*To* DAWN.) Okay?

DAWN. Yeah. Let's go.

BILL (*to* JEFF). Hey, if you see William around, tell him Bill says hello.

JEFF. Sure thing.

   They go outside and exit. JEFF *picks up his book, but he can't concentrate and throws it down. He does nothing for a while.*

   WILLIAM *enters onto the street and comes into the lobby.*

   Hey, William. How you doin'?

WILLIAM. Hello, Jeff. How's it going?

JEFF. Pretty good. The police were just here, but they didn't ask about you, and I signed them right in. It was that cop Bill and his partner. He said tell William Bill says hi.

WILLIAM. Was that all?

JEFF. That was all.

WILLIAM (*sitting down*). Okay...

JEFF. Oh, yeah, and I told Manuel to clean up the desk.

WILLIAM (*takes out cigarettes*). What?

JEFF. I said, I told Manuel to clean up the desk – to straighten up the desk drawers –

WILLIAM. Oh yeah, yeah, thank you.

JEFF. I really laid into him, too, because this desk is disgusting. I mean, when you open this drawer it should be *spotless*. I told him I want to be able to eat my *breakfast* outta this drawer tomorrow morning. I told him you were ready to kill somebody about these drawers. I really did.

WILLIAM. Okay, Jeff. Thanks.

JEFF. You're welcome. Taken care of. (*Long pause.*) You're not very chatty tonight…

WILLIAM. What?

JEFF. I said you're not very chatty tonight. You're not really holding up your end of the conversation very well.

WILLIAM. Sorry, Jeff, I've got a lot on my mind.

JEFF. That's okay. We don't have to talk about anything. I'm just glad to see your smiling face.

WILLIAM. Same here, Jeff. You just keep talking. If I hear anything worth responding to I'll just jump in.

JEFF. Okay. (*Pause*) How's your brother doing?

WILLIAM. I don't know. I haven't spoken to him.

JEFF. Did you find out what he did? Oh no, you knew what he did, you just didn't want to tell *me* about it. That's okay. I forgot. That's completely fine. I don't mean to sound so inquisitive. I'm sorry. (*Pause*) So did you see where the Mayor says he's gonna shut down all the –

WILLIAM (*on 'shut'*). All right, let me ask you something, Jeff. Suppose somebody who's supposed to be near and dear to you was accused of doing some kind of terrible crime, and was trying to use you as an alibi. What would you do, for example, if it was a false alibi? That is to say, you weren't with the person when they said that you were?

JEFF. I don't know. I guess it would depend on who they were and what...

WILLIAM. Yeah, see, we already part company. I like to tell the truth.

JEFF. Well, so do I –

WILLIAM. What are you talking about, man? I didn't even get through the details of the hypothetical situation and you're already gearing up to perjure yourself.

JEFF. No I'm not. I was just – I mean if it was my *mother* or something –

WILLIAM. Right, because that's what everybody expects, right? But that's where I part company with ninety-five percent of the human race. So I'm a freak. But I wouldn't do it.

JEFF. Are you talking – I assume you're talking about your brother?

WILLIAM. It doesn't matter who I'm talking about.

JEFF. So but what did he do?

WILLIAM. I don't know what he did, man, because he hasn't been tried in a court of law.

JEFF. What are you, some kind of Robotron? What did they *accuse* him of?

Pause.

WILLIAM. They say – They arrested him and two friends for allegedly going into a hospital last night to steal pharmaceutical drugs, and some nurse apparently saw them and they attacked her –

JEFF. Oh my *God*...

WILLIAM. ...and they beat her up with a pipe or something like that, and now she's dead.

JEFF. Oh my God...

WILLIAM. ...And according to my brother's girlfriend, my brother told the police I was with him at the time at some movie.

JEFF. Wow.

WILLIAM. Yeah, gave her a whole made-up schedule what we were supposedly doing last night for me to memorize: What movie, who called who, what time we ate, who ate what, you wouldn't believe it. See, he can't handle getting a job or applying himself to go to school, but he has the wherewithal to come up with *that* shit on the spur of the moment when he's in the jailhouse under arrest for murder at two o'clock in the morning.

JEFF. Wow.

WILLIAM. 'Wow.'

JEFF. Well, would – I mean, God, I mean – do you –

WILLIAM. And it's not like... See, his girlfriend called me tonight, and apparently two of my brother's friends – these *real* criminals, mind – were identified by some doctor, and the cops picked them up and they named my brother as the third guy. But the doctor didn't really get a good look at him, so they're trying to dig up something substantial that would link him to the scene, and meanwhile my brother says he was at home alone, no alibi, and so would I say he was at the movies with me last night?

JEFF. Jesus Christ.

WILLIAM. See, I don't think *he'd* ever do anything that fuckin' heinous, but he's definitely done a lot of other shit. And I know these guys he's always with, and...You know, I want to be objective about it, to some degree. I want to... I can't just be saying, 'Well, seeing how he's my brother, it is therefore impossible for him to have done this ghastly thing.' You know what I mean?

JEFF. Yeah...

WILLIAM. I just wish I had more information. But who am
    I gonna talk to? His girlfriend? She just parrots everything he
    says; she's got no will of her own. And what's *he* gonna tell
    me? That he's guilty? He knows what I'll do then.

JEFF. Yeah... Wow.

WILLIAM. And I am not the type of person who sympathizes
    with the criminal element in this kind of situation. Not at all.
    But the fact remains that there's a lot of people in jail who
    don't belong there, a lot of black people in jail who don't
    belong there, and a lot of cops and prosecutors and what
    have you who would just as soon throw somebody in jail as
    nobody. And I hate to say it, but my brother is tailor-made
    for the part; and if he's being railroaded in some way, I don't
    know what right I may have to my private reservations. So
    it's an interesting dilemma. It's interesting. But I'll tell you
    something, Jeff, and you can quote me on this right now: If
    he had anything to do with killing that woman I'd sooner put
    a bullet through his head myself than lift a finger to help
    him. Because that is inhuman. Inhuman. Even if he was just
    standing *by*... Some innocent person... And all she did was
    show up at work that night? (*Pause*) But we're hoping it's all
    some terrible misunderstanding, right?

JEFF. Right. Right.

WILLIAM. So what would *you* do there, Jeff?

JEFF. Me? Oh, well, the first thing I would do is I would
    definitely try to find out if my brother was with those guys or
    not. Because that could really inform the whole situation
    right there.

    Pause.

WILLIAM. Well no fuckin' shit, Jeff. How in the world do you
    expect me to do that?

JEFF. Don't get mad at me,
    you asked me what   WILLIAM. Well what the
    I would do!   fuck do you expect me to
                                   do? 'Find out if he was

there or not.'

All right, all right!

Hot *dog*, I never would have thought of *that*.

JEFF. All right!

WILLIAM. If I could just find *that* out the rest of this shit might just fall right into place!

JEFF. Well can't you go see him? Can't you talk to him? You'll be able to tell whether or not he's lying –

WILLIAM. No I can't go see him, Goddamn it, he's locked up in fuckin' Rikers Island! I can't go see him till after the arraignment!

Okay, what about his girlfriend? Maybe you should go see her –

I already talked to her, Jeff! Look, look, I don't actually expect you to solve this for me. Let's just forget I brought it up.

JEFF. I'm sorry. This kind of problem is not exactly within my forte.

WILLIAM. Which is what?

Pause.

JEFF. Okay, you don't have to get nasty, I'm only tryin' to be –

WILLIAM. What is your forte, man? What is your forte?

Pause.

JEFF. I don't have one. Losing money.

WILLIAM. All right, never mind, Jeff. Thanks anyway.

Pause.

JEFF. Do you know if the nurse was white or black?

WILLIAM. No.

JEFF. Because that could –   WILLIAM. What difference
                                    does that make?

JEFF. It's just if she's white there's probably gonna be a big
  stink about it in the papers, and if she's black they probably
  won't play it up as much.

WILLIAM. Well, I don't know what color she was… I just better
  figure out what I'm gonna do before the cops catch up with
  me, because I'm not gonna get two chances to do this right.

  WILLIAM *gets up*.

JEFF. Is there anything you want me to tell the cops if they
  show up?

WILLIAM (*stops*). What?

JEFF. If the cops come by and ask me if I've seen you?

WILLIAM. Tell them you saw me.

JEFF. What if they ask me if you talked about your brother?
  What should I tell 'em?

WILLIAM. Maybe it'd be better if you didn't mention any of
  that till I figure out what I'm doing.

JEFF (*a joke:*). Well – I don't feel comfortable *lying* to them.

WILLIAM. Okay. Well… In that case, just –

JEFF. No I was just – I'm just kidding.

WILLIAM. Oh.

JEFF. Sorry.

  Pause.

WILLIAM. What the fuck do you find funny about this, man?

JEFF. Nothing. I'm really sorry. I really apologize.

WILLIAM. All right. I should get going.

They see BILL *and* DAWN *enter onto the street.* BILL *says a word to* DAWN *and comes into the lobby.* DAWN *stays outside.*

Hey there, Bill.

BILL (*shaking hands*). Hey William. How you doin'?

WILLIAM. Oh, I'm all right. Do you know Jeff? Jeff, Bill.

JEFF. Yeah, we met before.

BILL. So how you doin' these days, William? All right?

WILLIAM. I'm pretty well. Can't complain.

BILL. Yeah? Things goin' all right?

WILLIAM. More or less, yeah.

BILL. Good... Good... That's good. So listen... Could I talk to you for a minute?

WILLIAM. Sure.

BILL *takes* WILLIAM *aside.*

BILL. So listen... I heard about the whole thing with your brother, and I was in the neighborhood, and I just thought I'd come down and just talk to you a little bit in case I could be helpful. But I don't want you to feel nervous; this is totally unofficial, okay? You know what? Don't even say okay. Just listen to me: Now I understand he's possibly putting you in a very bad position –

WILLIAM *starts to speak.*

Please! Don't say anything. Just listen for a second. I just want to say that I don't know if you were really with him the other night or not, and I don't want to know. It's not my case, it's not my problem. Now, I'm sure you heard what happened to that nurse, so I'm not gonna go into that, but we're talking about a twenty-seven-year-old single mother, three children. Okay? And I just want to say, if you were *not* with him last night, you're gonna need to talk to somebody. And I want you to know I'm available any time of the night or day. Okay? I'm not gonna – you know – there's only so much I can do, of course, but I want you to know I'm here, I'm not judgin' you, I wanna try to help you out, and I'm gonna do everything I can for you within the law and maybe a little bit around the edges, okay? Just don't quote me on that. Now, I'm gonna give you my beeper number (*Writing on his card*.) and this is my *home* number. Okay? And I want you to *use* this. All right?

He gives the card to WILLIAM.

WILLIAM. Hey, Bill –

BILL No no, just think about what I said and gimme a call. Okay? I'll stop by tomorrow, maybe we could just have a cup of coffee and talk. Okay? Don't even say okay. Just say goodnight.

WILLIAM. Goodnight, Bill.

They shake hands.

BILL. Now if you don't mind, I just wanna talk to your friend here for a couple of minutes. Okay? Just need a little privacy.

WILLIAM (*surprised*). Oh – No – All right. I'll just, uh, I'll just go on about my rounds.

BILL. Okay, buddy. See you later. And *call* me.

WILLIAM. See you later, Jeff.

JEFF. Goodnight, Will.

WILLIAM *goes onto the street and exits.* BILL *and* JEFF *are alone.* DAWN *is still outside on the street. She can't quite hear what's going on inside but she can get the gist.*

What can I do for you, Officer?

BILL. Jeff, right?

JEFF. Yeah.

BILL. Well, listen to me, Jeff. I don't appreciate people discussing my private business when I'm not around. Okay?

You got anything to tell my partner about me or my friends or the people I visit in this building or anywhere else, say it in front of my fuckin' face, so I could get a chance to stick up for myself and not spend the rest of my night defending myself against a bunch of bullshit that was dumped on me by some fuckin' idiot when I'm not even around to defend myself. Okay?

JEFF (*muttering, intimidated*). Yeah…

BILL. What?

JEFF. I said yeah! I'm sorry. I didn't…

BILL. What do you think it makes you a big man, tellin' her my business?

JEFF. No.

BILL. How do you know what I'm doin' up there?

JEFF. I don't.

BILL. That's not what you told her.

JEFF. I don't know what I told her…

BILL. Okay: Let's ask her. Hey, Dawn!

JEFF. Oh is that her name?

BILL. What?

JEFF. Nothin' – We don't have to call her in here –

BILL. What's the matter? Why not?

> *During this exchange, on the street* DAWN *has turned toward them.* BILL *gestures for her to stay put. She hesitates, then stays put.*

JEFF. – You really – You made your point.

BILL. All right. Now you listen to me. Look out there: What do you see out there?

> JEFF *looks out at* DAWN.

JEFF. I don't really know what you –

BILL. What do you see out there?

Pause.

JEFF. I'm sorry. I don't understand what you m–

BILL. Do you see a police officer? You see a piece of ass?
I mean, what?

Pause.

JEFF. I see a police officer piece of ass.

BILL. What do you think I'm joking with you?

JEFF. No.

BILL. You think it's some big joke?

JEFF. No.

BILL. You want me to tell you what I see out there?

JEFF. Sure.

BILL. I see a little girl wearin' a police uniform. Okay? I see a
little girl from the neighborhood who some moron told her
she could be a cop. But she's not a cop right now. But if
somebody takes a shot at her, or somebody else's life
depends on her, they're not gonna know she's not a cop.
They're gonna think she knows what she's doing. She walks
around the corner where somebody's trying to rob somebody
or rape somebody or kill somebody, they're not gonna know
she's a little girl in a cop suit; they're gonna see a badge and
a uniform and a gun and they're gonna blow a hole through
her fuckin' head. Somebody runs up to her and asks her to
help 'em she's not gonna help 'em, she's gonna look around
and say, 'Where's Bill? Where's Bill?' – That's me: I'm Bill.
Now, I could tell that girl likes me. It's only natural. I'm her
partner, I'm a big strong father figure, whatever, gotta lot of
experience, gotta lotta confidence, I know what I'm fuckin'
doin' – and that's attractive to a woman, it's attractive to
anybody. So she's attracted to me. That's okay. She's human.
I'm human. But maybe part of what I'm doin', part of
buildin' her confidence is makin' her feel like I'm interested

in her too. Maybe that makes her feel impressive. Makes her feel cocky, makes her feel like she's got something on the ball. Makes her feel like she's really a *cop*. Now, do I need you tellin' her I'm upstairs havin' *sex* with somebody on my *shift* so she can think I'm some kind of fuckin' *maniac* who's just messin' with her head, so she can lose all her confidence in me and consequently all her confidence in herself? Because of your big fuckin' flappin' fuckin' mouth? And then go out and get herself killed? Or me? Or somebody else? This is not a game. We're not *door*men. We're *police*men. Yeah, I know, we're terrible and everything, but we're playing with our *lives*, and the lives of the people we're supposed to protect. So I don't appreciate the fun I guess you're havin' at my expense and more importantly at her expense, while you're sitting around here twiddling your fuckin' thumbs and waiting for, uh, William to come around and make his rounds so you can go to *sleep*. Okay?

JEFF. Yeah.

BILL. You know what I really feel like doin'? I really feel like smacking the shit outta you. But I'm not gonna do that, because I don't do that. Just when I come around here in future, just be aware that you don't know what I'm doing here, you have no idea, and keep your fuckin' nose outta my business. You understand me?

JEFF. Yes.

BILL. Okay. The discussion's over now.

> BILL *goes outside.* JEFF'*s buzzer buzzes. He answers it, talks briefly into the phone, then hangs up. During the following, although he can't hear what they are saying, he edges closer to the lobby door and waits for an opportunity to go outside.*

DAWN. You have a good time?

BILL. Take it easy –

> BILL *takes her arm and tries to walk her away from the building. She shakes him off.*

DAWN. Get offa me.

BILL. All I did was tell that guy to mind his own business.

DAWN. *I* don't care what you're doin' up there –

BILL. Well, maybe I'm nuts, but I do. I care what you think of
me and it's pretty important to me that you believe me when
I talk to you. Okay? 'Cause I may do a lot of other things,
but I care enough about your opinion of me that I don't want
you to think I'm not being straight with you.

DAWN. Straight with me!

BILL. Dawn. I swear to God – I got no reason to bullshit you:
So I don't know why I'm goin' through this with you, but my
friend Jim lives upstairs with Amy Heinvald; it's her
apartment – And that's all there is to it. I hardly even *know*
Mrs Heinvald, and anyway, she wasn't even *there* tonight.
She's outta *town*. You don't want to believe me, there's
nothin' I can say to you.

DAWN (*slowly*). Well… How come you were up there for so
long?

BILL. I didn't really think it was so long, but if you really want
to know, I had to talk to Jim about something private which
doesn't concern you and which I'm not at liberty to talk
about with you. He's goin' through a hard time and some
really weird, really upsetting shit, and I can't talk about it
because it would be a breach of privacy. You don't want to
believe me, there's nothing I can do.

DAWN. I don't.

BILL. All right. Only personally, I think that's a shame, because
I really thought we really had something goin' between us.
At least that's how I felt. I don't know: Maybe you didn't
feel that way. So maybe it's for the best, you know? Because
the way things have been goin' between us, I wouldn't know
how else to stop it. It doesn't help that my wife and I are like
– I don't even know what – like we don't even know each
other any more. I respect her, she's my wife, she's the
mother of my children, I'll never say a word against her as

long as I live, but it's like we're strangers. And it's been like that for three years. If it wasn't for the kids, we wouldn't be together and that's the truth. You want me to be honest? I'll be honest: (*Pause*) This is very difficult for me to say. But I haven't felt like this about somebody since – I don't even know when. I don't know if I *ever* felt this way about somebody. You know, I think I'm a little bit like you: I could walk into a room and face down twenty bad guys and I wouldn't blink an eye. But somethin' like this, and the whole world starts goin' around in my head. Because when I'm with you, I really feel like you are the real thing, and everything else seems like bullshit to me. You want me to be honest? That's as honest as I get.

JEFF, *having now edged his way to the door, pokes his head out.*

JEFF. Excuse me, Bill?

BILL. What.

JEFF. Um – Mrs Heinvald just buzzed down. She says you left your hat upstairs and she wants to know if you want her to bring it down or if you want to pick it up tomorrow.

Pause.

BILL. You're a pip.

JEFF. I'm sorry – I –

BILL (*moving toward him*). Get – *back* –

JEFF *goes inside. Pause.*

All right. I'm busted. I don't know what to say. I'm sorry.

DAWN. Yeah, right.

BILL. No, I'm sincere about that. I really am. But you gotta believe me, I mean – I don't know what's the matter with me. I really don't. It's like I'm a sex addict. I think I need help. I really do.

DAWN. Hey! How *stupid* do you think I *am*?

BILL. No, wait a minute – it's like, whenever I meet someone could really care about, it's like I always gotta be doin' somethin' to mess it up, and I don't know why. You know? Why?

DAWN. Maybe it's because you're a dirty fuckin' liar.

BILL. Whoa, hey, Dawn: Slow down. Okay? I'm just trying to talk to you –

DAWN. I know what you're tryin' to do and you can forget it. We're workin' together, let's work together –

BILL – Okay –

DAWN. – I don't care what you do up there, I don't care what you do period. I *told* you this was a bad idea –

BILL. Okay. You wanna do it that way – ?

DAWN. – only don't expect me to sit down here and *cover* for you when the dispatcher wants to know where you *went*. I signed up to be a cop, not lookout patrol at the whorehouse.

Pause.

BILL. Okay, first of all, she's not a whore.

DAWN. Oh she's not?

BILL. It actually happens that the lady has a lot of class. So just be careful what you say about her.

DAWN. I don't *believe* this!

BILL. Second of all, I'm sorry if I hurt your feelings, but you don't come down here from the Police Academy in your little pigtails and tell me what to do. Okay? I tell *you* what to do. And if I want you to sit down here and wait for me all night, that's exactly what you're gonna do, every *night* if I want you to –

DAWN. No I'm not –

BILL. Oh yes you are. You're gonna sit down here with *Jeff* and you're gonna answer the radio for me, and if you don't like it,

Dawn, then – maybe you shouldn't be tryin' to be a cop.
Because that's what cops do, is they support each other. They
help each other, they're there for each other – and they don't
judge each other and they don't fuck each other up. Okay?
So before you go cryin' home to your mom and dad how
your partner was just mean to you, just remember I am not
the one who put some drunk in the hospital tonight for callin'
me names.

DAWN. That's not what happened.

BILL. I don't care what happened. My *three*-year-old coulda
handled that situation better than you, okay? So settle down
because you're totally outta control. And the way you're
acting now is completely unprofessional. Now, I'm gonna go
up there and get my hat. And you're gonna wait down here
till I come back.

DAWN. No I'm not.

BILL. Oh, you'll wait.

DAWN. No I won't.

BILL. All right. You wanna take off? Take off. Only see how
you do in this Division without me backin' you up. See if
things are a little different for you from now on. Because one
word from me and these guys'll make your life so miserable
I couldn't even begin to describe it.

DAWN. Look – Bill – I don't care about you and Mrs
Heinvald –

BILL (*overlapping*). No – you made your choice – I'm tryin' to
talk to you, you're givin' me all these ultimatums – !

DAWN (*overlapping*). – I just wanna do my job.

BILL. – That's okay: You made your choice. So see what
happens when you come to work tomorrow. Go ahead.

DAWN. Well – How do you think your friend Lieutenant
Finelli's gonna like it if I tell him what you been doin' every
night in the middle of your shift?

BILL. Oh. All right. Thank you. Now I know where I stand.
Before, I didn't realize. Okay. Yeah: You could do that. You
could do that right now. Only who do you think he's gonna
believe? You or me? And second of all, see what happens at
your hearing. See what I tell 'em in my report. '*I* didn't see
him rush her...' That's all I gotta say, 'I didn't see him rush
her...' and that will be It For You, Goodbye. Okay? And I
don't know when they're gonna schedule that fuckin' thing,
so if I were you I would be very, very *nice* to me for the next
few months, Dawn. Oh, I don't appreciate havin' to have this
kind of conversation. Uh, I got some flaws and that's the end
of me. Not good enough, right? So take off. You're never
gonna be a cop anyway. You're never gonna be anything. So
go ahead. Take off.

BILL *goes inside the lobby, past* JEFF, *and off toward the
elevators. The elevator dings.* DAWN *stays where she is.*
JEFF *looks out at her. She won't look at him.*

ACT TWO

Scene One

Late the next night. JEFF *is watching* WILLIAM *drink a cup of take-out coffee. Silence.*

JEFF. Does it ever strike you as stupid that you're 'the Captain?'

WILLIAM. No.

JEFF. No – ! I don't mean –

WILLIAM. How do you mean?

JEFF. I don't mean 'Don't you think it's stupid that you're the *supervisor*.' Obviously you're the *supervisor*; I just mean don't you ever think it's stupid that you're called the '*Captain*?'

WILLIAM. No, Jeff, I don't.

JEFF. But there's no other *ranks*.

WILLIAM. What?

JEFF. Well – Everybody else in the company is just a *guard*, but you're 'the Captain.' Do you know what I mean? Why aren't you a *corporal*? Why do they skip right up to captain? Or why aren't you just 'the supervisor?'

WILLIAM. Because this is a security company, Jeff.

JEFF. I know that –

WILLIAM. And occasionally some of the people who work for this company do actually have to provide security for the buildings we're working at.

JEFF. I know that –

WILLIAM. All right –

JEFF. – I do my bit.

WILLIAM. Well... I don't think it's inappropriate for a semi-military organization to borrow a little military vernacular.

JEFF. We're not a semi-military organization...

WILLIAM. Semi-military, semi-police, whatever you want to call it.

JEFF. I don't want to call it anything, I just –

WILLIAM. It's not like anybody's calling me 'captain' anyway, so what do you care about it?

JEFF. I don't. I'm just making conversation.

WILLIAM. Well, why you gotta be making conversation? I'm just trying to sit here for a minute. You feel like you gotta say stupid shit to me just because I'm in the Goddamn room, I'll be on my way and you can get back to your crossword puzzle.

JEFF. What's the matter with you? Lighten up. I didn't say anything.

WILLIAM. I'm sorry.

JEFF. How's your brother doing?

WILLIAM *does not respond*.

Well, I can see you probably don't want to talk about that. But I was thinking about it today, and *I* think... (*Off* WILLIAM*'s look:*) No, really. I was. And seriously, I don't mean to be – I'm not bein' cavalier about it. But I was thinking about it and I really think when you talk to the cops you should probably just go in there and tell the truth. Because – I realize you probably don't care what I think... but you did ask me my opinion last night, and I realize I wasn't very helpful, so I thought about it some more today and that's really what I think that you should do. For what it's worth. I know you probably don't even want to hear it... But I just want you to know, you don't have to worry about me. I mean... you took me into your confidence and I really appreciated that... 'cause it made me feel like you considered me as a friend. (*Pause*) You're not sorry you told me about it, are you?

WILLIAM. Yeah, Jeff, I'm a little sorry.

JEFF. Come on, man. You can trust me. What am I gonna do?
I'm not gonna say anything.

WILLIAM. Okay, Jeff. My brother's had a rough time. And he
just doesn't have the strength of character to meet a lot of the
situations he's found himself in. Which is no excuse... But
he didn't create those situations either. And I'm a great
believer in personal responsibility – as you know –

JEFF. Yes, yes, I know.

WILLIAM. ...so I don't usually like to say this, but sometimes
I think he just never had a chance, because he has a very
average personality. Now, I'm very disciplined. But that's just
my nature. I was always that way. So when all these criminals
used to come around our house and try to tempt me, I would
stay away. But I can't take a lot of credit for that, 'cause I was
just a little kid. So how am I gonna be patting myself on the
back for how I acted or didn't act when I was ten years old?
That's just absurd. But he was more like a regular kid. So he
got sucked up by these criminals and that was it. If they hadn't
been around he would have been a so-called normal kid and
now he'd be a so-called normal man, probably inflicting
lawful misery on someone in the corporate world, or what
have you. But I'm just exhausted with it, I really am.

JEFF. You must be.

WILLIAM. At any rate... I guess that's neither here nor there.

JEFF. When do you have to talk to the cops?

WILLIAM. Yeah – I already talked to them. I – I spoke to them
this morning.

JEFF. You did? Wow, I didn't realize that. So how did that go?

WILLIAM. It went fine, Jeff.

JEFF. Did you talk to your brother?

WILLIAM. No, but I spoke with his attorney. Which was very
interesting. And he threw kind of a whole new light on the
situation for me.

JEFF. Oh yeah? What did he say?

WILLIAM. Well, he said a lot of things, but I had a hard time following most of it because for the first fifteen minutes of the conversation he had my brother mixed up with another case.

JEFF. Are you kidding me?

WILLIAM. No. Didn't know my name, didn't know my brother's name – And then he's like, 'Oh, oh, you're *that* case, oh okay.' So after that I kinda lost track of some of the details of the defense he was outlining for me.

JEFF. Are you kidding?

WILLIAM. No. Then I went and talked to these two detectives for about, oh, I don't know, two and a half hours, something like that. Then I went home, called my parents, talked to my mother for a while, talked to my father for about five minutes. Talked to my wife, fended off *her* questions. Had to have a brief discussion about our relationship. Called my Uncle Paul, talked to him for a while. Then I took about a three-minute bath, ate some dinner, put on my uniform, came to work, and now I'm here. And Jeff, I'm glad to be here. Because believe it or not, I find your presence to be very soothing. You're probably the most easygoing person I've spoken to all day. Probably the most easygoing person I know. Which most of the time I find to be somewhat irritating, to tell you the truth, but right now I find it very calming.

JEFF. I'm glad you're here too, man. (*Pause*) So, but, I mean, but, like, what did you tell them?

Pause.

WILLIAM. I – told them I was at the movies.

JEFF. Well, but – I mean – So – You don't think – Now you think your brother didn't do it? Or –

WILLIAM. I know he didn't do it because I was at the movies with him. All right?

JEFF. Yeah – No – I understand –

WILLIAM. Understand what? What do you understand?

JEFF. I understand you were at the movies with him.

WILLIAM. That's right.

JEFF. Okay. (*Pause*) No, it's just that –

WILLIAM. It's just what? (*Pause*) What? Do you have something you want to say to me?

JEFF. No –

WILLIAM. You have some helpful suggestions for me?

JEFF. No –

WILLIAM. I know you don't.

JEFF. All right.

WILLIAM. I know it's all right.

JEFF. No. I just – William, I just – I don't know: I don't like saying this, William... But I feel like it's my civic duty –

WILLIAM. Your what?

JEFF. No –

WILLIAM. Since when do you have a sense of civic duty, Jeff?

JEFF. Okay, not my civic duty –

WILLIAM. Since when do you have a sense of duty period?

JEFF. I have a sense of duty. (*Pause*) I just – you know... What if he really did it?

WILLIAM. What do you mean, 'What if he did it?' I was at the movies with him.

JEFF. Yeah. All right.

WILLIAM. They want to *prove* he did it, let them *prove* it! I can't participate in this. I'll participate in a fair trial... I can't participate in this!

JEFF. Yeah! No! I mean –

WILLIAM. I mean you hear about this shit all the time; you hear about guys who go to jail because their lawyer was asleep in court, or because they forgot to file some deposition or something because they have two hundred cases apiece and about five minutes for each one. And then these cops pull you in the room and you gotta make up your mind then and there what you're going to say, and I don't know if he did it or not but I just – I couldn't do it to him, Jeff. My whole life I've told the truth, I always tell the truth. Because I believe in that, okay? You don't worry about if the world is bad or good, because I know Goddamn well it's bad. You just do your best and let the chips fall where they may. But I couldn't do it to him, Jeff, I just couldn't do it. And you don't have to ask me 'What if he did it,' because that's all I can fuckin' think about!

JEFF. I know, I wouldn't know what to do either! I probably would have done the exact same thing.

Pause.

WILLIAM. I'm sorry. I apologize.

JEFF. You don't have to apologize…

WILLIAM. Anyway, so then I ran into Big Bill and he just asks me straight out, you know, if it was true – so I told him, 'Yeah, Bill, it's true.' And he looks at me, real tough and what have you, and he says, 'Don't bullshit me, William,' and I said, 'Bill, I'm not,' and then he just sat back and he said, 'Okay, man, I believe you.'

JEFF. What's he got to do with it?

WILLIAM. Nothing. He was just there – I guess – 'Cause he knows me…

JEFF. Well…What if you – I don't know…What if you –

WILLIAM. See, I was thinking – I was talking to my Uncle Paul – You've heard me mention him –

JEFF. Sure. You talk about him all the time –

WILLIAM (*on 'all'*). All right, well, I was talking to him, and
    he was saying how we should put our heads together and just
    try to find a decent lawyer to take my brother's case. Scrape
    together some money, or find somebody who'd want to take
    the case pro bono. But he assumes that I was with him…
    They all assume… They don't understand. (*Pause*) But if we
    had a halfway decent lawyer, somehow, then I could
    probably feel more confident just letting things take their
    own course.

JEFF. That sounds better to me. I think that's a really good idea.

WILLIAM. Anyway… We probably shouldn't talk about this
    too much more…

JEFF. Well… I mean… we already have. So…

WILLIAM. I know, but… Well, if by any chance anybody does
    ask you about it… you just hold off. If you're comfortable
    doing that. I talked to you about this and I shouldn't have.
    That's not your fault. That's my fault – But I still need a little
    time to try to find him a decent lawyer, so at least he has
    a chance.

    BILL *and* DAWN *have entered onto the street. They come
    into the lobby.*

BILL. Good evening, gentlemen.

WILLIAM. Hello, Bill.

BILL. Hey, buddy. How's it goin'?

WILLIAM. Okay. How are you?

BILL. I'm okay. You mind if I talk to you for a second?

WILLIAM. No, not at all.

BILL. Would you excuse us for a second please, Jeff?

JEFF. Um – Sure…

    BILL *takes* WILLIAM *aside.* JEFF *drifts toward* DAWN.

    How you doin'?

DAWN. Fine.

BILL (*to* WILLIAM, *aside*). So listen – I think you're gonna
get some interesting news tomorrow. I talked to the
detectives after you left, I told 'em I knew you, told 'em
I believed you... I even – this'll amuse you, actually, I even
went to the ADA's office and I told him I would vouch for
you – This guy was not exactly thrilled to see me either,
believe me. They don't exactly like strange cops walkin' into
their offices and tellin' 'em who to charge and who not to
charge, but I figure what the hell. Somebody doesn't stick up
for your brother they're gonna lock him up with some *really*
unpleasant characters and that's gonna be *it* for him.

WILLIAM. I really appreciate that, Bill. I just hope –

BILL (*on second 'I'*). Naw, don't worry about that: I just think
that what you and your brother both gotta think about is if he
didn't have an alibi, or if I didn't know you: You think about
this kid's character and you think, 'I could see him doin'
somethin' like that someday.' So if not this time, when?

WILLIAM. I know, Bill. It – I know.

BILL. Just somethin' to chew on. Okay, buddy. I'll see you
later. (*Calling out*.) Uh, Jeff, I'll be goin' up to 22-J. That's
22-J.

JEFF. Would you mind signing in? (*Off* BILL*'s look*.) Never
mind. I'll do it.

   BILL *exits toward the elevators*. JEFF *signs him in*.

WILLIAM. I'll see you later, Jeff.

JEFF (*sotto voce*). Hey, wait, so what did he *say*?

WILLIAM. I'll tell you about it later.

JEFF. Sure. If you wanna come by when you're done with your
rounds...

WILLIAM. Yeah, maybe I will.

JEFF. But is everything okay? What happened?

WILLIAM. I'll tell you *later*, Jeff.

WILLIAM *goes onto the street and exits.* JEFF *and* DAWN *are alone.*

JEFF (*pointedly letting her know he knows her name*). How's it goin' – *Dawn*?

DAWN. Fine.

Pause.

JEFF. So is he doing this just to torture you now?

DAWN. He's showin' me who's boss.

JEFF. Which would be – him, right? I assume?

DAWN. I guess so.

JEFF. Well... Your turn will come. Someday you'll be upstairs havin' sex with some guy, and your rookie partner'll be downstairs learnin' who's boss from you... I'm sorry. Seriously though, how are things goin' down at the station? Pretty tough?

DAWN. No. I don't care if people know about my private business. That's their problem if they think it's interesting...

JEFF. Hm.

DAWN. What really bothers me is the illegality of this.

JEFF. Of course.

DAWN. Do you *know* how much trouble he would be in if I *told* anybody about this?

JEFF. So why don't you say something?

DAWN. Believe me. You just don't do that. Now could we change the subject?

JEFF. Sure. Sorry... How's that guy you beat up? I'm sorry.

DAWN. That's okay. They think he's gonna lose his eye.

JEFF. Are you kidding?

DAWN. No.

JEFF. Why?

DAWN. Because I *hit* him in it, that's why. So now they think he's gonna lose the eye, or go blind in it, and him and his wife are suing me, the Police Department, and practically everybody who ever worked for the City of New York. He was totally chargin' me, he weighed about five hundred pounds, and he was drunk out of his mind. But who cares about *that*, right?

JEFF. But they can't win, though...

DAWN. If nobody backs me up they can.

Pause.

JEFF. How long have you been on the Force now?

DAWN. Three months.

JEFF. You've racked up quite a few accomplishments in a short time.

DAWN. I know, right?

JEFF. Well... You missed a really great game today...

DAWN. Oh yeah?

JEFF. Actually it was only so-so. They fell apart in the second half.

DAWN. Yeah. I watched some of it on TV...

JEFF. I thought you didn't like basketball.

DAWN. I don't. My father had it on.

JEFF. Oh, do you live with them?

DAWN. Who, my parents? No. *No...* I was just visiting. (*Pause*) I looked for you in the crowd on TV, but they didn't show you.

JEFF. Yeah, I told 'em to stop filming me all the time. You know? People want to see the *game*. They're sick of watching me all the time. 'How did Jeff react to that play? What did Jeff think of that call?' It's enough already.

DAWN (*smiling*). Yeah…?

JEFF. To tell you the truth I couldn't really concentrate on it too well. I can't really concentrate on anything so well lately. I guess my mind is too distracted.

DAWN. Oh yeah?

JEFF. Yeah, I been very – my best friend is getting married on Saturday – my friend Scott – and I'm supposed to organize this bachelor party… so that's been a big pain in the ass.

DAWN. What are you gonna go to a topless place or something?

JEFF. Who knows? I hate bachelor parties. Bunch of guys sitting around some apartment drinking beer and watching porno movies – it makes me sick, it really just disgusts me.

DAWN. I thought all guys liked porno movies.

JEFF. Well, we do. It's just the thought of all these guys together, sitting around doing this stuff that makes me uncomfortable.

DAWN. What do you mean?

JEFF. I don't know. I just don't like it. Like I don't like the way groups of guys – the way men behave in a group. Like the way some guys get when they think they're playing sports. Or pretty much any bunch of guys anywhere making loud noises and screaming and impressing each other with what bunch of morons they are. I really don't like it. It makes me sick.

DAWN. You'd love the Police Force.

JEFF. No, I don't think I would. (*Pause*) Hey, did I tell you I saw a really nice apartment today? See, I've been – I live with my brother Marty – I didn't tell you about this?

DAWN. No.

JEFF. Well, I live with my brother Marty and his wife and two kids, in Astoria. (*Pause*) I rent a room from them. (*Pause*) And they're great, but now that I'm gettin' back on my feet a little bit, I've been thinking I really want to get my own

place. So today I saw a place that seems really nice, so if
everything goes well I think I'm gonna be able to move in
the first of the month, which is gonna be – amazing. My own
little kitchen... Do you like to cook at all?

DAWN. Not really, not that much.

JEFF. Yeah, I really enjoy cooking.

DAWN. My mother's a good cook. Really good... Only it's not
like it's free... You know?

JEFF. No, what do you mean?

DAWN. No, it's just always like, 'Gee, Ma, is there anything
about my life I'm doin' *right*?'

JEFF. Oh, really?

DAWN....She's always making these little comments...

JEFF. That's too bad...

DAWN. Oh but not just to me: to everyone. Like, there's always
something wrong with every little thing you do. She has all
these little ways of puttin' everybody down. And then she's
miserable because nobody wants to hang around her. I swear
to God she's nuts.

JEFF. Yeah, my old man was very –

DAWN. And my dad just sits there, right? Like nothin's
bothering him, right?

JEFF. Uh-huh?

DAWN. And she's sittin' there makin' all these little backhand
remarks about everybody: about his mother and father, and
everybody in his family, about his personal habits, right?

JEFF. Uh-huh?

DAWN. And he just lets it wash over him, like he doesn't even
hear it. And I asked him, I said, 'How can you listen to that
shit all day long?' And he says, 'Listen to what? What am
I gonna do, get divorced? Let her make herself miserable,

I can't stop her. I just think about other things when she's talking.'

JEFF. See – That is the great attitude to have.

DAWN. I sure don't have it.

JEFF. No, me neither. But I can really relate to that because my old man was a little bit like that, too –

DAWN. What do you mean, like puttin' everybody down...?

JEFF. Not putting people down exactly, but just very very hard to get along with.

DAWN. Uh-huh...

JEFF. And I'll tell you something: I really used to resent it –

DAWN. You're Goddamn right you resent it.

JEFF. Yeah, only except now that he's gone, and I don't have to listen to it anymore, you start to reevaluate things a little bit. Like he had a lot of really good qualities I think I could really learn from. And just in general, there's a lot of things I admire about his whole *generation*...

DAWN. Oh, definitely...

JEFF. Like he was tough. I mean he was *really* tough. And when he said he was gonna do something, he did it. He didn't just talk. Which is fortunate in a way, for everyone, because when he talked he didn't actually make a lot of fucking sense, if you know what I mean. I mean his opinions were pretty undeveloped, you know? But you have to admire that kind of character.

DAWN. Definitely. Definitely.

JEFF. My goal is to acquire that type of backbone and that kind of self-assurance without becoming as ossified as that. You know what I mean? Like, can you inspire that kind of admiration in people and really stand up for what you believe in, and still be like an open-minded person? That's my question.

JEFF. But like –
  I'm sorry –
  I didn't mean to interrupt –

DAWN. I don't know. I know
  people who –
  That's all right. No, go
  ahead. I don't even know
  what I was gonna say.

JEFF. No, I was just gonna say… I was gonna say… Well, I had
  some really interesting thing I was gonna say, but now
  I forgot.

DAWN. That's okay. You don't have to be interesting all the
  time. I'll still like you.

JEFF is momentarily embarrassed.

JEFF. Anywa… Anyway… What I was gonna say… I was
  gonna say, I think that's – for some people that's a form of
  *weak*ness…

Pause.

DAWN (*not following*). What… is?

JEFF. No – yeah – I mean in another way – For other people –
  if you look at it another way – Take your partner, for
  example.

DAWN. What about him?

JEFF. Nothing. He's just very self-assured, obviously, but he's
  also like a total scumbag and I'm just wondering if you can
  have one without the other. You know what I mean? (*Pause*)
  Anyway… Maybe you don't want to talk about that right now.

DAWN. I don't care… Must be nice to have it all be a theory.

JEFF. What do you mean?

DAWN. I mean it must be nice to sit here and watch other
  people gettin' squeezed to death by their own dumb-ass
  mistakes and sit around and think about how interesting it is.

JEFF. It's not all theoretical to me. Don't be like your mother.

DAWN. I'm not like my *mother*…!

JEFF. I'm just a very

empathetic person, and to tell you the God's honest truth, Dawn, I feel a little bit responsible for the mess you're in. Because if I would've –

DAWN. You're not responsible. *I'm* responsible. I'm *totally* responsible.

JEFF. Yeah, but if I would have kept my big mouth shut, it probably never would have escalated to this point. I just hate to see guys like that get away with stuff like that, because that's the kind of stuff that *I* wanna get away with only I can't figure out how it's done.

DAWN. That's how you wanna be? You wanna be like him?

JEFF. No, not exactly, but yeah, in a way. The guy has no qualms about anything, he does whatever he wants, he gets everything he wants, and as far as I can see he feels just fine about it. So yeah, I wouldn't mind being a little bit like that, would you?

DAWN. I don't *know*...! I don't wanna *talk* about this. Do you have any idea what I been *goin'* through...?

JEFF. Okay, you're right, I'm sorry.

DAWN. I don't know what I'm gonna do. He's gonna come back down in a few minutes – I don't know what to do. I don't know what he wants from me. All I did was tell him I don't wanna wait down here while he's upstairs with her when he's supposed to be working and he went fuckin' nuts. I don't know what to do.

JEFF. What can you do?

DAWN. I don't know. Maybe he won't go through with it.

JEFF. Through with what? (*Pause*) Go through with what?

DAWN. He said...

Pause.

JEFF. What?

DAWN. He said he's gonna get me kicked off the Force unless I'm really 'nice' to him.

JEFF. Nice... *Nice*, nice? Or – What does he mean?

DAWN. Uh, gee, Jeff, I don't know. What do you think he means?

JEFF. Are you serious?

DAWN. Oh yeah, we got a big date after work tonight.

JEFF. But isn't that like, sexual harassment or something?

DAWN. Uh, no, actually, I think it's called rape.

JEFF. Rape?

DAWN. Rape, sexual coercion... I don't know what it's called.

JEFF. What do you mean you don't know what it's called? You're a cop: Aren't you supposed to know the names of all the different crimes?

DAWN. Jesus Christ, what difference does it make?

JEFF. Yeah, but can't you *tell* somebody about this? Don't they have some committee or something you can talk to?

DAWN. Uh, yeah, only I don't think they'd be too sympathetic.

JEFF. Why not?

DAWN. Because I was already *with* him, Jeff. And everybody knows about it. Okay? So two days later I'm gonna turn around and complain about it?

JEFF. But God *damn*!

DAWN. What's the big deal? I got myself into this. Now I'm in it. Maybe he won't go through with it. You know? Maybe he'll be too tired. I still can't believe he would do something like that. But let's face it, I gotta be the worst judge of character in the history of the fuckin' earth. I mean can you believe this shit? Three days ago I'm practically in love with the guy and now he's tellin' me – Well, that is not gonna happen. I don't know what's gonna happen when it doesn't, but that is not happening. Let him get me kicked off the Force. Let him try. It's not worth it, I'm not gonna be one of those, 'Oh yeah, I let him rape me because I didn't know what else to do...' I'd rather be *dead*, okay? But I gotta find some way outta this, man. I don't know what I'm gonna do, but I gotta do something. I just gotta figure out what it is.

JEFF. I wish I could do something to help you.

DAWN. Yeah, so do I. That's all right. I gotta calm down... (*Pause*) Did your friend William tell you what happened to his brother?

Pause.

JEFF. He told me his brother was arrested.

DAWN. Nice, huh?

JEFF. It's terrible.

DAWN. I don't know, Jeff... You just can't believe some of the people in this world. You know? You can't even believe what they do to each other. And I only been doin' this for three months.

JEFF. Well... at least you can do something about it. You know? I mean, at least you can, like, help them, sometimes.

DAWN. Yeah, well, that's what they tell you. But it really depends on... Depends on a lot of things. Depends on who you're working with, for one thing. That's what's so crazy about this thing with Bill.

JEFF. How do you mean?

DAWN. Because the guy is supposedly like this genius cop. Like he just got on the list to get a gold shield? You know: to be a detective?

JEFF. Yeah, I know. I watch TV.

DAWN. All right, but that's not so easy if you didn't go through Narcotics or some of the other branches. He's always goin' out of his way. Like this thing with your friend's brother? Bill totally diffused that whole thing. He didn't have to do that. That's not even his case. Everybody's talkin' about it.

JEFF. Yeah. (*Pause*) How do you mean he diffused it?

DAWN. Well – you know – 'cause they were ready to hang this kid... I just hope he's *right*, you know?

JEFF. Yeah. What do you mean?

DAWN. I hope he's right, because if he's not, he's helpin' this kid get away with murder.

JEFF. So, but – So – I don't understand. What happened? Now they're gonna release him?

DAWN. Yeah, supposedly.

JEFF. Why would they do that?

DAWN (*confused*). Because his alibi checked out. Because your friend was with him on the night in question. Or so he said. Why? You know somethin' about it they don't?

JEFF. No. I don't know anything about it. We didn't talk about it. You know, he just told me, you know, that he heard his brother was arrested...

DAWN. Oh.

JEFF....he didn't tell me any of the details. (*Pause*) So do they just *release* the guy if Bill tells 'em to? That doesn't seem very systematic.

DAWN. No, no, they obviously don't do that: They ask you a million questions, especially a family member. But they obviously believed him. And Bill believes him. And that definitely helps... And this one was horrible. You know they *all* raped her, they beat her up so bad her own best friend couldn't ID the body, and then they stuffed her in the closet and just let her die.

JEFF. Yeah. Jesus Christ.

DAWN. You know she had three kids?

JEFF. Yeah... I overheard Bill sayin' something about that.

DAWN. What are they supposed to do now, you know?

JEFF. What will they do?

DAWN. Far as I know they're all goin' to Social Services.
There was no other relatives.

JEFF *does not respond.*

Want to know what *else* happened in the neighborhood this
week? 'Cause I can just go down the list.

JEFF. No thanks.

DAWN. They say summer's when it really gets bad. At least
that's what everybody's telling me. So I can't wait for that...
If I last that long.

JEFF. You will.

DAWN. But I'll tell you something, Jeff: Whoever did that, if
just once in a while I could have something to do with
catching somebody like that, making sure they could get
what they deserve, I would definitely feel like my life was
well spent. You know?

JEFF. Yeah... It's weird... Like, I watch you guys goin' back
and forth and it's... I don't know. I gotta get out of this
situation. I just –

DAWN. What situation?

JEFF. This *job* situation. I think it's startin' to drive me crazy.
I know you're having some problems at work right now –

DAWN. Uh, slightly.

JEFF. Well, okay, but at least you're *doing* something. You're
trying to *do* something important with your *life*. But I got no
family, I got... I don't know. I just feel like I want to do
something. To help somebody. Or do something. Contribute.
I don't know. Work with kids. Or – I mean, I don't particularly
like kids, but you know what I mean.

DAWN. Well – There's all kinds of ways to be useful. It doesn't have to be your life's work.

JEFF. Yeah, but that's what I'm saying, that's what's so great about you guys is that it is your life's work. It's your *life's work*. It's not just your spare time… And that's – It just makes me think that's the kind of thing that I would like to do… See, I always thought I'd just be a Navy guy, because of my dad… And that would be something: You know: Defend the country… But I couldn't stand it. Too many guys. All around. Guys guys guys. Groups of guys. That is not for me.

DAWN. Yeah, I remember you were tellin' me about that…

JEFF. No way, not for me.

DAWN. Yeah, I think maybe you got a little thing about that? Like a psychological fixation or something you might wanna look into.

JEFF. I don't want to look into anything, I just don't wanna be around a bunch of screamin' guys.

DAWN. Well… Thanks for sayin' all that.

JEFF. Oh. That's all right. I mean, you're welcome.

DAWN. No seriously, I really need to hear that kinda thing right now…

JEFF. And I know you're havin' a hard time now, but I want you to know, I really admire you… Even though you're havin' trouble… I feel like it's inspiring to me, to see somebody goin' through all that stuff because they want to do something to make a contribution.

DAWN. Thank you…!

JEFF. Friends?

DAWN. Definitely.

Pause.

JEFF. So listen: I have a hypothetical situation I want to ask you about.

DAWN. Okay.

JEFF. This whole thing with William kind of reminds me of this, so I wanted to ask you... Suppose you have a friend, and a close relative of his is arrested for a very serious crime...

DAWN. Yeah?

Long pause.

JEFF. So a close relative of his is arrested for a serious crime, and that relative is using your friend as an alibi – like William's brother did, only in this case it's not really true: Your friend was *not* with the relative at the time of the crime. But that doesn't mean the guy *did* it; it just means he doesn't have a good alibi, and he's worried he's gonna go to jail. Are you with me?

DAWN. Yeah...?

JEFF. Now, ordinarily your friend is a very upright kind of a guy. Again, kind of like William, but hypothetical – somebody who would never ordinarily lie for this relative. But he doesn't know if his relative is guilty or if it's a frame-up or what. And then he meets the relative's *lawyer*, and it's one of those court-appointed lawyers, and the lawyer is just completely incompetent and out of it, like he's drunk, and he doesn't know the client's name, and can't remember any of the details of the case... Like you might as well not even *have* a lawyer, this guy is so bad... Are you following me?

DAWN. I'm following you.

JEFF. So *now*, my friend – hypothetically – he starts talking to the cops, and without realizing it, he's backing up his brother's story because he just can't bring himself to just throw his brother – his relative, whatever – to the wolves, and on the strength of his interview, or for whatever reason, the detectives decide the relative is a solid citizen and the charges won't stand up in court and they decide to release him. Okay? A lot of similarities to the William thing.

DAWN. What's your question?

JEFF. My *question* is – How is anybody supposed to expect the brother – my friend, my imaginary friend or whatever – not to back up his relative's story? Considering that he's a human being and he has feelings, and no matter what he thinks the right thing to do is, he's gotta answer to their parents and all the rest of it. And by the same token, what do you think – My question is: What if *I* – me – *I* know the story is bullshit because my friend told me so, but nobody even knows I know anything. This is all for an idea for a novel I have, see. And for the character that would be me, see, I'm not sure what he should do. It's not *his* brother – *my* brother. But now the relative is being released and potentially he's a murderer but there's no way to tell.

DAWN. Well… that's why they have such a thing as trial by jury, Jeff.

JEFF. Yeah, but they *don't*, because the lawyer is no good.

DAWN. Then you do something about *that*. But you can't just lie to the police.

JEFF. Okay, good, that's good. Like what?

DAWN. Well, you can ask for a different lawyer, if the guy was really drunk; you can try askin' the judge –

JEFF. But, okay, but what if he wasn't literally drunk? What if I just said that as an extreme –

DAWN. If he wasn't drunk, or you can't prove he was drunk or something really serious like that, they're probably *not* gonna give you another one because they have no *reason* to give you another one. They don't offer you a *selection*. If you can't afford a lawyer they appoint a lawyer. Period. So –

JEFF. But then why should my friend tell the truth? Or why should I?

DAWN. Because you have to, that's all. Because there's no other way to do it. It's not your responsibility –

JEFF. It *is* my responsibility, it's *somebody's* responsibility –

DAWN. It's your responsibility to tell the truth –

JEFF. Why? If the city doesn't care about its responsibility to provide a decent defense –

DAWN. Because the city didn't *deliberately* give him a shitty lawyer. That's just an individual flaw in the system –

JESS. It's *not* just a flaw in the system, it happens all the time; it happens *all* the time, unless you have a lot of money and you can afford your own lawyer – But somebody made up the *law*, didn't they? Some *people* made up the law. A bunch of people like you and me literally sat down and wrote it up and made up a salary for the court attorneys that wasn't very high, and made up rules about whether you were allowed to switch lawyers if the guy was no good –

God didn't make up the rules –

DAWN. But it's still your responsibility to tell the truth and obey the law. You can't just make it *up* when there's some part of it that you don't like. You can appeal the decision, you can –

Yeah, and if you don't like the –

Yeah, and if you don't like the rule, you can appeal the decision, or you could run for office, I guess, and try to change the law. Or you could vote for somebody you think would do it better or a lot of things. But you can't just go in and lie about a murder –

But by the time I do that my friend's relative is gonna be getting stabbed and raped in jail and maybe he didn't *do* anything because he didn't get a fair trial!

DAWN. I don't know what to tell you, Jeff. You can't just lie to the police. I don't know why. You can't.

JEFF. What if we lived in Nazi Germany? Could you lie to the police then?

DAWN. We don't live in Nazi Germany!

JEFF. *We* don't live in Nazi Germany, but what if we did? Would you still say you have to obey the law – ?

DAWN. It's not the same as Nazi Germany!

JEFF. It's not the same in *theory*, but if you look at the statistics of who gets arrested and who goes to jail and who gets sentenced to the death penalty – what do you mean 'come on?'

DAWN. Oh come on!

DAWN. Well, if you think it's so unfair then why are you tellin' me about it?

Pause.

JEFF. I'm not telling you about anything! I'm outlining a hypothetical situation for this thing I was gonna write. Try to write.

DAWN. Why are you tellin' me about it?

DAWN. It bears a really suspicious resemblance to your friend and his brother, don't you think?

JEFF. Just in general. The details are all different – Like I added the thing about me knowing something about it... The guy isn't a security guard, they weren't at the movies. It's very different in the details. All I did was outline a hypothetical situation.

Long pause.

DAWN. What do you mean they weren't at the movies?

JEFF. No – I mean – In my hypothetical... thing, nobody was at the movies.

Pause.

DAWN. Oh, you mean because William and his brother were supposedly at the movies?

JEFF. Yeah.

DAWN. I thought you said he didn't tell you about it.

Pause.

JEFF. Thought I said – I'm sorry. I'm confused. Thought who said they didn't tell me about what?

DAWN. I thought you said William didn't tell you about it.

JEFF. He didn't.

DAWN. Then how did you know they were at the movies?

JEFF. Well – He told me *that*.

DAWN. What.

JEFF. Told me – This is so stupid. I was just outlining a hypothetical situation based on what William… This is really stupid.

DAWN. That's okay. Told you what?

JEFF. Told me – He told me that he heard his brother was arrested… And that it was something – I don't remember – Like for something that happened some night they were at the movies… And that it was really fucked up, and he knows his brother's done a lot of bad stuff, but he knows he didn't do this because he was at the movies with him.

DAWN. But then why'd you tell me that he didn't talk about it?

JEFF. Well, that was it. (*Pause*) What I said just then. (*Pause*) I wouldn't call that 'talking' about it, but maybe that's just a difference of words… He didn't *really* talk about it. He didn't talk about it at great length, the way I probably would, or like your partner would, because we're more long-winded. But he told me what I told you.

DAWN. Which is what.

JEFF. That – you know – his brother was in trouble.

DAWN. Okay, Jeff? If you know anything about this, you gotta tell me, and I mean right *now*.

JEFF. But I don't know anything, Dawn. I know I sound like I'm lying, but that's just because – It's that thing where if somebody thinks you're lying, even though you're not, you start to feel guilty like you're lying even though you're not? (*Pause*) It's like that.

DAWN. Okay... I don't believe you, Jeff. So, um, I'm gonna go tell the detectives I think you know something and you can talk to *them*.

JEFF. No, don't do that, I don't know anything, you're just making me nervous –

DAWN. Hey! They're gonna release that kid tomorrow *morning*. And if he had anything to do with murdering that nurse that's gonna be on *your* conscience. And if I can tell you're lying, those detectives are gonna rip you to fuckin' pieces, okay?

JEFF. But I'm not, Dawn, I'm not.

DAWN. Do you wanna see what they did to that woman? You wanna come down to the station and look at the pictures?

JEFF. No, not really.

DAWN. Read your paper! It's on page twenty!

JEFF. I don't need to read it. I already read it.

Pause.

DAWN (*softer*). Come on, Jeff. Nobody's gonna blame him for trying to protect his brother. But – I mean – You don't want to be helping somebody get away with *murder*, Jeff. Like a real *murder*...

JEFF. I'm not.

DAWN. Do you?

JEFF. No. But I'm not.

DAWN. ...Just tell the truth. That's all. That's all you gotta do. Just – truthfully – just tell me what he said.

JEFF. But I can't – I don't know anything. Honestly.

DAWN. Hey… I understand if you don't want to be goin' against your friend… And I know he's your boss. But that woman had friends too. She had three little kids. Now why is your friend and his brother more important than them?

JEFF *does not respond.*

And I also – I just wanna tell you, we can totally try to keep you out of it. Whatever you tell me, I can take it right to the detectives. They could just use it as background information. You understand? They're still gonna have to substantiate it…

JEFF. You just said they were ready to hang him.

DAWN. Okay, I know I said that. But they still gotta place him at the hospital. And Jeff, if he wasn't at the movies then he probably *did* fuckin' do it. All I'm sayin' is you gotta say whatever you know, regardless. That's just *basic*. And if they can place him at the hospital anyway, there's a really good chance we could keep you totally in the background. I mean I probably couldn't promise that, but you got my word, we could definitely try.

JEFF *shakes his head.*

Hey, Jeff. I really believed you when you said all that stuff about wantin' to do something. Don't you think that lady's kids deserve for you to tell the truth? You want to make a contribution, Jeff, here's your big chance.

Pause.

JEFF. Well – He, uh…Well… I don't think they were at the movies…

DAWN. Okay. Why not?

JEFF. Because he said – 'Cause he said he wasn't.

DAWN. Okay, just tell me exactly what he said.

JEFF. He said he heard his brother was arrested –

DAWN. From who?

JEFF. From his brother's girlfriend...

DAWN. Did she say he *did* it?

JEFF. No. No. Definitely not.

DAWN. Are you sure?

JEFF. Yes, definitely.

DAWN. But he definitely wasn't at the movies.

JEFF. No. Not with William.

DAWN. And when did this all take place?

JEFF. Last night.

DAWN. Okay.

JEFF. The *conversation* took place last night.

DAWN. I understand... (*Smiling.*) Okay...

JEFF. What are you *smiling* about?

DAWN. Nothing. It's – I'm not.

JEFF. And then just now he came in and he told me that his
brother's lawyer was such a bum he didn't know what to do,
so that's why he told the detectives or the cops or whatever
that they were at the movies.

WILLIAM *enters onto the street.*

DAWN. Okay. Great. (*Seeing* WILLIAM.) All right. I'm, uh,
I'm gonna – As soon as the detectives get to work, I'm
gonna tell 'em what you said. I'm gonna –

WILLIAM *enters the lobby.*

JEFF. Hey.

WILLIAM. Hey, Jeff.

Pause.

DAWN. How you doin'?

WILLIAM. I'm all right... What are you guys talking about?

The elevator pings, off. BILL *enters. Everyone turns and looks at him. He stops short.*

BILL. What's goin' on?

DAWN. Uh, nothin' too serious, Bill, I'm just doin' some police work right now. You can go back upstairs.

BILL. What kind of police work?

DAWN. Oh, well, it turns out while you're up there with 'Jim,' your buddy William here has been lyin' his ass off to the whole Police Department – !

BILL. What?   JEFF. Hold on a second!

DAWN. – and gettin' away with it, because of you!

WILLIAM. Excuse me?

BILL (*to* WILLIAM). All right – whoa, whoa, wait a minute. (*To* DAWN.) First of all, calm down –

DAWN. You calm down.

WILLIAM. What did you just say?

BILL. Second of all – Just a second, William –

DAWN. I don't have to calm down.

BILL. Second of all, what makes you say that?

DAWN. Because that's what he told *Jeff.*

   WILLIAM *and* BILL *look at* JEFF. *Pause.*

JEFF. Thanks a lot. That's great.

DAWN. And you just made a tremendous jerk outta yourself with your buddies on the detective squad and the DA's office, and tomorrow morning I am personally goin' to the ADA myself and tell him

BILL. That's what he told Jeff?

what a moron you are for
stickin' your nose in where
it doesn't belong and
practically getting the case
thrown out. And then   Okay – okay –
everybody in the precinct
is gonna know what a
lousy, stupid, dishonest   Okay, settle down!
fuckin' cheat you are. So
tell 'em whatever you want
at my hearing, you mother-   Calm down!
fucking piece of *shit*.
Because after tomorrow
nobody's gonna believe a
word you say about me
for the rest of your fuckin'
life!

DAWN *goes out onto the street and exits.*

BILL. What is she talking about, Jeff?

JEFF *shakes his head.*

(*To* WILLIAM.) Somebody wanna tell me what she's talking
about?

WILLIAM *starts for the door.*

Where do you think you're going?

WILLIAM *walks out onto the street and off.*

What the hell is going on?

JEFF *throws his newspaper in the trash can.*

Scene Two

The next night. JEFF *is alone in the lobby, asleep.* BILL *enters onto the street, carrying a bouquet of flowers. He looks at* JEFF *for a moment and then bangs on the door.* JEFF *wakes up, sees* BILL, *and hesitates. Finally he goes to the door, unlocks it, and steps back quickly.*

BILL. Hello, Jeff.

JEFF. Stay away from me.

BILL. Take it easy. I'm not gonna hurt you. You seen William?

JEFF. No.

BILL. He didn't come by yet?

JEFF. No. He's usually here by now.

BILL. All right, I'll just wait.

JEFF (*referring to the flowers*) If those are for me, I don't want 'em.

BILL. Don't push me, Jeff. (*Sits down.*) So you know what they did to me this afternoon, thanks to you and your girlfriend?

JEFF. She's not my girlfriend.

BILL. They bumped me off the list for my gold shield. Seven years I been waiting to get on that list, and now I gotta wait another year at least. Or maybe two. Or maybe more, before I could get back on it. And maybe never. That's a loss for the community. Okay? It's a personal loss to me, but it's a primary loss for the community, and I don't mind sayin' that. And all because that fuckin' bitch does not understand what it means to behave like a professional.

JEFF. Yeah… I'm sorry to hear about all that.

BILL. And you know what else she did?

JEFF. No.

BILL. She made a bitter enemy of every uniform cop in the city. She is ostracized in this department as of now. Forever.

Because maybe the brass'll get on my ass for making a little mistake, but the rest of the guys, they don't give two shits about that. What they care about is backing people up, sticking to your man, and not selling him out to the ADA because you think he's cheatin' on his wife with somebody else besides you. And okay, I got a little overzealous and sometimes I put my two cents in where nobody's asking for it, but is that some kind of crime? I only do it 'cause I care. Yeah. I know that sounds corny, but I do. I care. I cared about William and what happened? All he had to do was tell me to mind my business, or anything like that, and I would have stayed out of it. But no. He's gotta abuse my confidence and with the help of my partner, the *sleuth*, he's gotta make me look like an asshole in front of the whole Goddamn division and every muckety-muck I been kissing the ass of for the last seven years. I mean I just can't believe it. I can't believe the sense of betrayal. I really can't.

JEFF. What happened to William?

BILL. What happened to William? He won't recant, that's what happened to William. His brother still says he wasn't there, and personally I believe him. They're gonna charge all three of 'em. And it's all thanks to you, Jeff.

JEFF. So now I gotta testify?

BILL. You're gonna testify, he's gonna testify, everybody's gonna testify. There's gonna be a lotta testifying.

JEFF. I never said I could testify. I just said I'd make a statement.

BILL. Uh, yeah, they don't usually give you a choice. That's, like, the Law? You know: The Law? It has rules? Right and wrong? You're not allowed to break it?

JEFF. The detectives said they thought he would recant.

BILL. Well, I guess the detectives don't know everything. And I'll tell you something else, Jeff. I have a lot more respect for what he's doin' than I do for you. Because where I come from you stick up for your friends no matter what, and you don't sell 'em out for a piece of ass.

JEFF. A piece of ass…!

BILL. I'm sorry. I'm sure you had the highest noblest motives –
I shouldn'ta said that.

JEFF. I didn't do *any*thing for a piece of ass… I didn't even *get*
a piece of ass.

BILL. You wanna know what I think?

JEFF. No.

BILL. I think the both of youse are a coupla fuckin' rats as far as I'm concerned – Good for you! Now what time is he supposed to get here?	JEFF. I don't care what you think.

JEFF. I don't know. Maybe he's not comin' tonight.

BILL. All right. I can't hang around here all night. I have
important police duties to perform. (*Heading for the
elevators.*) I'll be upstairs. Buzz me when he comes by.

JEFF. Um, Bill? Sorry – She's not home.

BILL. Who's not home?

JEFF. Mrs Heinvald. I think she –

BILL. What do you mean she's not home?

JEFF. I was just gonna say, I think she went away for the
weekend.

BILL. Oh yeah? And what makes you say that?

JEFF. Because about an hour ago she got in a big car with some
guy and told me to have a good weekend.

BILL. What do you mean, 'with some guy'? What'd he look like?

JEFF. I don't really like to talk about the tenants' personal
business.

BILL *takes a step toward him.*

All right, all right, take it easy – I don't know what he looks like, I didn't really see him.

BILL. Was he an older guy? Older guy?

JEFF. Could be. I didn't really notice, Bill.

BILL. All right... I know who it is. It's no big deal. All right... Always be honest with yourself, Jeff. It's the only way.

BILL *goes out of the lobby just as* WILLIAM *enters onto the street. They both stop.*

Hello, William.

WILLIAM. Hello, Bill.

BILL. I been lookin' for you.

WILLIAM. Is this an official police inquiry?

BILL. Oh do me a favor...!

WILLIAM. Is this an official police inquiry?

BILL. No. Nothin' like that. But I love the arrogance. I really do. And after your brother goes to jail for the horrible thing he did, maybe you'll think about takin' it down a notch or two. Maybe. That's all I gotta say. Oh, and by the way, your boy in there's been sleepin' on the job.

BILL *exits.* WILLIAM *takes a moment, then enters the lobby and crosses to* JEFF.

WILLIAM. Jeff, have you been sleeping on the job?

JEFF. No.

WILLIAM *rips* JEFF's *badge off and grabs him like he's going to beat the shit out of him. Pause. He releases him.*

WILLIAM. You're fired. Now go get your stuff and get out.

JEFF. I'm sorry.

WILLIAM *waves him away.*

I guess you don't want to hear what happened.

WILLIAM. I don't care, Jeff.

JEFF. Well – but – I mean, are you really firing me?

WILLIAM *does not respond.*

Because… I mean, are you really firing me because you think I've been sleeping on the job? Or because… Because it doesn't really seem like you are – since I don't know why you think that.

WILLIAM. Go home, Jeff.

JEFF. Well… I'd like to tell you what happened, if you want to hear about it.

WILLIAM. I *don't* want to hear about it, Jeff. I just want you to get your stuff and get out of here.

JEFF. Well… okay. But I'd still like to tell you what happened –

WILLIAM. I said get OUT of here, Jeff!

JEFF. All right.

Silence.

Please don't fire me. I don't want to live with my brother anymore. I just put a deposit on an apartment *today*. Please don't fire me. (*Pause*) I know you think that I'm a frivolous person. But I didn't just lightly tell that lady cop what you said to me… no matter what you may think of me. I wouldn't do that. And I know what you're saying about the lawyer, which is a very serious problem –

WILLIAM. Jeff. You want to tell that little cop – You want to sit here and tell everybody in the world about everybody else because you don't have any life of your own, that's your own problem, but I don't want to hear about it.

JEFF. Well, I don't think that's what I was doing… I've thought about it and thought about it, and I don't think that's what I was doing… I was trying to do what I thought *you* woulda done, if it wasn't your brother.

WILLIAM. I wouldn't have done it behind my back.

JEFF. That's just the way it turned out. (*Pause*) But if you're
firing me for sleeping on the job, then I think you should tell
me why you think I was doing that. And if it doesn't have to
do with anything to do with how I do my job, then I don't
think you should be firing me.

WILLIAM. Well, Jeff, somebody *told* me they saw you
sleeping on the job. Is that true?

Pause.

JEFF. No.

WILLIAM. It's not?

Pause.

JEFF. No.

Pause.

WILLIAM. All right. Pick up your badge.

JEFF. Pick up my –

WILLIAM. Pick up your badge. I shouldn't have hit you. I never
should have confided in you in the first place. Pick up your
badge now.

JEFF *picks up his badge.*

JEFF. I'd still like to tell you what happened, but thank you.

WILLIAM. Well, I'm not gonna fire you for something I didn't
see you do, because I don't believe in that. I don't believe in
that, and not you, or my brother, or those cops are ever
gonna make me into the kind of person that believes in that.
Now I don't want to talk about this anymore. I want you to
pin that badge back on your shirt and sit back down behind
that desk and try to do your job. And I don't care if you think
it's all a joke. Because it's not a joke to me. I'm gonna finish
up my rounds and then I'm going home. I have a lot of calls
to make in the morning, and I gotta figure out what I'm
gonna do next.

JEFF. Well... I just want to say, I really admire you.

WILLIAM. You admire me.

JEFF. Yes.

> WILLIAM *exits.* JEFF *sits down at his desk and pins his badge back on his shirt. Pause.* DAWN *appears and enters. She is in her street clothes. She comes into the lobby.*

DAWN. Hello. (*Pause*) I been waitin' across the street. (*Pause*) I didn't know if you'd be on.

JEFF. I'm on.

DAWN (*attempting a joke*). Yeah, I see that... (*Pause*) Well... I just came by because I wanted to apologize for the way I handled everything last night... I didn't mean to sacrifice your confidence – your confidentiality like that... but I guess I really wanted to show him, and I guess I got a little carried away –

JEFF. But are you gonna be able to patch things up with Bill okay? Because that's what I been concerned about.

DAWN. Jeff, I'm really sorry –

JEFF. But are things gonna be okay with you guys now? Because I been kind of worried about it –

DAWN. Hey, Jeff, I came here to apologize: If you're gonna stand there and be an asshole about it why don't we just forget the whole thing?

JEFF. Well, that is a really first-rate apology, I gotta hand it to you.

DAWN. What do you want me to *say*!?

JEFF. I don't want you to say anything! I want you to get out of here, Goddamn it! Man, you are nothin' but trouble!

DAWN. All *right*! I didn't come outta this too well either, I want you to know! My career is probably *over*!

JEFF. Yeah, good! Because you're a fucking *menace* and you oughta be stopped!

DAWN. Well, you're all gonna get your wish, so you can all just relax.

JEFF *does not respond.*

Well, you obviously don't wanna talk to me right now so –

JEFF. Right!

DAWN. – I'll just see you later.

JEFF. Okay.

Pause.

DAWN. Well, they're changin' my tour, so I might not see you around too much. They're puttin' me on days for a while. So that'll be easier... Except no one'll work with me... Everyone's supposedly out to get me now. (*Pause*) I don't care. I didn't join the Police Force to make friends.

JEFF. Well... judging by how you've been handling yourself that's probably just as well.

DAWN. I don't care if people like me. I'm not just doin' this for my own amusement. (*Pause*) Jeff, I'm really sorry –

JEFF. Let's just forget it.

DAWN. Okay. Thank you. (*Pause*) Did you get a date to your friend's wedding yet?

JEFF. No.

DAWN. Well, I'm still available. When is it, Saturday?

JEFF *does not respond.*

Well... You probably wouldn't want to bring somebody who didn't know anybody... You know, with all your friends there...

JEFF. Yeah... You wouldn't really know anybody...

DAWN. Yeah, no, that's true... (*Pause*) So what are you gonna do now? You gonna stick it out here, or are you gonna... What are you gonna do?

JEFF. I don't know. (*Pause*) I was thinkin' about it… I was kind of hoping this whole experience would encourage me to rise to greater heights.

DAWN. What do you mean, like the advertising thing…?

JEFF. Yeah. (*Pause*) I just don't want to be one of those pathetic guys in the lobby who are always telling you about their big plans to do some kind of shit you know Goddamn well they're never gonna do. I'd rather just be in the lobby and just *be* in the lobby. (*Pause*) To tell you the truth, sometimes I feel like I was worn out the minute I was born.

DAWN. But you shouldn't say that about yourself. I think you got a lot of potential. I think you're a great person. (*Pause*) I don't know, Jeff: How are you supposed to know if you're right and everybody else is wrong, or if you're just wreckin' your own chances?

JEFF. I wouldn't know. I never tried to do anything before.

Long pause. JEFF *hesitates, then reaches out tentatively and squeezes her shoulder.*

The End.

www.nickhernbooks.co.uk

facebook.com/nickhernbooks

twitter.com/nickhernbooks